The Liquid Continent

The Liquid Continent

Travels through Alexandria, Venice and Istanbul

by
Nicholas Woodsworth

HAUS PUBLISHING
London

 ArmchairTraveller

This edition first published in 2010
First published in three volumes by Haus Publishing in 2008 as
The Liquid Continent volume I: Alexandria
The Liquid Continent volume II: Venice
The Liquid Continent volume III: Istanbul

HAUS PUBLISHING LTD.
70 Cadogan Place, London SW1X 9AH
www.hauspublishing.com

ISBN 978-1-906598-75-4

Typset in Garamond by MacGuru Ltd
info@macguru.org.uk

Printed and bound in the UK by
CPI Mackays, Chatham ME5 8TD

A CIP catalogue for this book is available from the British Library

To my mother, Julie Woodsworth

One

Ancient cities are hardly ever as you imagine them. In my mind the train to Alexandria was a slow train and time barely counted at all. I pictured it as a string of aged railway carriages swaying imperturbably towards the port-city, heat and sun penetrating open windows, flies and dust-motes circling the aisles, passengers lolling half-asleep as if getting there hardly mattered. But of course getting there does matter – the whole world is rushing away from the past, and even if the place it is going is unknown we are all in a hurry to arrive. At the Cairo station the Alexandria train turned out to be no slow train at all, but a silver express that hurtled its way to the sea in a whoosh of mobile telephony and refrigerated air.

Outside my window the damp, spreading fan of the Nile Delta flew by. Was it rushing away from the past, too? It was hard to say. Fields of newly sprouted wheat glowed a bright, electric green in the January afternoon sunshine. Women crouched low in vegetable plots. Men hoed. Dark and dripping water-buffalo stared dumbly up at the rushing train from muddy ponds. There was splashing water everywhere, canals and sluices and irrigation ditches bringing new life to an old landscape.

The Delta might have been out of time altogether. But the closer one got to the homes of the makers of all this beauty the less idyllic their wet and fecund life appeared to be. From the train window one only had to follow loaded donkeys tottering their way home on worn paths, their bodies invisible, their legs skinny appendages scissoring back and forth beneath domed cargoes of swaying fodder. At the end of the paths lay mud-brick villages in foetid shambles – houses crumbling, refuse and plastic bags scattered far and wide, open sewers running through unpaved village lanes. Gangs of small, dirty children ran and waved as the train passed. Strewn here and there were chunks of rubble, sections of concrete drainage pipe, odd lengths of rusty steel. They looked left over, like bits discarded from a large and ambitious construction scheme. I couldn't see where any recent work had taken place.

'Are they finishing some kind of rural development project here?' I asked the Egyptian sitting beside me. He was a business student at Cairo University and on his way home to Alexandria to visit his family. He wore a little goatee and dark glasses, and his glistening hair was combed slickly back over his head. He'd told me he was not looking forward to a weekend in Alexandria. The city was boring and hopelessly provincial. There was nothing to do.

He looked up from the mobile telephone on which he had been relentlessly thumbing text-messages. Glancing out of the window, he vaguely shrugged his shoulders and answered my question. 'In the Cairo newspapers they celebrate the completion of rural development projects every day,' he said. He thought a little bit more, then smiled, pleased with his rhyme. 'Out here they're not completed. They're defeated.'

The train rushed on, a passing village vanished behind us, and the rural idyll, green and ordered and peaceful, resumed.

I dozed, short of sleep after a late flight into Cairo the night before. I was woken by a slow, lurching halt and the squeal of the train's brakes. Waiting for a free platform, the express had stopped short of the station. But it couldn't have been far away, for we were surrounded by buildings. They were not mud-brick, but Alexandria's urban equivalent – grimy apartment blocks of raw grey concrete. Blooming with satellite dishes and hung with flags of drying laundry, they ran along the railway line in either direction. Outside a vegetable shop I watched a boy unloading cauliflowers from a cart mounted on a car chassis and pulled by a horse. Opposite, on a greasy black pavement in front of a row of garages and body-repair shops, men in overalls banged away at Ladas with ball-peen hammers.

But what caught my eye in the midst of the shabbiness and the clutter was a villa. It stood close by with its back to the tracks, an old Italianate construction that had once been beautiful. And somehow, in its decrepit dignity, it still was.

The windows on the ground floor were tall and narrow and topped with pointed arches. Most of the glass panes were smashed. Wooden shutters to either side hung at odd angles, broken beyond repair. Balcony balustrades were cracked and iron railings had streaked rust down a stained marble entranceway. Once a rich ochre-yellow, the moneyed tint of old Italian architecture, the building was peeling and leprous, so weathered by summer heat and winter rain that a dozen dirty hues billowed back and forth across its walls. Outside, emerging from a wilderness of a garden untended for decades, rose a single, luxuriant palm tree. I'd never seen a place of such abandonment.

The train sat, the minutes passed, and I gazed on. What was the point of this slow slide to ruin? In Rome or Naples a villa like this would be highly valued; here it seemed to have no value at all. But if I was intrigued no one else was. On the far side of the aisle the man who'd so energetically mashed his tin-tray railway lunch of fava beans a short time before was now sucking his teeth in satisfaction. A couple of rows ahead three *nouveau-riche* Alexandrians, fleshy females with eyes beady and observant behind designer glasses, continued their gossipy cackling. Neglect, it seemed, was a known condition in Alexandria.

The student beside me looked up from his text messages to shoot me a glance. He was not interested in the villa himself, but I could see he was wondering why I was.

'It is nothing,' he said, dismissing it with a wave of his hand. 'There are hundreds of buildings like that in Alexandria. Rich foreigners used to live in them. Italians, Jews, Greeks, Armenians, Lebanese, French... they were all sent away. Now their houses are disappearing, too. Soon this one will also be knocked down. What does it matter anyway? It's old.'

His eyes flicked back down to his mobile telephone and I could see he wasn't really expecting an answer. But the question about old things mattering hung there.

Why, indeed, should the decaying remains of the past mean anything at all? It was a question I had been asking myself for some time. It was a matter, in fact, that had worked away at me so persistently that at last I had finally packed a bag, boarded a plane and set out for the shores of the eastern Mediterranean.

'Maybe it doesn't really matter at all.' I said. 'But I like old Mediterranean places. I live in France not far from the sea in a town called Aix-en-Provence. It's charming. It's filled with restaurants and trendy boutiques and summer opera festivals. It's so charming that every now and then I get completely fed up with it. When that happens I go down the road to Marseilles.'

My student-friend looked doubtful. I carried on.

'It's only half an hour away. But it's different. There's nothing trendy about it. It's poor and crowded and noisy. It's lively and full of immigrants. There are docks and ships. And plenty of bars. There are always sailboats out in the bay, and in hot weather Arab kids dive from the quays at the mouth of the harbour.'

'So apart from diving into dirty water,' said my companion, 'what else is there to do?' Obviously he was not impressed.

I shrugged. 'I don't have to do anything at all. I can spend whole days wandering around the waterfront. I guess I just like hanging around old Mediterranean ports.'

The young man yawned. 'There's not even a new library. That's why tourists come to Alexandria. It sounds like there's even less to see there.'

I thought of the Vieux Port, the heart and soul of Marseilles. He was right. There wasn't a lot to see. It wasn't like Rome – there were no monuments, no ruins, no ancient walls. The city had been invaded, besieged, pillaged by brigands, decimated by plagues, burned down, blown up and sacked so many times that there wasn't much left that was old. Which made it all the more curious that you could feel the distant Mediterranean past in every crack and cranny of the place. Along with the sea the past was what made Marseilles. You could feel it even in the people. Twenty-six centuries of harbour-life had made them, too.

I shrugged. 'Sometimes you have to imagine it. For me the best ports aren't the modern, busy ones like Rotterdam or Yokahama. They're the old ones in the oldest parts of the world – the ports that were great a long time ago but aren't so great today.'

We sat there in silence for a while, the train perched motionless and waiting on the track in the still, sunny afternoon. My new friend was clearly dubious about what I was saying. But I found myself unable to go any further, to be more convincing about my reasons for this trip. It wasn't that I didn't want to tell him. But my real motivation for wanting to travel around the eastern shores of the Mediterranean wasn't something I could readily explain. Even to me it sounded odd. To a stranger it would have sounded ridiculous. What could I have said? That I possessed no real history of my own? That I wanted the Mediterranean to give me one?

If the train had sat outside the Alexandria station for an eternity, if my travelling companion had grown talkative and pressed me for an explanation, I suppose I would have tried to tell him. One summer years ago, I'd have begun, I met a young woman travelling on holiday in Europe. She wasn't like me at all. Emotional, demonstrative, deeply rooted in the place and the life she'd been born to, a big user of her hands when she talked, she was southern French, a Mediterranean. By the end of that summer I had returned to my own northern home in Canada. But by mid-December I found myself pulled back to her and Aix-en-Provence, the town where she lived. A two-week Christmas break there turned into a month, and a month into a year. In the end I never went home.

Eventually, I would have said, Jany and I were married. I became a foreign correspondent for a British newspaper. I could have grown biographical for my railway-friend, appended a background CV of assignments and bureau postings for him. Or I could have become intimately emotional, and explained that although I spent much of my life moving between one distant place and the next I was never happier than when I found myself back in the Midi. If Provence became an adopted home it was because I found things there I hadn't found elsewhere.

And what would I have said of the results of such an unforeseen grafting? As a couple we were unlikely. My own family, unlike Jany's, was never settled – they were global gypsies, their past a series of random displacements. My father had been a diplomat, and we followed him from one mission and one capital to the next. I developed a taste for wandering early on. New York, Saigon, Cape Town, Addis Ababa ... one after another places came and went. I liked the cities where we lived, but never stayed long enough in any one of them to feel a part of it. No single landscape, no country, no continent had greater pull than any other.

Jany's family was different. They had their feet planted deep in the red soil of Provence. They were country people, a Gallic tribe of small-hold farmers who'd scratched away in the same tilted fields of the Vaucluse hill-country for the last five hundred years. And although courgettes and melons hadn't made them wealthy, there was such ritual in their daily existence, such a depth of feeling for the land and for family and the past that their lives were rich. From that first Christmas dinner on Jany's uncle's farm – the entire clan had sat down to tiny grilled thrush and wild boar and truffles sniffed from the earth by the family dog – I had never felt such strong and valued attachments. From the beginning they were worth more than all the capitals in the world to me.

What else could I have added for my fellow rail-traveller's benefit? That one day, not so long ago, I had finally gone to ground. For the moment had finally arrived when I'd had more than my fill of life on the go with a laptop. What I really wanted, I decided, was less of the wide world and more of those close attachments.

The things that attracted me didn't come from the Provence of renovated farmhouses and well-heeled, urban Anglo refugees. They weren't to be found in fashionable Aix-en-Provence either. The Mediterranean I was interested in was older and more elemental, and lay hidden away in unexpected corners. Free of deadlines, I could look around, use my eyes in ways I'd never had time for. With Jany I spent long days poking about the harbour and immigrant quarters of Marseilles. With Jany's cousin Gérard I tended flocks of ducks and chickens on his poultry farm in the Vaucluse backwoods. In the company of easel-toting painters, admirers of Paul Cézanne, I tramped the slopes of Mont Sainte-Victoire. On a plateau high in Haute Provence I cloistered myself with black-robed monks in a Benedictine monastery. I hung around with bearded hippies in valleys deep in the Cévennes, sweltered beside a kitchen-range in a small-town restaurant near Vaison-la-Romaine, hauled nets from a fishing boat on the rocky Provençal coast.

And in all these places I came to the same conclusion: true Mediterraneans, if lesser in number these days, continue to use their physical senses in ways that most of us have forgotten. There is a kind of *faux*-peasant, goat-cheese-and-lavender sensuality about Provence, most of which emanates from glossy lifestyle magazines. But the Mediterranean also has a real sensuality, its own developed life of the senses. It comes from a direct contact with the immediate world, from the intimate attachment of individuals to simple things around them. Mediterraneans answer to the strong flavours and sensations of the landscapes they grow up in, to family and community, to the cyclical rhythms of the seasons, to routines of daily work, to old habits sustained through the ages.

In the end it is such ties which weave the web that gives Mediterranean life its strength and texture. I would have insisted to my railway friend that there wasn't any magic about it – I wouldn't have argued for some sort of loopy, New-Age Mediterranean spirituality. But from that life of the senses comes a capacity for connection, a sense of attachment and belonging, that in most places in the western world is fast unravelling. Here was a quality, I would have said, which these days we all seem to be in urgent need of. Myself especially.

But on the afternoon that our train lay waiting to pull into Alexandria station I didn't say anything like this. I didn't say anything at all. I doubted if the young man beside me would have been receptive to such argument. In fact he seemed to have forgotten me altogether. It was only after a few minutes that he finally turned to me and said in a knowing voice, 'You say you like old places. I think maybe you like nasty, shabby places, places with bad reputations. Perhaps that's why you like run-down ports – people can do things there they can't do in nicer places.'

So that was it – I was off to wallow in the mire of Levantine sinkpits. Clearly I was failing to capture my companion's imagination. But at the same time he wasn't altogether wrong. I *was* drawn to down-at-heel places with seedy reputations. They had their own sort of romance. It wasn't the pimps, the petty crooks, the professional drinkers and other harbourside fauna that attracted me. There was something in the air of dissolution and decline blowing through seaport life that I found irresistible – with it came regret and a faint whiff of things long gone and now irretrievable.

'Some of them may be shabby now,' I admitted. 'But in the past there was nothing like the ports of the eastern Mediterranean.' I looked at the scuffed-up, threadbare street outside the window. 'Two thousand years ago Alexandria was one of the greatest cities in the world, a place of luxury and learning.'

My friend closed his eyes and emitted a mock snore and a whistle.

'It wasn't the only one. Take Istanbul, the capital of an empire that stretched across half of Asia and Europe. Or what about Venice, home of the most powerful merchant fleet in the Mediterranean? Do you call that shabby? Those are the places I've come to see. A long time ago they were sophisticated, complex cities, but sophisticated and complex in ways we've forgotten about. Maybe we shouldn't have.'

At the mention of the Italian city in the lagoon my companion's face brightened. 'Why not just fly straight to Venice?' he suggested. 'That way you can bypass all the dumps between here and there.'

I shook my head. 'I'm going overland,' I said. 'There are other ports in between, maybe not so great but just as old. I don't want to miss them either.'

My fellow-traveller sighed. 'You want shabby, you get shabby,' he said. 'Which way will you go?'

'I'm going to have to play it by ear,' I replied, 'but the Syrian coast sounds good. There's an old port there, the home of President Assad's family, called Latakia. Nearby is the dead city of Ugarit, one of the most ancient harbours in the world. I thought I might visit Izmir, the Turkish port – it used to be Greek Smyrna. Just next door is the island of Lesbos; it's the opposite – it's Greek but it used to be Turkish. Then of course there's the Adriatic – the Balkan coast is opening up fast. And what about Gallipoli in the Dardanelle Straits? In the First World War it was the ...'

'O.K., O.K., I get the picture,' my student-friend cut in. 'You want the whole thing, the entire armpit of the Mediterranean.' By now he was convinced I was beyond remedy – I clearly didn't know the first thing about life's priorities. He leaned forward.

'Let me get this right,' he said. 'You live near Cannes? Where they hold the film festival? You are not far from the casinos in Monte Carlo? You're close to Saint Tropez, where there are women who remove everything they're wearing, except maybe their sunglasses, right in front of you on the public beach?' I nodded. Both of us noticed that the three fat Alexandrians in front of us had gone suddenly silent.

'Are you out of your mind?' he said, lowering his voice to a fierce whisper. 'Do you know that young women in this city cannot be persuaded to remove even their headscarves unless they are behind closed doors in the company of their fathers? You could be happy in the south of France, living like Omar Sharif. If I could get a visa I would be there tomorrow. But instead you leave. And for what? To walk around dirty and bad-smelling ports in the Middle East thinking of things everyone else forgot a long time ago?'

'That's one way of putting it,' I said. 'But ... yes.'

My companion gave up and slumped back into his seat.

We sat in silence a little longer, aware that the women ahead of us were still listening hard. Then the train lurched abruptly and started slowly moving off to the station platform. It was only when the far side of the ruined villa came into view that I saw it was still partly inhabited. On a ground-floor terrace, suspended from a length of cord strung between two columns, hung a row of men's shirts and underpants. They'd been washed a hundred times, and drooped from the line a uniform and dingy grey. They lacked Italianate elegance. They lacked elegance of any kind at all. But they showed that the villa, decrepit as it was, still lived. Of course trains and landscapes and cities all over the world were charging headlong into the future – they'd never stopped charging. Of course Alexandria was in a hurry to get where it was going – it was no different than anywhere else. But even in this gorgeous ruin of a house the past had not been entirely abandoned. To me it felt like a good sign.

My friend got on his mobile to announce his imminent arrival. The train picked up speed, the villa disappeared and we plunged on into the swirl and confusion of the modern city.

Two

All travellers to Alexandria are drawn sooner rather than later to the city's most alluring feature, its waterfront Corniche. It runs for much of the city's attenuated, fifteen-mile length, a sinuous ribbon of asphalt backed by a wall of high-rise buildings. At night, with its lights twinkling and palm trees waving in the sea breeze, it can make Alexandria look as glamorous as Miami Beach.

But that is only at night. It was still late afternoon when I stepped down from the train and began looking around the cheaper hotels lining the seafront. They were so unglamorous that by sunset I was still walking the pavement. In keeping with the idea that this was a trip of unadorned Mediterranean simplicity, I'd decided on avoiding big hotels and the kind of places used by foreigners on holiday. I'd wanted the feel of eastern ports.

By the time darkness fell I had started to form an extensive and nasty picture of all the dumpy hotels in all the dumpy cities that lay between me and Venice – my railway friend's counsel about bypassing the whole lot of them was beginning to look good. It was those discoloured, not-so-faint aureoles left on the walls above the beds, the oily traces of former occupants' heads, which put me off most.

It wasn't much before nine o'clock when I came across the Union Hotel. It stood on the waterfront just two short blocks down the Corniche from the Cecil Hotel, a place I had scratched off my list hours before. Alexandria's oldest and best-known establishment, the Cecil had a rich history and a room rate to match. In 1942, with the German army sitting not far along the coast at El Alamein and poised for a final push to Cairo, it became a headquarters for Allied military intelligence. General Montgomery kept rooms there and British Eighth Army staff officers, their accents as clipped as their moustaches, strode purposefully about the hotel's high-ceilinged hallways. More romantic still, the Cecil had been a pre-war watering hole for Alexandrian sophisticates – it was here that Justine was sometimes to be seen swaying sensuously about the lobby's potted palms, en route to a lover's tryst.

Even today there are visitors who put up at the Cecil in the half-hope of seeing her. But it is useless – the characters of Lawrence Durrell's *Alexandria Quartet* are now relegated to a past so ephemeral and rearranged by imagination that the Cecil is incapable of producing even evocative mood, much less flesh-and- blood literary inventions. These days it is part of an international tourist chain and favoured by foreign groups who sit in Monty's Bar avidly recounting the day's visits. Justine wouldn't have dreamed of setting foot in the place.

The Union Hotel, on the other hand, had no history at all. I doubt if Justine would have set foot in it, either. It was housed on the sixth floor of a building that looked like a concrete waffle-iron, and in the evening's failing light the side-street by which it was entered looked decidedly dodgy. Like most Alexandrian streets it was run down and dilapidated, its façades stained and neglected, its doorways grubby and paw-marked by an unrelenting press of humanity. On the far side of the street a gym's windows were hung with lurid posters of muscle-bulging weightlifters in American-flag bikini briefs – inside, under bright fluorescent lights, a couple of skinny Egyptians were peddling furiously away on exercise bikes. In the hotel building's dimly-lit lobby a family of cats, the mother with a missing eye, were sleeping by the lift shaft.

I pressed the lift button and stood looking for a moment at the thick pile that lay at the bottom of the shaft, the accumulation of years of refuse tossed down from business premises above. There was a sudden clanking noise above and a lift cage descended on a greasy and vibrating cable. I was sure that in two minutes I would be on my way back down again. But I wasn't.

'Shower! ... Toilet! ... Sink!' Five minutes later I was being toured around a room by an aging, hollow-chested retainer with a pronounced tubercular cough. His bellboy's jacket was several sizes too large – his finger-tips barely showed beyond its sleeves. Ali's English was slight, but he knew his sanitary installations. In the attached bathroom he reeled off the words for the fittings on offer. He ran the shower, flushed the toilet and turned on the sink taps. When I cast an eye over the bathtub he even managed to hunt down a missing drain plug. Ali's vocabulary failed him only when it came to the small-diameter pipe that pointed upwards from down inside the toilet bowl. I was stumped, too – such things do not exist in the English-speaking world. But it also worked.

When Ali turned a tap I stepped back in surprise as a jet of water gushed into the air, rising high in a graceful arc above the toilet before it fell to the floor. It soaked the bathmat, but Ali paid no attention. As an exhibition of superior Egyptian plumbing it was worth it.

The room was clean and carpeted. It didn't smell of damp or old food. There were no oily head marks on the wall above the bed. It cost the equivalent of $9.50 a day, with a 15 per cent reduction after the first ten days. After he'd turned on the lights and television there were no more demonstrations for Ali to make. But in an inspired bid to seal the deal he ran out, returning a moment later with a brand new bedspread. He tore the old beige bedspread off the bed, ripped open the plastic wrapper of the new blue-and-white one, and with a flourish unfurled it on the bed. Woven into the cloth was an image of a long-limbed, almond-eyed beauty wearing a square-cut head-dress. It was Cleopatra, seducer of Caesar, lover of Mark Anthony, the last ruler of the Greek Ptolemaic dynasty to reign over Egypt.

As images go it was schmaltzy – all over Egypt Cleopatra lends her name to everything from filter cigarettes to belly-dancing cabaret cruise-boats. But just over twenty centuries ago, in a seaside palace that had lain a stone's throw from the Union Hotel, the real Cleopatra had lived. The bedspread seemed a good sign to me, too. I took the room, brightened Ali's face with a tip, and went out to find something to eat.

I slept badly that night, my half-waking dreams full of suffocating crowds and the panicky feeling there was no room left on earth for all its people. I had gone out for dinner and seen a night-time Alexandria so densely packed that not a single open place remained. I walked along brightly lit main streets where at 11 o'clock shops were still heaving with customers. I picked my way through back-alley cafés where little brass tables and backgammon games and long-stemmed water-pipes clogged the route. I strolled jammed bazaars where street-hawkers were bulked up in blankets against the night cold and the air itself was cluttered with tinny music. Alexandria's policemen had not even tried to cope with the throngs that spilled off the sidewalks – they only stood and watched as people, buses, horse-drawn caleches and cars that never stopped honking negotiated their separate ways. There was no free space anywhere – it was a luxury Alexandria couldn't afford.

The sensation remained so oppressive that on waking early the next morning I got up and immediately pulled back the curtains and the sliding glass doors that lay behind them. Suddenly the room was filled with light and there was more air and empty space than I could imagine. Out on the balcony I was no longer earthbound. I was high over the water, the land at my back invisible. I had left not just Alexandria, but all Africa, behind. Spread out before me and filling the entire horizon lay the Mediterranean.

It was the middle of winter, and the Mediterranean of the imagination, that dazzling sea of hot and flawless blue, lay months away. Instead the day was cool, and small, white, racy clouds were sailing overhead on a fresh wind. They mottled the surface of the sea – one moment the patch of water in front of the hotel was as dull and lustreless as green lentil soup, the next a sparkling ultramarine.

But it didn't matter what the weather was. In the weeks that followed I came to look forward to this moment at the beginning of each day, this drawing back of the curtains, for it was a constant, dramatic surprise. There were mornings when the air was misty, the edges of the shoreline soft and blurred, the water pearly-grey. On others heavy and featureless cloud lay stretched over a leaden plane of water. And sometimes I would be met by squalls of dark rain racing in across the harbour. Short, angry swells would ram the sea wall that edged the Corniche below my room. It was all a bit like Ali's demonstration of the toilet-geyser: great sheets of water would fly skyward, drenching the road and causing startled waterside pedestrians to make sudden sprints landward. After these storms scummy rafts of empty bottles, old planks and bits of plastic appeared from nowhere. They would slosh about the harbour for days, slowly breaking up, until the next south wind finally flushed them out and away. The sea that awaited me behind the curtains was always the same sea, and always different.

But on this first morning it was the harbour itself that held my gaze. It wasn't just the bright fishing boats swinging around on their moorings or the little dinghies dropping red buoys for a small-boats regatta later in the day. I had never seen a port so regularly and evenly formed – it could only have been arranged by the hand of man.

From the Union Hotel the Corniche and the solid wall of high buildings that lined it swept away on either side in a smooth curve. To the west a neck of land continued evenly on around in an arc to what had once been an offshore island; long ago Alexander the Great had joined the island of Pharos to the mainland by a stone causeway, so forming a sheltered anchorage on this otherwise low and harbourless coast. To the east at Chatby, where Cleopatra's royal palace had once stood at the opposite end of the port, a thin peninsula mirrored the same regular concavity. A long mole curved across the harbour mouth, leaving two narrow entrances and completing the whole. The port formed a pleasing, perfectly uniform oval. It was like looking at a small inner sea, egg-shaped, enclosed, and cosy.

There was a knock at the door, followed by a deep, racking cough that resounded down the hallway. It was Ali. He had brought towels. After he'd put them in the bathroom he hung around the doorway, hacking mournfully, letting me know that in this part of the world any service, no matter how small, called for remuneration.

Perhaps I tipped him too well; he must have sensed he was on to a good thing. The second time he knocked he brought soap. It was also appreciated, but although Ali's cough was louder and more pathetic than before, his tip was smaller. He arrived yet a third time with a wide smile and a roll of toilet paper. He was playing his strongest card – in return for relieving me of dependence on the mighty waterspout that erupted from the toilet he was hoping for vast gratitude and a matching tip. I was grateful but I could see this kind of game might go on forever – his last bit of baksheesh was a pittance.

Still, Ali was not one to be easily dissuaded. He continued to bring me the same trio of soap, towels and toilet paper almost every morning for weeks. It wasn't long before I was running out of places to stack it. Several times I had to ask him to take it all away.

Of course that service, too, came for a small consideration. Ali was nothing if not a creative generator of tippable events. Certainly the pitiful cough helped, although when it suited him it disappeared altogether, a medical miracle.

When Ali had gone for the last time I took a final look across the harbour and then went out myself. I was no longer thinking of Alexander, the man who'd built the magnificent harbour. I was thinking of the European residents who two thousand years later had made fortunes shipping cotton from it. If they'd left their architectural traditions behind perhaps they'd left their breakfast traditions as well. I wanted a croissant and *café au lait.'*

At the bottom of the shuddering lift-cage I strolled up the street and across the tram tracks on the rue Chambre de Commerce, the broad boulevard that ran a block back from the Corniche. It was after eight o'clock, but traffic was still light and there were few pedestrians about. Like their fellow port-inhabitants all around this sea, Alexandrians are slow to get going in the morning.

But immediately I saw what I'd been unable to see in the noise and the crush of the night before. There were hundreds of foreign buildings here. Transplanted and incongruous, downtown Alexandria was a European metropolis shipped to the Arab side of the sea.

Odd and exotic constructions ran block after block. A mix of a dozen styles, they were in better condition but as anachronistic as the Italian villa by the railway station. There was the curvilinear grace of art-deco cornices and the formality of neo-classical columns and pediments. On one side of the street lay the whimsy of art-nouveau apartment décor, on the other the stylised towers of a neo-Gothic office block. Stranger still were the Islamic arches, Ottoman cupolas and Pharaonic friezes reinterpreted through western eyes – they displayed the sort of eclectic orientalism that Edwin Lutyens, imperial architect of the British Raj, would have enjoyed.

Breakfast forgotten, I continued walking. If Lutyens were to tour New Delhi today he'd be proud of the legacy it had preserved. But the oddest thing about Alexandria's past was that while it was everywhere it was nowhere at all. You had to consciously look to see these things – at any busier time of day these buildings would have disappeared altogether. Their ground floors were converted to garish shop-fronts. Their façades were festooned in tangled telephone wires, their roofs hidden in jungles of advertising and sign-boards. And what was visible was hardly recognisable. Decades of dirt and dilapidation had bestowed on everything the same gritty film and suggestion of slow, unstoppable decline. It didn't surprise me that tourists arrived and left in a day. Alexandria, a place of desperate rural migration and shoddy Egyptian holiday-making, was a city of some pathos, perhaps. But of its fabulous past there wasn't a single convincing sign.

I wandered for a long time, from a turbaned bronze horseman on the city's central square to once-grand mansions on leafy residential avenues. Finally, back on a major thoroughfare, I found what I was looking for.

The Brazilian Coffee Stores was the kind of establishment good enough to have its collection of morning regulars. Some of its patrons, in that time-honoured tradition maintained by old farts in coffee shops the world over, had their own personal cups kept on shelves behind the counter. I didn't even have to go inside to know it was that kind of place. I could see the men from some distance down the sidewalk – they stood at the shop's open door nursing their coffee and gassing away in Arabic, as easy and familiar in their manner as if they had stood there surveying life every morning for years. Which they probably had. Retired, well off, and unoccupied, they were like people everywhere with time on their hands – they enjoyed nothing more than hanging around together, comparing notes and handing down acerbic judgement on the world and all its works.

But what struck me most as I approached these characters was their physicality. Their gestures were animated. Their facial expressions were vigorous, their voices lively. They talked with their whole bodies. Suddenly I realised I had seen these men before.

They weren't sipping pastis, but in their jokey bravado and mocking affection for each other they were the spitting images of the pastis drinkers I'd seen propping up bars in the back streets of Marseilles. They didn't have a shady bench to sit on, but in their sharp-eyed surveillance of the street they were just like the old gaffers I'd seen sitting in Sicilian village squares. Even their brassy stories, recounted in a language I couldn't understand, were somehow familiar – the stories might differ in detail, but in their bantering delivery they were the same ones I had already heard in waterfront cafés from Piraeus to Valencia.

Alexandria may sit on the edge of Africa and, looking out to the sea, barely belong to the continent. In the prickly post-Suez era it may have an even harder time acknowledging its historical ties to the European landmass across the water. But of its essential nature there could be no doubt. The city's character exists most markedly in its people, and they have no trouble at all expressing it. There is an intimacy, a garrulous warmth and near-tribal sociability that belongs to this city and is shared by all others on this sea. It is not African, nor European, nor Middle Eastern, either. But it is identifiable. It is Mediterranean.

And it is infectious. Could it have been these elderly men who made me feel just a little bit livelier, a little younger and more engaged with the morning around me as I ate my breakfast? Or was it breakfast itself? The *café au lait* and croissants were as good as any I'd ever had in Marseilles.

Three

Like the ancient Greek city it is built over, modern European Alexandria is laid out on a right-angled grid of avenues and boulevards. Its more important commercial establishments – airline offices, *pâtisseries*, cinemas and banks – sit on these wide thoroughfares. Always busy, their plate-glass display windows shiny and well garnished, they give the city, or at least the downtown area behind the Corniche, whatever air of middle-class prosperity it can muster. The filler that lies in between is something else.

You don't have to wander very far off the main grid to bump into another Alexandria, a city that belongs not to its small, westernised Arab elite but to its real owners, the great mass of new Alexandrians. Today less than a third of the city's five million inhabitants are Alexandria-born; the others, mostly from the fly-blown towns and villages of the nearby Nile Delta, have pitched up in the great waves of rural migration that continue to wash over the city. Just a few yards down the alleys separating Alexandria's principal European streets an altogether more crimped and cheek-by-jowl existence begins. It was in one of these side streets, a place of hole-in-the-wall restaurants favoured by Alexandria's poor, that I discovered the little restaurant called Petros.

Petros must have been a modest establishment even when run by its eponymous Greek owner. Down on the Corniche, where cold winter waves were smacking into the seawall in the black night, there were better places to eat. But in this season they were dead and depressing, inhabited only by gloomy waiters who stood in doorways waiting for better days. There was not even a doorway to Petros, but one of those roll-down metal blinds that take the place of outside walls in small shops across the Middle East. There were just five tables crowded inside, and so little space left over that there was no room for the usual blaring television. Instead there was a radio on the cash desk. '*Habibi, Habibi*' – my love, my love – the voice of Fairouz, darling of the Arab world, floated out into the busy night.

A man in his sixties, a bristly, unshaven Egyptian wearing a ragged woollen hat, beckoned me in. He said nothing, but pointed instead to one pot after another on the gas cooker before writing down the price of dinner for me. I checked my dictionary to make sure I had the Arabic numerals right. Chorba soup, half a roast chicken with cooked vegetables, a tomato and cucumber salad, hummus, flat bread and tea cost the equivalent of $1.50. I sat down, and after that evening rarely ate dinner anywhere else.

It wasn't the food, but the company that I ended up coming for. Petros had long ago passed into Egyptian hands. Abbas, the man in the woollen hat, tended a smoky sidewalk grill and washed dishes. Mahmoud, the slim, light-complexioned Alexandrian who owned the restaurant, ran the kitchen. The waiter who served the tables had darker, coppery skin, a reflective, intelligent face, and kinked African hair. His name was Mamdouh.

All three men at Petros became my friends, and Mamdouh has remained so ever since. I still talk to him from time to time over the telephone that sits at Petros on the shelf opposite the gas cooker. Often I hear something like the sizzle of eggs in a hot frying pan. But it isn't the cooker, just a cheap phone and a bad line. As Mamdouh shouts 'Aiwa! Hello? Yes? Aiwa! Hello! Hello?' into the receiver I can hear other noises in the background – a faint clatter of plates and the sounds of Egypt from the crowded alley outside. All Alexandria comes buzzing over the line to me.

Abbas spoke rarely and preferred to make things known with his hands. Mahmoud had only a little English. Mamdouh, though, turned out to be a subtle communicator. His contemplative nature was evident as soon as he spoke. He hadn't a huge vocabulary, but he took the time to carefully put together his English words so that they meant what he wished them to mean. Never rushed or careless, he was deliberate in thought. He was principled, in fact, not just in language but in everything he did – he was receptive in outlook, judicious in his observations, finely attuned to the sensibility of others. His entire life, I think, was based on a regard for the primacy of human relations. These may seem curious observations to make about a waiter encountered by chance in a back-alley Alexandria restaurant. On the other hand perhaps they aren't – during the First World War the British novelist E M Forster fell in love with a conductor on an Alexandria tram. Nothing quite as radical happened to me, but in my friendship with Mamdouh I was reminded that Alexandria, historical world-spanner of cultural divides, has always been a place of curious encounters.

I didn't talk to Mamdouh a great deal that first evening. The place was busy and he had his hands full. But I had never seen, in restaurants like this at least, quite as meticulous a waiter. Modest Egyptian eating places are generally something less than spic-and-span – up and down the street plates were getting peremptory wipes with dish towels that spent most of the evening hanging around their owner's sweaty necks. Mamdouh, though, was fastidious in his work, and I wondered why.

I, too, had my hands full that evening. When my dinner arrived three or four street-cats suddenly materialised on the floor around my feet. Soon they were in my lap. They were spoiled and not easily chased off. It was Abbas who showed me the simplest method for getting rid of them. Picking up a handful of chicken bones from a plate by the sink he hurled them out into the street. The cats tore after them. 'Hah!' he said softly, his only locution of the evening. When they returned a few minutes later I pitched my own chicken bones out. None of the other diners thought any the less of me for it.

But on following days I would sit after the evening rush was over. As Mamdouh tidied up, or finally sat wearily down with a cup of tea, we would talk. Sometimes he would tell me about himself. He was a practising Muslim, sincere in his belief, and with enough of that Egyptian fatalism that he could bear life's vicissitudes without bitterness. But that didn't mean he wasn't aware of the injustices and waste around him.

'I hate my job. I will not go to work tomorrow – I will tell them I am ill,' he would sometimes say decisively. At the same time he would shake his head, smiling to himself at the impossibility of such an idea.

Mamdouh was only moonlighting at Petros. By day he was an Alexandria restaurant inspector with the city hygiene department, an organisation that was, to say the least, challenged. Not only did the job provide a miserable salary; Mamdouh was regularly pressed to take the bribes and backhanders that most minor Egyptian functionaries regard as their due. Inspectors came and went, the flies remained. Mamdouh detested the whole thing.

'If only I could find another job,' he assured me, 'I would leave.' There was one thing, though, Mamdouh wouldn't do. He came from a family that was neither rich nor privileged, but that had always lived in the city. Mamdouh loved Alexandria, and now wouldn't leave it for anything. He had tried better jobs elsewhere, but quit within weeks to return home. There was no Corniche in Port Said, he told me, no sea breeze in Cairo. I felt sorry for him, a man consigned by fate to practising by night the things he couldn't get others to do by day. After a while even my own transgressions of hygiene embarrassed me. I stopped throwing chicken bones out into the street, and started sharing dinner with cats.

Mamdouh soon got used to my asking nosy questions about himself and the lives of other Alexandrians. In return I'd told him of my itinerant existence and about finally washing up in Provence. I'd explained my need to find a past of my own in the Mediterranean past. But if Mamdouh was discreet about asking further questions, I could see he remained perplexed. Why would anyone, he finally asked me one night as the cats mewed hungrily and circled about our feet, go far from home to spend months travelling among strangers in distant ports? Wasn't Provence Mediterranean enough?

'It was the sea,' I replied. Of all the places I had visited in Provence it was on the Marseilles waterfront that I thought I saw most clearly where the special character of the Mediterraneans comes from. 'What makes Mediterraneans,' I said, 'is the Mediterranean itself.'

'Well, what else would?' Mamdouh, amused, smiled and shook his head. He got up to bring us tea. In the alley outside the stream of human traffic was finally slowing down, the night-noises of the city growing softer.

'It's obvious, and then perhaps it isn't so obvious,' I said. For a sea more than two thousand miles long, I had to admit to Mamdouh, the Mediterranean is remarkably uniform in makeup – for centuries its inhabitants have shared the same rocky coasts, adapted in the same ways to the same climate, lived in the same kind of houses, practised the same occupations, eaten the same foods.

But it wasn't that simple. This was also a sea that had spawned three of the world's major religions, several of its greatest empires and many of its bloodiest and most intractable disputes. The more time has passed, I said, the more the Mediterranean has come to seem divided. There are conflicts of nations – Israelis and Palestinians, Greeks and Turks, Serbs and Albanians. There are conflicts of continents – economic migrants bobbing northwards in small boats towards a Europe that wants to know nothing about them. There are conflicts on single islands – Cyprus – and even conflicts over single rocks – Gibraltar. And now, spread about the globe but centred on that Mediterranean buffer zone where Islam meets the West, was the most alarming prospect of all – a conflict over two separate visions of a world that for all practical purposes has become one. Sometimes there seems little that Mediterraneans are capable of sharing except sunshine.

'What's astonishing, given the history,' I said, 'is that wherever you look in the Mediterranean life is basically the same. I don't mean in the hinterland or in the capitals lying far in the interior – their agendas are different. I mean the people and ports on the sea itself.

'It's really odd if you think about it. Just take France and Egypt. They are thousands of miles and civilisations apart – two completely different places. No one could say that Paris is even vaguely like Cairo. Yet

Marseilles is very much like Alexandria. I'm not talking about income or health care or how often they pick up the garbage. But in their character, their spirit, Marseilles and Alexandria have the same way of looking at the world. Barcelona, Thessalonica, Tangier, Palermo, Beirut, Valetta ... walk down the street in any of those ports and you feel the same thing. Why is that?'

I was settling into my stride. Mamdouh, knowing by now he was going to get an answer whether he wanted it or not, merely stirred more sugar into his tea.

'It's simple,' I said. 'Trade. These places have been buying and selling from each other for thousands of years. Their ships have been sailing in and out of each other's harbours long before history began to record it. Greeks, Phoenicians, Catalans, Carthaginians – these were the original mercantile peoples. Commercial exchange is what gave birth to these cities – it's what they have always depended on for their existence.

'What's interesting, though, is what they exchanged,' I went on. 'It wasn't just commodities. Along with the grain and wine and olive oil and all the rest of it there were invisible cargoes. They unloaded entire cultures in each other's harbours. Strange languages, foreign ideas, new philosophies, peculiar foods, unknown music, odd religions, weird hairstyles – all these things came ashore on the quayside. The people who lived around the ports couldn't help but absorb it all. And that's saying nothing, of course, of that other invisible cargo that also got absorbed – human genes. Sailors being sailors and women women, DNA was probably the first thing they unloaded after the ship itself.'

In my enthusiasm for my subject I had sugared my own tea twice. But I didn't care, for I was now coming to my point. 'And that common civilisation, the product of a dozen shared cultures, is where it began, I think. It's all about cosmopolitanism.

'If Mediterraneans have these vital ties, if they share this basic sense of connection to each other and the world around them, it isn't because they are different from any other people in the world. Like everyone else they take their nature and outlook from their surroundings – in their case from

24

the sea they grow up on. For the people of the classical age the Mediterranean made up the entire civilised world. They called it "*Mare Nostrum*", our sea. Its cultures, races, and languages were different, but for anyone who lived on its shores the entire world really *was* connected. Sitting around its periphery, binding it together in a dense network of maritime links, lay the great ports. They were a bit like a prototype of the Internet. Here were countless places, all attached to countless other places, each feeding into the life of the other across the sea. If individual Mediterraneans still feel a strong connection with the world around them, maybe it is because an entire civilisation used to be held together that way.'

I had spilled some tea on setting my cup down. From this sticky puddle I drew out an oblong, vaguely Mediterranean-shaped territory with the back of my spoon. It lay on the scarred surface of the table with no borders and no landmasses around its edges.

'I'm starting not to think of the Mediterranean as an empty space surrounded by Europe, Asia and Africa. You can look at the sea as a single entity, a place from whose coastlines people look not outwards, to this country or that capital, but inwards over the water to each other. This sea has its own cities, its own life, its own way of being. Jean Cocteau, the French writer, loved the Mediterranean. That's the way he looked at it fifty years ago. Of all the world's continents, he said, it is the only one that is liquid.'

But Mamdouh, who knew a thing or two about accepting things for what they are, just smiled and shrugged. 'That was fifty years ago. Look at Alexandria fifty years ago. Look at it today. It's gone. Who cares about all that now?'

Here, once again as on the train, was that question about things mattering. It was my turn to shrug. Abbas had finished washing the dishes and Mahmoud, on his feet since morning, was wearily preparing to close up. It was time to leave.

'Maybe we should care,' I said, standing and slipping on my jacket. It had grown chilly outside. 'The Mediterranean is no longer at the centre of things and culture doesn't get off-loaded any more. It gets down-loaded.

But I still enjoy thinking about how the port-cities once connected an old world. Sometimes I wonder if they mightn't help us think about reconnecting a new world.'

Mamdouh raised his eyebrows. 'What do you mean?'

'I'm not really sure,' I said, 'apart from the fact that these are good places to think about globalisation. Everyone talks about globalisation and no one can agree on what it is or where it's taking us. A lot of the time it seems to be driving us apart. The only thing people seem sure of is that we've just invented it.

'I'm not at all convinced – when I walk through old ports I get the feeling that globalisation has been with us for a very long time. It began with exchange. Of course it is not today's high-tech version – it took other forms. And that's what interests me. Only the very greediest can believe that simply chasing corporate profits around five continents is what globalisation is really about. Just knowing that in old port-cities there were other ways of doing things might help us think that other options are possible today.'

We were outside, and the rolling steel shutter descended with a metallic rattle and a final loud clang. I made my goodbyes to Mamdouh, Mahmoud and Abbas in an alley that was now dark and quiet. Old or new, even global cities must sometimes sleep.

Four

EM Forster, bound for India in 1915, had the odd destiny to find himself marooned in Alexandria for three years. He ended up liking the place in two stages. It was only after he allowed himself the time and reflection to enter into the city's deeply hidden past that he began admitting a real fascination for the place. His affection for Alexandria in his earlier days was shallower. 'One cannot dislike Alex,' he wrote, 'because it is impossible to dislike either the sea or stones. But it consists of nothing else as far as I can gather: just a clean cosmopolitan town by some blue water.'

The Alexandria that I found myself wandering about some ninety years later was no longer either clean or cosmopolitan. But still I had to agree with Forster – disliking Alexandria was impossible, at least as long as that blue water was somewhere nearby. Once through the door of the Union Hotel my feet, almost of their own accord, would lead me to the far side of the Corniche and alongside the water of the Eastern Harbour.

I say 'almost' because anyone who let their feet alone do the thinking wouldn't have lasted three seconds. In Forster's day the Corniche was less than a decade old, a genteel seaside stroll complicated at most by horse-drawn carriages and a few ambling motorcars. Today it has been widened, in some places to twelve thundering lanes, and getting to the other side of it in one piece involves speed, timing and luck. For all their charming ways, rational driving is as absent in Alexandrians as it is in any other Mediterraneans. Once behind the wheel they're all lunatics.

Safely on the other side, I would hesitate. The Union Hotel sat almost at the centre point of the great sweeping curve of the harbour. If I turned left a half-hour's walk beside the water would take me out along the promontory, once Alexander's stone causeway but now long silted up and heavily built over, to the medieval Arab fortress of Qait Bey. If I turned right a stroll of equal length would lead me along the edge of the modern city to its most popular tourist attraction, the new Alexandria Library.

The idea of a second library replacing the great Ptolemaic library that had disappeared some fifteen hundred years before had historical glamour. But the sea, the great dish that is a captor of all the life and vitality surrounding it, exercised too strong a pull on me – its gravity was greater than a mere repository of words.

There was a constant play of light and movement along the walk to Qait Bey – wind and sun on the water and the work of the people who made a living from it. There were boats everywhere – out in the harbour, overturned on the sandy shore, pulled up in repair yards where naked wooden ribs were clothed only in the sound of hammer and saw. In Anfoushi, the old Turkish town that spread across the promontory, there were fishwives who had the same rough voices and humour as their colleagues on the Vieux Port in Marseilles. But there was less of the West here. Bellowing crowds, over-loaded donkey carts, strange and stomach-turning smells, choked lanes, crumbling Eastern architecture, odd bits of animals hanging on hooks, baffling market-goods whose use and provenance I could only guess at ... there were oriental mysteries in Anfoushi I was just as happy to leave unsolved.

One glittering, breezy day I made my way through Anfoushi and kept on walking until I could go no further – I ended up at the narrow, rocky tip of the promontory where Qait Bey lay guarding the entrance to the harbour. A towering structure of sandstone walls and crenellated towers, it had been built by Egypt's formidable Mameluke slave-dynasty and was five hundred years old.

Far more imposing, though, was the thought of the building that rose in precisely the same place twenty-three centuries ago, seventeen hundred years before Qait Bey was ever dreamed of. For early Alexandrians the great lighthouse of the Pharos was more important than a simple fortress. It was much more, too, than a basic aid to navigation. The seventh wonder of the ancient world, it was a glorious symbol of the city itself.

I arrived just as a bus was pulling in and tagged discreetly along behind a group of visiting Europeans. Later Alexandrians, I could see as we walked along a seaside terrace towards the fort, did not assign the place quite the same central and symbolic role as early ones did. For strolling couples and families taking the air, the open spaces around Qait Bey were a refuge from the overcrowded city life that began closer to shore. Buffeted by cool, fresh wind, surrounded by a white-capped sea on three sides, this part of Alexandria felt as much a creation of water as of land. It was a maritime escape, an open doorway to an endless, bright blue city park.

I followed the group through the fortress's turnstiles and up rough, stone-carved steps. High on the battlements overlooking the courtyard the group's young guide got down to business.

She was vivacious, knowledgeable, and covered the ground well. We couldn't see Lake Mareotis for all the buildings, she said – it ran parallel to the shore just behind the city. These days the lake was silted up and no longer used. But under the Greek Ptolemies it was one of the keys to the city's greatness. Then it had been navigable, and from the eastern end of Lake Mareotis a freshwater canal had been cut to the Nile River. Cargoes could be carried from here to the up-river city of Memphis, and from there along another canal joining the Nile to the Red Sea. Thus more than two thousand years before Ferdinand de Lesseps dug his own canal at Suez, Alexandria was not just the greatest commercial port in the Mediterranean – it was a city that joined the old commerce of the Orient to the new wealth of Rome. A major link between East and West, Alexandria grew very wealthy indeed.

But the port-city was not simply rich. It was sophisticated and celebrated, a meeting place for races from around the globe. Its population for the time was unrivalled. If eventually the Roman capital was to outstrip the Hellenistic capital, Alexandria was for three centuries before the Christian era the largest city on earth – in modern Europe urban life was not to be replicated on a comparable scale until the 18th century growth of London and Paris. Alexandria, our guide proudly declared, was the world's first true metropolis.

Edward Gibbon, who wrote about the port under Roman imperial rule, also seemed to have been impressed by it. 'The beautiful and regular form of that great city, second only to Rome itself, comprehended a circumference of fifteen miles,' the guide read a photocopy taken from *The Decline and Fall of the Roman Empire*. 'It was peopled by three hundred thousand free inhabitants, besides at least an equal number of slaves. The lucrative trade of Arabia and India flowed through the port of Alexandria to the capital and provinces of the empire. Idleness was unknown. Some were employed in the blowing of glass, others in weaving of linen, others again in manufacturing the papyrus. Either sex, and every age, was engaged in the pursuits of industry, nor even did the blind or the lame want occupation.'

Gibbon, though, was less than impressed by the character of the city's inhabitants. 'The people of Alexandria, a various mixture of nations,' he had gone on to write, 'united the vanity and inconsistency of the Greeks with the superstition and obstinacy of the Egyptians.'

It seems an unkind appraisal. But Gibbon, a man who would have preferred to see Rome live forever, had his reasons. For not long after the city was integrated into the Roman empire after the death of Cleopatra, it became an influential centre for the new cult of Christianity – Saint Mark established one of the earliest congregations here, and succeeding city bishops were no less active in early ideological struggles to decide what was heretical and what was to become part of the established Christian canon. Adopted by Rome as the state religion in the 4th century, Christianity was a creed that Gibbon ultimately blamed for the demise of his beloved empire.

But not even Gibbon himself, I was sure, could have failed to be moved by Alexandria's most astonishing physical achievement, the lighthouse to which the guide now turned her imaginative attention.

'The Pharos was the tallest building ever conceived in the classical world,' she marvelled. 'It stood more than four hundred feet high.' To emphasise her point she gestured straight upwards. The sky above Qait Bey was quite empty, but we all craned our necks to look into the highest, bluest part of it.

The Pharos was built, she went on, in the 3rd century BC by Sostratus, a Greek architect from Asia Minor. It stood in a vast colonnaded court, and was made of four stages. The lowest was square, the second octagonal, and the third circular. Beneath the fourth part – a stone cupola supported on eight columns – burned the lantern itself, a signal visible up to seventy miles out to sea. In the bottom section were three hundred rooms – housing for the engineers, technicians and tenders of the light. Hydraulic machinery is believed to have lifted the wood to light the beacon at the top. Figures of tritons stood on the cornices above the structure's base, and a great statue of Poseidon rose from the cupola above the light.

'How could a hot fire burn if there was a stone cupola with a statue above it?' a sceptical Scandinavian in the group asked. 'Wouldn't it have cracked?'

'Yes, you are right, there are problems,' the guide admitted. 'When we try to picture the lighthouse we don't in fact have much to go on. A century ago a German scholar named Hermann Thiersch conceived a model for the Pharos that we still employ today. He used written descriptions and pictures found on old coins and mosaics. He used a picture of the lighthouse on the wall of Saint Mark's Basilica in Venice. He even used the little clay vase of a lighthouse found near Kabul, a sort of tourist knick-knack brought back from Alexandria by an ancient traveller. The trouble is that nowhere are the details very precise.'

When invading Arabs took Alexandria nine hundred years later, she said, they did not know the secrets of maintaining the Pharos. Like the city itself, it fell into disrepair. But the conquerors' delight in all things mechanical kept many stories of the lighthouse alive. There was supposed to have been a statue whose finger followed the course of the sun through the day. There was another statue that called out the hours, a third that indicated the direction of the wind, a fourth which warned of the approach of a hostile fleet.

The higher one climbed the lighthouse, the guide added, the fuzzier and more fantastic the details became; by the time one got to the beacon itself almost nothing was known. There were descriptions of the firelight being magnified by mysterious mirrors or polished steel. There were even accounts suggesting that the Alexandrians, as skilled in mathematics as they were in glass-making, had invented some sort of telescope – they tell of an operator sitting under a curious glass disc by which he could follow the progress of approaching ships long before they became visible to the naked eye.

'That is ridiculous. No one could forget such a thing,' a doubting German spoke up. 'How could the Alexandrians discover the optical lens and then lose it? It is very careless. Could these stories possibly be true?'

Once again the guide had to admit ignorance. She didn't know where the truth left off and legend began, she said. Nobody did, not even that eminent historian of the Mediterranean, Fernand Braudel. But there was at least a real basis to the stories. Apart from their theoretical learning the Alexandrians were so technically accomplished, Braudel had believed, that if they hadn't had slaves to rely on they could have begun their own industrial revolution.

What was certain, the group was told, is that the Pharos was so impressive that it came to be seen as one of the crowning achievements of the ancient world. Physically, it marked the planetary axis about which the rest of the world was arranged. It was through the Pharos and that other towering monument to the north, the Colosus of Rhodes, that the Alexandrian geographer Eratosthenes traced the earth's prime meridian – for the first time the earth was given a coherent spatial order. But the lighthouse had a metaphysical dimension, too. Long after its destruction its memory continued to remind the world what human imagination had been capable of. A tribute to Alexandrian Hellenism, it was a triumph of both rationalism and spirituality.

I sat on the battlements looking out to sea long after the tour party had continued on inside the fortress. The remains of the Pharos, toppled by earthquakes in slow stages over seven centuries, now lay on the sea floor beyond the harbour mouth. Apart from a few select items rescued by a French underwater archaeological team, most of it would remain sunken below the waves forever.

But that didn't mean that even today the light of the Pharos had stopped glowing in men's minds. In the recent past there had been at least half a dozen plans, most of them hopelessly unfeasible, to rebuild the lighthouse.

I wouldn't have minded eating in a revolving restaurant at the top of a second Pharos, but I didn't have the time to see if that particular project would ever come to anything. The story of the lighthouse had whetted my appetite for the Alexandrian past. But I was frustrated. It was difficult to understand what the ancient city had been all about – it seemed either to be built on fantasy or to be lost altogether. I certainly couldn't go tagging along behind tour groups every day.

But then I didn't need to, I realised, as I turned around to look back across the harbour at the city. There on the waterfront rose a low, disk-shaped form. If the old Pharos had yet to be reconstructed, a new Library already had. The very next day, I decided, I would turn right instead of left on the Corniche, and consult it.

Five

It is, apart from the sea itself, the most arresting sight in the city. The Alexandria Library came into view as I strolled along the harbour towards the waterfront at Chatby, and not even the royal palace of the Ptolemies that once stood there could have surprised me more. It sat facing the Mediterranean, a glamorous and alien edifice rising unexpectedly from the city's shabby dilapidation.

A vast roof of glass and aluminium, disc-shaped and upward-tilting, emerged from below ground to angle a hundred feet up into the air. Surrounded by a reflecting pool of blue water, it climbed the sky like a dawn sun rising out of the sea. Its symbolism was not limited just to a traditional Egyptian past. Evoking international scholarship's high-tech future, a complex geometrical arrangement of metallic bas-reliefs on the roof made it resemble a gigantic silicon chip as well. Nor did architectural metaphor stop there. Recalling its global literary mission, the Library's walls looked like the surface of an exotic alphabet soup – they were incised with characters from almost every known written script in the world. By any reckoning, this was a building of grand lexical ambition.

Outside the doors I stood for twenty minutes. There were more foreigners queuing here than I'd seen during my whole stay in Alexandria. They weren't visiting scholars unless, like the man in front of me, academics had recently taken to pinning red plastic nametags to their shirtfronts. 'My name is Todd,' his tag said. Todd was from Cincinnati. He wanted to see papyrus scrolls. When he was a kid, he was telling another man in his group, he'd spent a season keeping Cincinnati Red batting scores on scrolls of rolled-up birch bark. 'Even better'n papyrus,' he said. The new Library, a paying attraction, had put Alexandria on the tour circuit.

We passed through the doors and the chatter ceased. The Library was even more impressive inside than out. Beneath a luminous, sloping ceiling supported on thin columns, terrace after staggered terrace of desks descended into the largest reading-room in the world. If the open space seemed far bigger than it appeared from the exterior it was because only three of the Library's seven levels sat above ground; the others sloped away beneath us, the last one lying well below the surface of the sea outside.

The 'oohs' and 'aahs' of arriving visitors were of the subdued kind usually kept for cathedrals. The lavishness of the place went far beyond anything offered by hard-used libraries of the ordinary sort. Did it seem especially breathtaking, I wondered, because it was so different from the scruffy and grime-coated world that lay just outside? Here everything was new and slick and polished. The floors were decked in glowing Californian oak. The fittings were of burnished steel. The walls were encased in smooth black Zimbabwean granite. And on every desktop where students and researchers sat working lay a new, on-line computer console. With a price tag of a quarter of a billion dollars, the Library would have been an extravagance for any city, much less a resource-strapped one like Alexandria.

I peered around, not sure where to start – there was seating for two thousand here. Beginning from the top, Computer Sciences, I slowly made my way downwards, each level taking me further from modern technology and closer to the origins of civilization.

Applied Sciences and Communications; Social Sciences; Economics; Literature; Music ... Lower and lower I went; on the last floor I bottomed out at Religion, Philosophy and History, and found a free desk.

The world has grown too complex for any new library to aim at the goals of the old Library of Alexandria – twenty-three hundred years ago it was the first institution anywhere to consciously set about amassing the entire world's recorded knowledge in a single place. So eager were the

Ptolemies in their collecting that they had all ships in port systematically searched from stem to stern for written works. Copies were made and returned, the originals kept. Today there is simply too much information in existence; not even the American Library of Congress – with 120 million listings the biggest, richest library on the globe – could hope to achieve those old aims.

This library didn't even come close. It couldn't afford it. Although it aimed eventually at creating a world-class institute of learning and academic research, funding was short. Construction for the prestige project had been mostly paid for by oil-rich Middle-Eastern states. None of them, ironically, would themselves have tolerated a hint of the intellectual freedom the Library stood for; one of the largest cheques came from Saddam Hussein, and cleared just before the beginning of the first Gulf War. And while the Library was working hard on establishing a huge digital collection, books themselves came largely through donation – in a building designed to hold eight million volumes, at the moment there were only two hundred and fifty thousand.

Still, it seemed to me there was something of importance that had been revived in the new Library – the memory of the old Library's grand ambition. Through it the Bibliotheca Alexandrina, as it was loftily christened, was attempting to salvage a part of the city's original identity.

It was a taste of that identity that I was now after. I took a stroll through the stacks. I wasn't surprised not to find scrolls of papyrus neatly stored in pigeonholes. But I was looking for works on old Alexandria, and I found them. After several exploratory trips I had my desk piled high enough to keep me going for months.

I didn't have that long. Where do you begin reading about a library that among all the libraries of the ancient world – Pergamon, Athens, Rome, Antioch and half a dozen others – was acknowledged as the greatest? You don't. How can you delve into the intricate workings of the Mouseion – the Temple of the Muses – the scholarly Palace institution to which the Great Library was attached? You can't. What you can do is dip into the remaining fraction of the four hundred and ninety thousand works that once made up the collection there. You can read of the lives of the most notable of the learned men who, from every corner of the civilised world, were attracted to the pampered life offered by the Mouseion's Ptolemaic patrons. And you can rely on the commentaries of scholars who have devoted their lives to the study of such things.

For who, apart from a historiographer of mathematics, is going to plough his way through works like the thirteen volumes of Euclid's *Elements*? Never mind that this Alexandrian mathematician's theory of numbers and plane geometry was so brilliant as to immediately supersede all previous work in the field. Never mind that from the 3rd century BC until very nearly our own times it remained the standard reference on the subject. Did it really matter how Euclid established the mathematical axiom by which two entities that are each equal to a third entity are themselves equal? I never decided if it did or not, for I never looked into it – it is the kind of thing that makes my eyes glaze over straight away.

Nor did I feel any deep sense of loss when I discovered I could no longer look into the complex astronomical theories of one Aristarchus of Samos. Most of his writings had disappeared long ago. But it was a great pity for the medieval world, for sometime around 280 BC this Alexandrian astronomer became convinced that the earth revolved around the sun. Of course the notion ran counter to the established wisdom that the earth was the centre of the universe, and it certainly wasn't popular with the Church in the Middle Ages. The idea wasn't to gain currency again until it was rediscovered by Galileo almost two thousand years after Aristarchus.

No easier to contemplate, either, was the famous correspondence between the Greek mathematician Archimedes and three renowned mathematicians of Alexandria: Dositheus, Conon of Samos and Eratosthenes, the man who had used the Pharos to reconfigure the world's maps. Today's learned men like to point to this correspondence as an example of the spirit of international scientific co-operation that originated in Alexandria (Archimedes lived, and finally died by a Roman soldier's sword, in the Sicilian city of Syracuse). In these letters the world's experts batted mathematical ideas about like shuttlecocks, arguing the best way to demonstrate as yet unproven theorems. Once again, though, the mere idea of Archimedian texts like *The Method of Mechanical Problems, Addressed to Eratosthenes* left me cold.

But of all Alexandria's scholars it was to Eratosthenes that I warmed most, perhaps because there were small bits of his work I felt I could just about understand. The third chief Librarian to be appointed by the Ptolemies, Eratosthenes was not just the man who with his three-volume *Geographica* turned geography from a Homeric art into the rational study it is today. As a *philologos* – a lover of all knowledge – he was a philosopher, poet and literary critic as well as a mathematician and cartographer. He wrote dialogues that subtly blended propositions on Platonic philosophy and mathematics. He authored a work on musical harmonics. He produced a twelve-volume study on ancient comedy, as well as two Greek grammars, technical glossaries on ships and chariots, and collections of epic poetry, mythology and legend. He also gave the world *Eratosthenes' Sieve*, a work on the identification of prime numbers.

The achievement for which Eratosthenes was best remembered, though, did not involve extracting slippery and elusive numbers from a mathematical colander. It was far less abstract, and had to do with the measurement of the planet itself. Even I could appreciate the ingenious method by which Eratosthenes, without ever leaving the Mouseion, had been able to accurately measure the earth's circumference.

This is how he did it. Eratosthenes had heard of a deep, dry well in Aswan in southern Egypt down which no shadow was cast at noon on midsummer's day – the sun, in other words, stood directly overhead. But further north at Alexandria, another point on the same meridian, the sun *did* cast a shadow at the same time on the same day (by such comparisons Eratosthenes had already deduced that the world was round). Using a tall Alexandrian obelisk, he measured the sun's rays off the vertical at noon, and found that the difference in angles between the two towns came to seven and a half degrees – that is, one fiftieth of a complete circle. Eratosthenes sent out his surveyors; they calculated that the distance between Alexandria and Aswan was five hundred miles. Multiplying that distance by fifty, he estimated the circumference of the earth to be 25,000 miles, and its diameter 7,850 miles. Only fifty miles out, the latter calculation was extraordinarily accurate for its age.

And so I spent my time – not just one day, but several succeeding days – entertaining myself with a haphazard ramble through old Alexandrian learning. The city's achievements were not just scientific. On following visits, for example, I read of Zenodotus. The Mouseion's first Librarian, he undertook a comprehensive study of *The Odyssey* and *The Iliad*. In bringing together and evaluating divergent Homeric texts, in removing, annotating or correcting doubtfully inserted words or lines, he became the first student of literature to try to establish definitive editions. It was Zenodotus who introduced critical literary scholarship to the world.

I also came across the story of the Alexandrian rabbis who translated the Hebrew scriptures of the Torah – the first five books of the Bible – into Greek. Popular legend had it that the Ptolemaic ruler Philadelphus, wanting to know the religious law of the city's large Jewish population, had seventy rabbis sequestered in seventy huts on the island of Pharos. Miraculously, they all emerged at the same time, having produced seventy identical translations of the Old Testament – thus the name of Alexandria's most famous translation, the Septuagint.

If in reality the task was laboriously accomplished over many decades, the consequences were none the less earth-shaking. There were many other religious translations made in Alexandria – two million lines of Zoroastrian texts, for example. But without the Greek translation of the Torah the course of Western history would have been entirely different – the Hebrew scriptures on which Judeo-Christian traditions were built would not have penetrated the Greek-speaking Hellenic world, nor through it reached the Roman Empire which finally adopted them. Christianity itself would not have existed. Without the Septuagint, as one modern historian put it, 'London and Rome would still be pagan and the Scriptures would be hardly better known than the Egyptians' "Book of the Dead".'

I thought about that proposition for a while. It had its pluses and minuses – no Christian crusading from the White House, no Bellini

Madonnas in the world's art galleries. Would we all be sun-worshippers? The implications were endless. Who knew what the world might have become without Alexandria bridging the ancient and modern worlds?

But it was as I was reading of Callimachus that I began thinking not just of the consequences of Alexandria's achievement, but of its causes. Callimachus, a sort of Jorge Luis Borges of the ancient world, was a man who delighted in exploring the great labyrinth of knowledge the Library had become. Deep in its furthest reaches he examined obscure works, half-forgotten legends, rare words, arcane usages. And he collected them. *The Collection of Wonders of the World, arranged Geographically* was typical of his erudite efforts at all-encompassing compilation and synthesis. No detail was too insignificant – gathering material from every branch of study, he wrote volumes devoted to wind and to birds, to the names of towns, to the habits of barbarians.

But his greatest work of assemblage was devoted to the Great Library itself. Callimachus set out on a systematic exploration of its nearly half-million volumes, classifying them, commenting on their scholarship, providing biographies of their authors. This early effort of bibliography was all-inclusive – Callimachus' *Tables of Persons Eminent in Every Branch of Learning, Together with a List of their Writings* ran to a whopping one hundred and twenty volumes.

It was a phenomenal undertaking, one never attempted before. From what source, one could only ask oneself, did Callimachus draw this deep desire to unify and collate all knowledge? What was the driving force, for that matter, behind any of these scholars' efforts to systematically collect the world's learning? As the city's most celebrated institution, the Library could only reflect the values of Alexandria as a whole. The answer had to lie somewhere in the origins of the great metropolis itself.

To find it I had to go back to the very oldest of Greek stories, for in creating his capital Alexander the Great had looked for inspiration to Homer. At least that's the way the Roman historian Plutarch recorded it in his *Life of Alexander*.

According to centuries-old tradition, said Plutarch, Alexander's architects had already chosen another place to build a great capital for him not long after he conquered Egypt. But the night before they were due to begin work on it the young Macedonian king had a dream. In it a wise and ancient man stood beside him reciting a passage of poetry. Alexander recognized the verses immediately – they were from *The Odyssey*, and described the stranding of the Greek hero Menalaeus on an island off the Egyptian coast. Menalaeus had offended the gods, and in order to discover which divinity he now had to placate, he wrestled down Proteus, the immortal and all-knowing sea god who came to sleep on the island. His struggles were not so frantic, however, that he didn't notice that the island would make a very fine harbour.

The old man in Alexander's dream was, of course, Homer, and the island named by Menalaeus in his verses, Pharos. In the Alexandrian legend, inevitably, the world conqueror headed off to Pharos the morning after his dream and immediately decided the place would make an excellent port and capital. And so Alexandrians believed that from the beginning their city was divinely sanctioned, that Greek heroes and immortal gods, speaking through Homer and Alexander, had long ago decided on its unique destiny.

Other stories go on to confirm that destiny. When Alexander set out to trace the plan of the city on the ground he found his surveyors had run out of chalk. So he used barley meal instead, and was greatly disturbed to see vast flocks, birds of every species, flying in from the marshes of Lake Mareotis and circling overhead, attracted by the food. Was it a bad omen? Not at all, said his seers. It showed that this was no ordinary site – it would become a place of abundance, a city that would attract every kind of man. Shortly afterwards Alexandria's special role as a world capital was ordained not just by Greek oracles, but local ones as well – like all Egyptian rulers from the earliest pharaohs, the city's founder was proclaimed a divinity.

So much for the myth. In reality, modern historians say, it was unlikely that Alexander ever saw the city as his world capital. Not even its name indicates a special role – over years of war and conquest the conqueror bestowed it on many places, some of them no more than miserable garrison towns lost in the high wastes of Central Asia. In fact, Alexander never saw his new city at all – having subjugated the West, he embarked immediately on the conquest of Persia and the East. Egypt was now part of a vast Hellenistic empire, and Alexandria simply a defensive buttress on its Mediterranean flank.

But all that changed when it became apparent to his leading generals that if Alexander was a god, he at least shared some of the attributes of mortal men. Following his invasion of India, Alexander, alcoholic and exhausted at the age of thirty-one, died of fever in Babylon in 323. It wasn't long after that his great empire began to break up, his squabbling generals claiming vast territories over which they became local satraps. Few did well – some lost their kingdoms through internal conflict, others through ambitious plans to reunify Alexander's empire with themselves at its head.

Ptolemy Soter, the Greek general who founded the dynasty that was to last until Cleopatra's death, avoided both of these pitfalls. In waylaying Alexander's Macedonia-bound funeral cortege and having his body buried in Egypt instead, he affirmed Alexander's divine Egyptian credentials. The act also legitimised rule over the country by Alexander's Ptolemaic Greek successors.

But if the Ptolemies had persuaded Egypt's theocratic elite of their right to rule, the challenge posed by the Hellenised world outside was different. How were the Ptolemies to project an image as the rightful inheritors of Alexander's mantle?

They were well aware of the errors of military adventurism made by other leaders of Alexander's fractured empire. The Ptolemies' solution was far gentler and more successful. Alexandria would assume its destiny by becoming the world's first universal metropolis, a place unexcelled in learning, multicultural in make-up and plural in attitude. No longer a mere port, the city would become Hellenism's showpiece. Alexandria would look to the entire world, and in return the entire world would look to Alexandria.

And so it happened – Alexandria became a place of opulent splendour woven from the threads of many cultures and civilisations. Nothing lasts forever and neither did Alexandria's greatness – eventually its unifying spirit of rational enquiry was overtaken by zealous Christian theological debate and its greatness diminished. But for three hundred years it was the most accomplished metropolis in the world. In its universalist dream Alexandria, the world's earliest model of the globalised city, was unique.

That, at least, was what I was able to gather about old Alexandria as I sat deep in the heart of the Library. In the end what was intriguing about the city's ancient institution was not so much the specifics of its scholarship, but its entire, remarkably curious attitude towards the outside world.

If there is a human tendency to look to the familiar, I thought, a desire to want to see one's own reflection in everything and everyone, there is also an opposite tendency. It is possible to welcome difference as well, to include rather than exclude it, and from new kinds of syntheses to go off in new directions. It is not an attitude that has shaped our own current outlook on global culture. But adopting an inclusive world view, or even a multiplicity of views, had not weakened the Ptolemies – it had worked to their advantage. What is extraordinary today about this 2,000-year-old dream of universality is our own continued curiosity about it. That, and our willingness to believe that such a thing might still be possible. The more time I spent on the shores of the Mediterranean the more I found myself intrigued by just such an idea.

Six

It was dark when I emerged from the Library one evening after a long day's reading. Perhaps I had been at it too long. I was feeling restless and couldn't settle to anything. I ate dinner at Petros, but shortly afterwards said goodbye to Mamdouh and made my way out into the street again. I stopped at a café to drink tea and puff on a water-pipe, but the bright fluorescent lights and noisy babble drove me away. It was growing late. Still I wasn't tired, and began strolling aimlessly about the city.

I couldn't say, exactly, where I wandered that evening. I must have crossed my own trail numerous times, and only ended up back at the Union Hotel in the small hours when all of Alexandria lay silent and asleep. But something happened that night. I walked not through the city I was expecting, but through a second Alexandria, a shadowy and insubstantial city far more splendid than the first.

Was it because I had spent days in a subterranean refuge, surrounded on the lowest floor of the Library by the buried vestiges of the ancient city? Alexandria seemed to rise up out of the darkness and the silence of the ground beneath me. The crowds had disappeared. The kebab shops and bazaar stalls, the grim housing blocks and the refuse that littered the streets, all faded into obscurity. Across the city a calm fell and the darkness smoothed over everything distracting or ugly. And what emerged from the gloom in its place was Alexandria's past.

Down by the water, in the dark shadows of the square fronting the

Cecil Hotel, I reconstructed the Caesareum. Once it had stood here as a temple dedicated by Cleopatra to Mark Anthony, the lover she had declared divine. Loving no one, Caesar Augustus, Anthony's victorious enemy, had later rededicated it to himself. A patron of sailors, he encouraged prayers and supplications by thankful mariners who'd sailed safely into Alexandria's port. Now not a trace of it remained. Even Cleopatra's Needles, the two tall stone obelisks which had marked its entrance, had been carted off as booty – one now stands on the Embankment in London, the other in Central Park in New York.

But on this night the needles rose in front of the sea for me once again, as did the ghostly temple courtyards and sacred groves that had lain beyond. In the daytime the square is full of shouting shoeshine boys and noisy souvenir hawkers waiting to pounce on guests emerging from the Cecil Hotel. In their absence I thought I could just make out fainter, foreign voices. Was it the sound of seafarers recently sailed in from distant places? Perhaps it was just the sea itself.

Further inland I found myself on the rue Fouad, a broad avenue that by day is a chaos of horn-blaring, exhaust-spewing traffic. It is a thoroughfare that has known repeated incarnations as regimes and rulers have come and gone. It is sometimes called Sharia El Horreya. In the past it has been known both as Sharia Gamal Abd el-Nasser and the rue Rosetta. But now, well after midnight, it was for me what it had been in the very beginning, the Canopic Way, a broad ceremonial promenade lined with marble colonnades running from the Gate of the Sun in the east to the Gate of the Moon in the west.

It was here the Ptolemies held their processions. In my mind's eye I saw it all again, reviewed the parades as they passed by. What had become of the towering statues of the divine Bacchus that once rolled by on four-wheeled chariots? What of the poet-priests, the devotees dressed as satyrs, the female initiates whose heads were crowned with living snakes? What of the famous golden phallus, one hundred and eighty feet long and mounted on a star? The two thousand golden-horned bulls herded in the procession? The giant wine press containing a choir of fifty satyrs, accompanied by flautists, who trod grapes as they sang? The virgins in purple tunics and gold belts, the young boys driving chariots pulled by oryx and ostriches, the falconers with their rare birds, the hunters parading a pack of 2,400 leashed hounds?

They had marched, all of them, into Alexandria's memory, and there they remained in its furthest, darkest recesses. I looked down the silent, sleeping street. Of the 2,400 noble hunting hounds there wasn't a single one left – as far as I could see there was nothing moving but one lame and skinny mongrel.

And what of the greatest, earliest memory of them all? Not far from the corner of rue Fouad and Nabi Daniel I paused. This oldest of city intersections had long been thought the site of the Soma, the tomb of Alexander himself. It was at this place, long before the Mosque of the Prophet Daniel was built here, that Alexander was supposed to have been interred in his royal crypt.

The Soma may have been destroyed, as some historians believe the Library itself was destroyed, in the riots that in the late 4th century saw Christian zealots rampaging across the city in their determination to obliterate all traces of paganism and the Greek philosophic tradition. But Alexander's body, wrapped in gold and encased in a crystal coffin, is rumoured still to lie in the place where the Soma once stood.

He continues to haunt the city. A story still in circulation has it that once the ground by the mosque opened up and a bride in a wedding procession disappeared, swallowed up forever in the passages and cisterns that riddle the city's substrata. It was deemed useless for the bereaved groom to search for her – the great conqueror himself had called her down to lie with him. More recently a local Greek named Stelios Coumoutsos, a café waiter obsessed by the memory of Alexander, began digging underground for the king's body. It was a fevered search that was to last until his death years later.

It all came to nothing – Alexander the Great has never been found. I had read myself into my own fevered search, and now I had to ask a question. Did ancient Alexandria ever really exist at all? As an idea – the universal city – Alexandria was accessible; the myth had a bright, undying life of its own. But as a physical place the old city seemed to exist merely as the faintest of memories, a ghost that could be brought to life again only in the depths of a dark and quiet night. I contented myself with passing a hand over the base of an ancient stone column, perhaps Greek, incorporated into a gatepost opposite the prophet Daniel's mosque. It was cold and hard and damp – at least one old object in this vivid night was real. Then I made my way home along echoing streets to bed.

Seven

A couple of days later I dropped earthwards from my seafront perch at the Union Hotel. I had an invitation to lunch. It was a lengthy hike down the old Canopic Way but I didn't mind. As I walked I was considering a certain film genre – the archaeological action movie – and one of its glaring shortcomings.

There is no film called *Indiana Jones and the Tomb of Alexander*. There should be. All the elements were there – an ancient, exotic Levantine city, once glorious and now shabby, sitting forgotten by the sea; an extravagant mausoleum, legendary and lost, containing the body of antiquity's greatest warrior king; a host of locals, shadowy and rapacious, who would stop at nothing to achieve their foul ends. Never mind that this last bunch were only Egyptian property developers whose evil crimes consisted of pouring foundation slabs over any construction site they could get their hands on – Hollywood would have them wearing fezzes and looking fiendish in a jiffy. The important thing was that in a city where unknown treasures were at risk of disappearing beneath concrete forever there was one man ready to try to save them.

By the time I reached my destination I had already fleshed out a movie plot. But who, I wondered as I rose claustrophobically upwards in a lift barely bigger than a sarcophagus, would be the best man to direct the thing?

The elegant figure who met me at the top, Jean-Yves Empereur, wouldn't have needed much help from Spielberg or anyone else. His own sartorial conceits did not run to Harrison Ford's felt hat and bull-whip. Instead he favoured a Panama and held his trousers up with colourful braces. He also wore longish, swept-back hair, glasses on a cord around his neck, and a foulard – items the rugged Harrison Ford might just possibly have considered sissy-stuff, and far too French besides. But beneath the scholarly mien he had that same determined air, the same appearance of readiness to throw himself into risky, high-stakes ventures at a moment's notice. Jean-Yves Empereur, Alexandria's best-known archaeologist, was unmistakably a man with a mission.

Being French, Empereur was also a man who appreciated the sociability of the dining-table, and he liked to invite guests visiting the Centre for Alexandrian Studies to eat with him. Was it Cousteau who began making meals – long, winey feasts in the galley of the *Calypso* – look not simply congenial, but absolutely integral to archaeology's intricate workings? It was the same on dry land in Alexandria. Most of Empereur's headquarters was given over to offices, research libraries and conference rooms. But as far as I could make out it didn't matter what happened in any of them – the real heart of the operation, the place where issues were debated and courses of action hammered out, was in the rooftop dining-room over copious piles of food and drink. It was here, at a long wooden table covered with a Gallic-looking tablecloth of blue and white checks, that we sat down to lunch.

We were not alone. From the end of the table I looked past vast bowls and serving dishes at fifteen archaeologists, all of them talking at the same time. There were a few grey heads, but most of Empereur's team were young. I found them admirable. All were dedicated, highly qualified professionals, but none had lost the enthusiasm that turned their work from a job into a passion. Even as they ate they continued to volubly argue the arcana of digs and dives. These were people to whom archaeology meant everything.

Over a pois-chiche salad I asked Empereur what archaeology meant to him, why he had opted to practise it in Alexandria. He might have chosen a dozen other places to make his reputation. A one-time secretary-general of the renowned archaeological French School in Athens, he had led underwater and underground excavations in Greece, Turkey and Cyprus. Yet he had given it all up for Alexandria – he had settled permanently in a city where more than a century before Heinrich Schliemann had quickly thrown up his hands in frustration and stalked away.

Schliemann, the discoverer of ancient Troy, had been looking for yet one more spectacular find; he came to Alexandria with the express aim of discovering nothing less than Alexander's tomb. But the city, Empereur began telling me in French, does not give up any of its treasures in so easy a fashion.

'Alexandria is not like Athens or Rome,' he said. 'There is no Parthenon, no Coliseum you can walk around and see as part of a living city landscape. The written works that survived the destruction of the Library have come down to us because they were copied time and again. But you cannot copy a temple or a palace. None of the buildings Alexandria was famous for – the Pharos, the Mouseion, the Great Library – have remained standing. We are not even exactly sure where most of them were located.'

However splendid it was, the lack of accessibility to the ancient city meant that from the beginning Alexandria was simply passed over. Egyptologists were understandably drawn to easier pickings. Disembarking at one of the oldest ports in the world, they immediately disappeared far up the Nile Valley to find fame and glory in even older Pharaonic tombs.

Alexandria's greatest problem, Empereur said, was its urban setting. It was one thing to dig in uninhabited desert. It was another to search for the ruins of an old city over the top of which a new city, densely packed and heavily populated, now lay sprawled.

'Still, it is an archaeologist's dream,' mused Empereur as we moved on to the main course. 'Imagine, the largest city in the Hellenistic world, the earth's first megalopolis, barely touched until now. Almost everything is left to do.

'Of course, there have been some very good archaeologists here over the years, both foreign and Egyptian,' he went on. 'There have also been some total madmen, mavericks who come up with all sorts of preposterous and unfounded claims. Because so little is known people can invent all sorts of nonsense. Sometimes they even invent themselves – they claim pedigrees and pasts that are non-existent. But that, too, is part of the myth of Alexandria. In the circumstances,' he smiled, 'one mustn't dig about too much in their past.'

But digging about in uncertain conditions is just what Empereur had specialised in. Salvage excavation, as he called it, is often the only solution left to archaeologists in a rapidly changing city like Alexandria. As one real-estate boom succeeds another competition is fierce and available sites limited. With residential property protected by social legislation, developers keep rare commercial properties – old cinemas, warehouses, hospitals and garages – squarely in their sights. And when one of them comes due for demolition there is an ungodly scramble.

So archaeologists had to be ready to scramble, too. Often the conservation orders granting them rights for exploratory digs last only a few months. 'The window of opportunity is tiny. You can't pick the moment and you can't pick the site,' Empereur said. 'And it's very exciting. You can never tell what you are going to come upon. Sometimes you don't find things where you were hoping to; other times you find things you never dreamed of.'

We talked about some of the discoveries the French team had made over recent years – Gabbari, the vast underground necropolis in the west of the city; Hellenistic floor-mosaics, part of the royal palace complex, uncovered on the site of the new Alexandria Library; the Macedonian-style dining-room found beneath the garden of the old British consulate. The most impressive find of all had been the remains of the earthquake-toppled Pharos out beyond the Eastern harbour – more than two thousand stone building blocks scattered across five acres of sea bed. There had been some astounding discoveries out there, the archaeologist said – Egyptian sphinxes from the 19th century BC, statues of Ptolemaic queens, marble columns imported from the Sea of Marmara, well-preserved cargoes from Greek and Roman wrecks.

Empereur was about to tell me of yet one more submarine find when dessert came along and he fished a handsome, bone-handled French clasp-knife from his pocket to slice open a piece of fruit. It was at this point that I thought I had better exploit my own small and shrinking window of opportunity. I had a mission, too.

I knew nothing of archaeology, I began. Instead, I told my host, I was afraid that I was becoming just one more victim of Alexandrian myth. I described to him my recent night-walk through the city. Here, by the bright light of day, in the company of empiricists who worked by methodical investigation, the idea seemed sillier than ever. Old cities simply do not rise up from the ground and abruptly materialise. My reading had gone to my head. But now, I said, I wanted something more than the written word. I wanted solid proof of the ancient city's existence.

It was all arranged before the archaeologist had finished peeling and paring his apple. A couple of days later, armed with the necessary government permits, I met Empereur's colleague Francis Choël outside St Sabah, the former Greek Patriarchate. Choël was burly and intense, a man in his late fifties who gave whatever he was doing his full energy. He talked so fast I could barely keep up with the detailed flow of his conversation.

We skirted around St Sabah's age-stained walls, a century and a half old and now abandoned for newer premises, and entered Patriarchate property through a rear gateway. The land behind the building had long ago been leased as a Citroën garage, and it, too, had now been abandoned. It was typical salvage work, Choël said – the Patriarchate was anxious to redevelop the site and the dig was now winding up.

We emerged from a dim hallway still grease-marked by the hands of car mechanics. Suddenly the ground was no longer there – what was once a walled lot was now a gaping square hole cleanly sliced thirty feet down on all sides. After the roar of traffic outside it was quiet here. The only sound was a thunking of picks and a scraping of shovels issuing from the pit below.

Choël laughed at my surprise. 'You should have seen the junked car bodies piled here when we began. It took weeks moving them before we could even break ground.'

Beneath us spread a gigantic stone puzzle of right-angled geometrical forms; walls, wells, foundation buttresses, flagged floors, narrow passages, cisterns, stairs and courtyards. All of them fitted into each other in complex and mixed-up ways. They lay not just side by side, horizontally – there were intersecting planes lying one on top of the other as well. Egyptian workers carrying baskets of rubble made their way across the terrain at the bottom of the pit over a tortuous series of stairs and ladders. It was all horribly complicated, a bit like one of those Escher engravings where steps leading always upwards somehow finish by ending lower than they started.

'Look at the excavation's walls,' said Choël as we advanced to the pit's edge. 'There are fifteen different layers of archaeological sub-strata down there. In thirty vertical feet we have cut downwards through two thousand years of history. You can see that there is not much in the upper Ottoman and Mameluke layers. But lower down, as you approach Roman and Greek times things begin to get much busier. The challenge is trying to understand how it all comes together.'

'It's like a three-dimensional chess game,' I said, gazing first sideways and then from top to bottom.

'It's tougher than that,' Choël smiled. 'There's the fourth dimension as well – time. Long after the Roman era this site became a garden. By that point it was no longer flat, so its builders dug up earth in some places to level it out in others. You can't automatically date pottery and other artefacts from the levels they lie at – sometimes it's someone else's garbage, landfill from a different age and civilization. It's a constant puzzle of "where" versus "when".'

Choël began a discourse on techniques used to get around the problem, but I was looking all around the pit's sides, where walls, floors and passageways abruptly disappeared into the earth.

'Just one question,' I interrupted. 'Does all this underground construction extend on outwards past the limits of this hole?'

'Of course,' said Choël, nodding matter-of-factly. 'It runs off in all directions. It's the old city of Alexandria. It's huge.'

He carried on with his explanation, but suddenly I was far from technical matters. I was thinking of the stone maze which, thirty feet below the city's tram lines and ice cream parlours, fruit stalls and video rental shops, stretched away invisibly for miles. Wherever you were in modern Alexandria you were walking directly over an ancient Alexandrian courtyard or well, street or temple complex. I felt vindicated. I hadn't been that far wrong on my night-walk after all – a second city, more fabulous than the first, did indeed rise up from the silence and darkness of the ground below.

That afternoon, a mile or so further east, I passed through another gate and once again left the noise and swirl of city traffic behind. Terra Sancta is one of the prettiest spots in Alexandria. It is a place of trees and gardens and winding walkways, and over it all reigns a supreme silence. For its residents are the quietest in the city – they lie in crypts, beneath headstones, or inside marble mausoleums whose iron-grilled windows and little peaked roofs make them look like miniature houses.

Alexandria's contemporary city of the dead is vast and varied. In adjoining cemeteries on either side of Terra Sancta untold numbers of other non-Muslim Alexandrians are buried, each according to their own rites. Egyptian Copts, Orthodox Greeks, British Protestants, Armenians and Allied war dead all have their separate burial grounds here. There is even a walled plot reserved for agnostic Freethinkers. But Terra Sancta is the domain of the city's Italian Catholics.

My own rendezvous there was with a Frenchwoman who was very much alive. Sylvie Boulud was an archaeologist agile and athletic enough to scramble into even the deepest tomb. There was nothing morbid about Terra Sancta, she said when I asked her about digging among old bones – she had never worked anywhere as peaceful and relaxing.

We proceeded down long, tree-lined avenues and for the second time that day the ground abruptly dropped away. A massive cube lay below us, its sides twelve feet long, made from thick slabs of white stone. Its exterior was roughly carved and uneven. But inside, I discovered as we clambered down and entered it, the walls were smooth and polished to a glossy sheen.

'What is it?' I asked, passing my hand over the cool, marbled surface of the stone.

'It's called the Alabaster Tomb,' said Sylvie. 'It's not a new discovery, but it's the closest we've ever come to finding anything resembling the tomb of Alexander. It's built in the Macedonian style, it dates from the 3rd century BC, and it was intended for someone of wealth and influence. For a long time most archaeologists refused to believe that Terra Sancta might be the site of Alexander's Soma. But recently we've become convinced that it's his most likely burial place. What we're hoping to find beneath Alexandria's modern necropolis is an ancient royal necropolis.' A glint came into her eyes. 'And perhaps, somewhere in it, Alexander's tomb itself.'

Sylvie's own exploratory dig lay not far away. Angled to cause the least disturbance, a long trench had been cut between two rows of graves. Work had been difficult at first, slowed by several layers of human remains – with space at a premium, successive generations of Italians had been buried one on top of another. At first Sylvie had been encouraged by her discovery of a Greek cistern. But a year had gone by, and the trench was now nearly thirty feet deep. When I peered over its lip I looked far down onto the heads of Egyptians working in the earth below. But not the slightest trace of an ancient necropolis had been found. Even now Sylvie was preparing to abandon the excavation.

She didn't seem downcast by a year's fruitless labour – for her, hope always lay at the bottom of the next dig. Why, I asked her, do Alexandria's archaeologists spend so much time looking for such an elusive past? Physical finds can be exciting, Sylvie said, but they're not important in themselves: it's what you can do with the knowledge you're able to extract from them that is. Collected over years, an accretion of tiny details builds up pictures of long-vanished lives. What is so painstakingly sought after doesn't in the end necessarily have any material existence at all.

In fact, what is sought after sometimes sits out on the farthest, metaphysical edges of human existence. When I returned to his office to thank Jean-Yves Empereur for his help, I reminded him he had been about to tell me of one more intriguing discovery on the marine site of the Pharos. What was it, I asked?

For an answer he sent me down the hall to talk to Elizabeth Hairy. She was a major consumer of coffee and cigarettes, a serious, no-nonsense academic. But she had the most astonishing theory. I won't even attempt to reproduce the details of her argument, for Pythagorean mathematics have never been my strong suite. But the gist of it was as follows.

One of the more important vestiges to have been dragged up out of the waters beyond the harbour was a carved block of Aswan granite. It was a small portion of the Pharos' doorframe, a structure that at thirty-six feet high had formed an impressive entranceway. But for Elizabeth Hairy it provided a far more crucial form of access. From a study of the mathematical proportions and configuration of that block of stone she was reconstituting the entire Pharos in its correct dimensions. It was a bit like deciphering a genetic code in a single cell in order to know the shape and properties of a complex organism, she said; it was possible because of the mathematics and the creative genius of the architect Sostratus. And the Pharos she had in mind was a very different one from the Pharos of the German scholar, Hermann Thiersch.

For not only, she said, was it possible to extrapolate the entire nature of the Pharos from a single block of stone. More importantly, the Pharos itself was a simulacrum of something far larger – it was a working mathematical model whose own make-up demonstrated the make-up of the very universe. Inevitably that universe, based on the Greek Platonic principles of ideal forms, invited speculation as to the relation between science and the spirit. As far as this researcher was concerned, the ultimate intention of the Pharos' builders' was to light a path showing the way from mathematics to God.

As I walked back home along the old Canopic Way my mind was wobbling. For me an imagined and mythical Alexandria was now tied to a real and historical Alexandria by archaeology. But in a city like this that didn't make it any easier. If from a block of stone a complete 400-foot lighthouse could be reconstructed, and if from that lighthouse an entire universe could be deduced, there was no end to it. One day we might wake up to find that the universe is only an infinitesimally small part of the door jamb of a lighthouse. In the meantime the painstaking work of archaeology continues apace.

Eight

Dropping my key off at the reception desk one morning I bumped into a newly arrived visitor. The few guests staying at the Union Hotel at this time of year tended to be long-distance travellers – young people with large backpacks, small budgets and extended schedules. The man standing at the desk was young – twenty-four or -five, perhaps – but had none of the hair, the ear-studs or the red-and-white Arab *keffiya* scarves that such travellers wore. Clean-cut and fresh-faced, he was dressed in a wrinkled lightweight tan suit, a laundered white shirt, and scuffed desert boots. He had all the hallmarks of the freelancer, an ambitious writer-journalist who'd set out to make his name in the world.

We exchanged the usual good-morning greetings, and then my curiosity got the better of me.

'Are you a hack?' I asked, fairly sure of myself as I passed my key over to the receptionist.

'No,' he replied. 'Are you?' His voice was English public school, distinctly upper middle class but brisk and outdoorsy rather than languidly plummy.

'No,' I said. I supposed I deserved it for being nosy.

'Well, that's all right, then, old boy. Can't be too careful about the company one keeps. It's time for a drink, wouldn't you say?'

I glanced at my watch – it was barely 11 o'clock. Drinking in the middle of the day usually made me sleepy. But then it wasn't all that often that someone from the pages of *Horse and Hound* popped up in Alexandria.

Old boy, indeed. Why not, I thought. I was curious to see what this young man in his much-travelled suit was all about.

Once we were in the street Joseph took charge. He knew where he was going. He should know where he was going, for heaven's sake, he said – he knew every drinking establishment in Alex inside-out. Most were either dark and smelly dives or over-the-top, five-star- hotel cocktail lounges for rich Gulf Arabs on holiday. But the Elite, he promised, was different. We might even meet Madame Christina.

What was I getting into, I wondered? Was Joseph an aficionado of white-slave bordellos? Oriental transvestite bars? Opium dens? So far I hadn't run across anything even vaguely sinister in Alexandria, but who knew what was left over from the bad old days? At any rate it was too late to do anything about it – I could only follow as my new acquaintance strode purposefully ahead.

The moment I saw Christina I knew she wasn't that kind of madam. She was tiny and ancient and white-haired, and had greater notoriety in Alexandria that any mere procuress could have – as proprietor of the Elite Café she had chosen to stay on when her Greek compatriots had fled fifty years before. Like the Elite itself, she was the last of her kind.

Both were now anachronisms. Although she showed up every day her health permitted and sat faithfully beside the cash register, Christina lived mostly in her memories. In her polished French she could tell you about visits to the Elite by Edith Piaf and Josephine Baker. Through her cloudy eyes she could still see the elegant crowds that congregated in the café after the city's theatres let out. Greek and Italian cotton brokers, English ship-ping agents, Levantine factory owners, the socialites, café philosophers and sybarites of a score of nations ... for Christina they might have left the Elite only the evening before.

Now in the place of all these ghosts there was just me and a young Englishman who seemed cheerfully intent on getting plastered. Other-wise the place was empty. 'Why don't we have a spot of early lunch,' Joseph suggested as we slid into an old-fashioned booth beneath a faded theatre poster. 'That way we can tuck into a bottle or two of Omar Khayyam.

Egyptian red's a bit unpredictable, but Khayyam's the best of a bad lot. What about nosh? Does mezze and moussaka sound all right?'

Mezze and moussaka sounded fine, and the wine turned out to be not too bad at all. The only real challenge was Joseph. I couldn't figure him out. Was it a put-on, I wondered, the confident, gentleman's-club bearing, the chit-chat liberally sprinkled with 'old fellows' and 'jolly goods'? At times you got the feeling Joseph was taking a poke at his own class, playing a florid-faced country colonel who'd put down his *Telegraph* long enough to splutter about the lamentable state of affairs in the colonies. At other times you wondered if he wasn't the real thing, a genuine throwback to a manner and style of life that had long ago vanished. If Joseph was playing a young fogey he did it with aplomb.

Not even the drinking seemed real. Joseph was tossing it back by the glassful. But he was no rake – his clear, watchful eye gave the lie to his stories of drinking prowess. Only a few extra pounds' weight and a large appetite – he rapidly demolished his moussaka and ordered another plate – hinted at any self-indulgence at all.

By the second bottle I had wormed out of him a semblance of a life. His grandfather had fought with British forces in Iraq in the Second World War. His father, who'd died when he was young, had served in the Middle East as well; he'd even spent leaves in Alexandria. Joseph, brought up Catholic, had gone to a Jesuit boarding school in Lancashire. At university he'd decided to become an Arabist, and a language course had brought him, in his turn, to Alexandria.

'I hated every moment of the year that I spent here, old man, absolutely detested it,' he said. 'I couldn't stand the noise, the crowds, the dirt, the obsequious grovelling, the incessant pandering for baksheesh. But do you know, it was the oddest thing, when I got back to Britain I couldn't think of anything else but Alexandria. All I wanted to do was get back here.'

So now back he was; it was the latest of several visits over the last few years. As we moved on to our third bottle of Omar Khayyam Joseph seemed to loosen up and, like anyone revisiting old student haunts, revel in old memories. Never let anyone tell you Arab girls won't sleep with men, he told me – if she's from a wealthy and sophisticated family, if you're a westerner and she fancies you, well then, your odds aren't bad. There were other confidences along these lines. And Joseph did indeed harbour literary ambitions – one day, he promised, he would put his Alexandria down on paper. All in all he seemed little different from other travellers with a taste for the more adventurous parts of the world.

But there was one area of his life that Joseph grew immediately cagey about. When I asked him what, apart from trips down memory lane, he was doing with his life now he became mysterious.

He'd been doing some physical training in Britain, he said. In fact as soon as he returned he'd have to get back to it and shed a few pounds.

Territorial Army, I asked? Yes, something like that, he replied.

Had he, I ventured, been to Iraq? Yes, once or twice, he admitted. As part of the British occupying forces? Not exactly, he said – he really couldn't say anything more. And apart from a later casual allusion to the courage of men in tight situations he wouldn't talk about it.

Was Joseph in the SAS? In military intelligence? On his way home from some cloak-and-dagger operation in Falluja? Or was the Lawrence of Arabia persona just one more part of an old-fashioned, conservative romance he'd wrapped himself in? I never found out.

But what I did find out was that Joseph, a genuine and practising Catholic, had a detailed knowledge of the different religious groups that once made up Alexandria's foreign population. By the end of the meal we were both quite drunk, and Joseph proposed a tour. Where else but Alexandria, I wondered as we shambled out of the Elite, would a boozy lunch with a shadowy Englishman be followed by a church-crawl?

Joseph's Arabic was certainly fluent enough to impress the two soldiers who stood with automatic weapons outside Alexandria's main synagogue. Almost all important non-Muslim places of worship in Egypt are guarded against fundamentalist attack, but not against an onslaught of charm. After a minute or two of jokes and smiles, followed by the discreet presentation of a small wad of banknotes, the guards swung the rusty gates of the synagogue grounds open.

Don't expect an accurate description of the synagogue, nor of the various Anglican, Armenian and Orthodox churches that, interspersed with side-visits to bars, followed during the course of that afternoon. I had drunk less than Joseph, but far too much for anything like reliable recounting.

Some details remain. In Saint Mark's Coptic Church we gazed spellbound at a small silver reliquary that sat on an altar – in it lay the bones of the saint himself, returned to Alexandria only recently after having been stolen by Venetians and kept in the basilica there for a thousand years. In Saint Catherine's, Joseph's own church, we talked to the Somali clerics who were taking over as the last generation of Italian priests in Alexandria died out. In the Evangelinos, a dilapidated Greek church, we stumbled up a circular wooden stairway to a high, dusty pulpit, the better to stare into a single eye that stared back at us from inside a golden triangle at the top of the iconostasis.

But that is about all I remember. At some point Joseph said we were drinking in commemoration, lamenting the passing away of a hundred holy places. And passing away they were – I was left with the impression of vast and lofty buildings, edifices built for grand ceremonies, now cut from their moorings and drifting slowly to oblivion. The churches were full of dark shadows. They were damp and they echoed. And apart from a lonely custodian or minor religious official awaiting the next tiny and fast-shrinking congregation, they were abandoned.

Joseph and I eventually abandoned them too, and spent the early evening drinking beer in the Cap d'Or. Joseph really did know every bar in town. It wasn't a bad place in the daytime, he said, but after dark it became an Egyptian poofters' bar – you had to watch your backside. My backside survived the evening without incident, but I wasn't surprised to wake up the next morning with a roaring ache in my head.

Nine

What I needed after a bender with Joseph was coffee, and as far as I was concerned there was just one place for that. In the same way I was used to ending each day at Petros, I always started the next one at the Brazilian Coffee Stores, the café I'd run across on my first morning in Alexandria.

It was an odd place, and I'd grown to like it. Like the Elite, it was one of the few businesses left in the city with an atmosphere that was not just Mediterranean, but distinctly European. Redolent of the rich smell of roasting coffee, it also retained a faint whiff of bourgeois comfort left behind by an old-world clientele from the far side of the water.

There were no tables inside. The place was for buying coffee as much as for drinking it, and customers stood ranged along a marble-topped counter running along two walls. The other half of the room was occupied by ancient and bulky pieces of torrefaction equipment – creaky roasters and grinders and drums holding revolving metal paddles. Behind them was elaborate decoration: set onto a mirror occupying an entire high wall was a bas-relief pyramid made of clear glass and filled with coffee beans. On the mirror were also painted a bright tropical parrot, a large map of Brazil, and production statistics showing Brazil's dominance of the coffee market. 'Le Meilleur Café du Monde', trumpeted a gold-lettered inscription beneath the map. There was a founding date over the door of the shop – 1929. A Brazilian flag, with its motto 'Ordem e Progresso', was painted on the ceiling.

It didn't seem, though, that of late there had been much of either order or progress. The gold lettering was peeling. The statistics were seventy-five years out of date. The glass pyramid was chipped and leaking coffee beans. On the marble counter the hinged wooden boxes labelled 'Special', 'Français' and 'Extra Prime' remained empty and closed – instead an employee filled little ready-to-buy paper sacks with rapid flicks of a long-handled spoon. The whole establishment felt worn and a little scruffy.

My head pounding, I could have done without the shop's tedious routine for ordering. But in Egypt it is no good asking one person to do what three people might do more laboriously. Each morning I paid a man sitting behind a till, who gave me a receipt. I duly passed it on to another man working the espresso machine. I got another receipt for a croissant, which I handed to yet another employee standing behind a glass warming-case.

This morning the procedure was even slower than usual, and I passed an extra Egyptian pound over the counter. Instead of the bright smile the tip usually produced, the espresso-man virtually ignored me and kept on glancing out the shop's door and windows. Something was up at the Brazilian Coffee Stores.

I looked more carefully around the room. The place was fuller than usual, and there were faces I hadn't seen before. Outside, too, things were not entirely normal. At an hour when the streets were generally quiet, pedestrians were gathering. Even the poorest of them seemed to have dressed in fresh, clean clothing.

'Is this a special day today?' I asked the man standing beside me. He was bearded, and soberly dressed in a dark jacket and a shirt buttoned to the collar. In the middle of his forehead he had that puckered, faintly purplish weal of flesh one sometimes sees in fervent Muslims. It comes with years of prayer, the result of head-to-floor prostrations five times a day.

'Very special, a very happy time,' he said smiling, a man in cheerful, expectant mood. 'This is the last day of Id al-Kabir, one of our most important holy celebrations.' He didn't usually drink coffee, he told me. He lived just up the street – he had come to the Coffee Stores this morning for the conclusion of the festivities.

Id al-Kabir, no one could have escaped noticing, had been on-going in Alexandria for some time. Schools and government offices were closed. In the last few days Alexandria's weather-bound fishermen had been making extra money rowing parties of exuberant teenagers around the harbour in leaky rowboats. The drivers of horse-drawn carriages had been doing a brisk family business along the Corniche. In city streets wandering bands of young men banged away at drums and cymbals until late at night. At Petros Mamdouh had had his patience tested to the limit by gangs of naughty ten-year-olds who would order soft drinks and then rush away giggling when they arrived. Far from solemn, Id al-Kabir seemed as lively and antic as a religious celebration could get. Today, evidently, the whole thing was coming to a culmination.

Exactly what was planned, though, I couldn't find out. 'Let it be a surprise,' the bearded man would only say when I pressed him. 'We must wait.'

So I waited. The coffee finally arrived. It helped; the fog in my head gradually cleared. As I waited I gazed around, imagining how different this shop must have been in 1929. Like my church-tour, the place made me wonder – not about Alexandria's ancient history, but about its recent past. The minutes ticked by and the little crowd outside the door continued to swell. I fell to daydreaming.

It is at this point, perhaps as good a place as any, that I must admit a certain over-indulgence. Having a soft spot for the past, ancient or modern, I do tend to get caught up in it. It's not always the best way to proceed – a too-large regard for history can often get in the way of the senses, of spontaneous emotional responses to immediate physical surroundings. And those things, surely, are among the most valuable of all traveller's tools when it comes to looking for the spirit of a place.

But on trips like this I couldn't help myself. Despite the fact that history is sometimes tiresome and its place in lighter accounts of travel debatable, I simply couldn't keep my nose out of it. For in the Middle East there is no debate about it at all. In this part of the world the past is the beginning and the end of everything – it lies at the heart of its politics, its economies, its popular culture, its passions and prejudices, its religions and wars and ongoing injustices.

And so when I came upon a big chunk of history, as I did now, I didn't feel I had much of an option. To me, obscure and run-down coffee shops were just as interesting as lighthouses that no longer existed. I could always walk around the past, of course, pretending it didn't exist, and simply keep on going. But the risk was that I mightn't be able to make head or tail of anything that followed. Or I could confront history and try to take it on – the other risk being, of course, that history can swallow you up. On these shores once you begin turning over the stones of the past there's no end to it. In travel you can only hope that once you start asking questions, start trying to make some sense of a complex and unfamiliar past, you will be granted a little indulgence.

So I continued daydreaming. What kind of people in this rag-tag metropolis, I wondered as I sipped my coffee, had once had the sophistication to mull over a choice of extra-prime or French roast? I glanced at the date over the door again. In the years following the stock-market crash the price of raw materials had plummeted and markets vanished. Coffee reserves became so unsaleable they were used as fuel to fire the boilers of Brazilian ships. Global cotton markets were hit almost as hard. Yet as a lavish temple to consumer luxury the Brazilian Coffee Stores had survived and even prospered.

So, too, had the class of affluent European Alexandrians who patronised it. Their lives had been extraordinarily privileged – Alexandria, for a few generations at least, had been protected from the worst of the world's shocks and surprises. And yet Suez, a later and lesser world crisis, had obliterated that privilege entirely, destroying and scattering the city's international population forever. What kind of colonial society was it that could be so insulated and at the same time so vulnerable?

In fact Alexandria was never a true colonial city at all. If Great Britain had taken a controlling hand in Egyptian affairs at the end of the 1800s, its power had centred on Cairo. Alexandria was something entirely different. Detached from politics, a port dedicated to shipping, international commerce and profit, it didn't even see itself as a genuinely Egyptian city. Neither, on the other hand, did it hold to European ideas of nationality. Nationalism of any kind ran counter to its interests, and in a port-city marked above all by endless human variety, notions of identity and belonging were uncertain from the beginning.

Rather than a colonial enterprise in Egypt, Alexandria, I was coming to see, could be better viewed as a vessel conveniently anchored some distance off the Mediterranean coast. A lifeboat for people from all around the eastern edges of the sea, the city became a place to ride out a major historical storm that convulsed the entire region. The collapse of the Ottoman Empire was a long, agonised and often violent affair. But it brought rebirth to Alexandria and, more than two thousand years after its first flowering, a second golden age.

Few places rose and fell as suddenly. You only had to go back to the early 1800s and the rule of Mohammed Ali, the turbaned, bronze equestrian I'd come across on the city's central square, to see the beginning of the process.

Like the inhabitants of the city he recreated, Mohammed Ali, reformer and founder of modern Egypt, was a man of complex origins. And like them he was a product of the troubled Ottoman Empire. Born in the port of Kavala – now in northern Greece, then a place firmly inside Istanbul's imperial orbit – he was a Macedonian of Albanian ethnic origin. He was wily and acquisitive, and graduated rapidly from simple tax collector, to wealthy merchant, to ambitious mercenary leader. In the aftermath of the struggle between Britain and Revolutionary France for control over Egypt – neither came out a winner at this point – he managed to proclaim himself the country's Viceroy.

In theory Egypt, like all the territories of the broad Ottoman Empire, remained under the control of the Sultan. In practice Mohammed Ali ruled it as a virtually independent state, and had big plans for it. As a military man he had seen the kind of influence naval powers like Britain could wield in the world, and his dream was to remake Egypt into a modern Mediterranean sea power. It was Mohammed Ali who woke Alexandria from its long sleep.

Almost overnight he transformed it from the fly-blown fishing village it had become into an international city. He knew that maritime power could not be achieved without expertise, investment and commercial exchange, so he threw Alexandria's doors wide open to the world. The 'Capitulations', a system of treaties offering tax exemptions and other commercial advantages to foreigners, meant there was no lack of takers – as the city's prosperity increased decade after decade the migrants kept on coming. In the 1820s Alexandria had 13,000 inhabitants; less than twenty years later, 100,000; before the turn of the century, a third of a million.

Early on Alexandria became a model, modern city. Originally conceived as a naval base, its harbour was refurbished to become a thriving commercial enterprise. Long before they arrived elsewhere on the African continent, canals and water mains were dug, sewer and gas lines installed, train and tram tracks laid. Alexandria was also a place where a leisure culture found an easy and early blooming. Well before 1900 there were gardens, squares, theatres, operas, racetracks, clubs and grand hotels. In southern Europe only Genoa and Marseilles had busier, bigger ports. The streets that lay outside the Brazilian Coffee Stores might not look so elegant today, but by 1929 the city's 150,000 Europeans – a quarter of its population – had turned Alexandria into one of the most sophisticated places on the shores of the Mediterranean.

Once again I looked around the Brazilian Coffee Stores. From time to time other tourists showed up here, but on this particular morning, even with the place crowded and continuing to fill, I was the only non-Muslim.

It had been different in Alexandria's heyday. From the beginning the modern city had been multicultural. Across a once-harmonious, now fast-unravelling Ottoman Empire there were all sorts of people anxious to escape growing tensions. Religious minorities were among the first populations welcomed by Mohammed Ali. Orthodox Greeks, later to form the largest foreign group in the city, arrived fleeing violent nationalist rebellion at home. But the Mediterranean's complex history had thrown up countless far-flung communities – from the Venetian Jews of Corfu to the Monophysite Armenians of Anatolia there were scores of lesser religious and ethnic minorities only too happy to find a safe haven in Alexandria. Thus all the churches I had discovered the day before. In an unpredictable world Alexandria had been a raft of prosperity floating buoyantly on the Mediterranean waves.

It was as I was gazing out the Coffee Stores' big picture window, trying to imagine a vibrant, mixed community against the backdrop of the city's now threadbare décor, that I noticed the cattle. None too enthusiastic, a pair of large black cows were being led down the sidewalk. Every time they came to a stop they were hauled onward by two men holding ropes running through their noses. Followed by a small horde of dancing children, they were finally tied up outside the Brazilian Coffee Stores. They stood there watching traffic flying by with large, frightened eyes.

Nobody seemed to find the tethering of two cows to a downtown lamppost out of place. A small but expanding lake of runny green cow dung on the sidewalk was discreetly ignored. Finally I couldn't hold back any longer. 'What's it all about?' I asked the bearded man at the counter beside me.

A smile lit up his face. 'Patience! Soon you shall see,' he said mysteriously, as if by revealing all he might spoil the excitement slowly building around us. 'It is a tradition of the Muslims. It is also, I think, a tradition of Jews and Christians, too. It is,' he said, looking for the word, 'a cosmopolitan tradition. But you will see, it will not be long now.'

I tried to recall a worldwide religious custom that involved cows and lampposts, but couldn't. But the word 'cosmopolitan' brought me back to the wealthy, multicultural Alexandria of the past. I ordered another coffee and croissant and continued to wait.

In modern parlance it is a fuzzy term – applied to New York or London 'cosmopolitan' these days generally means no more than urbane, varied and sophisticated. But in Alexandria the concept had precise significance, one upon which the city's well-being depended. It was its special brand of cosmopolitan life, in fact, that defined the city's entire existence.

For if Mohammed Ali created a metropolis that was part of a modern European economy, he built it on the traditional structures of a society that rejected Europe's national divisions. It was based instead on an old multicultural institution, the Ottoman *millet*.

Over centuries of conquest this was a system which had grouped the empire's citizens not by nation-state – a category which in the Ottoman scheme of things didn't exist – but by community. At first it had been a method of distinguishing Muslims from nonbelievers for tax purposes. Permitted to practice their faith, Christians had to pay for the privilege. But as the empire expanded and became more complex the *millet* also became a way of promoting supranationalism – each subject belonged not to a political entity but to a religious community that transcended old borders. A Bulgar, for example, was not above all Bulgarian, but a Bulgarian Jew, Muslim or Christian, and part of a larger religious community. The Sultan protected the rights and traditions of these communities, and in return the religious leaders of each group guaranteed the loyalty of their followers. Thus all subjects were Ottoman subjects, and encouraged to the service of a multicultural empire under a single authority.

This was the pluralistic outlook brought to Alexandria from the shores of a sea still Ottoman in name but increasingly influenced by the West. The result was a multiplicity of groups, each with its own traditions and internal organisations, each responsible for the administration of its own affairs. At the top of Alexandrian society stood a powerful financial elite – the heads of family-owned export houses – in which a half-dozen races rubbed along together. It was this clique, closely allied through personal business relations, that assured the bonding and social negotiation necessary for peaceful co-existence in the city.

But Alexandria was no new-world melting pot in which ethnicity slowly dissolved as one generation replaced another. Its communities were under no obligation to adapt to some vague set of universal social values. Instead the city evolved a society that at the same time was both global and local in makeup. If it was liberal and modern in its international economic outlook, it remained firmly attached to its different traditions and habits. 'Five races, five languages, a dozen creeds', Lawrence Durrell had written of the city's varied mix. Anyone could become an Alexandrian, but no one fell outside membership of its vibrant and varied communities. Even the Levantines, that commercial subculture of western Europeans who had long ago installed themselves in eastern ports, looked for identity not to their countries of origin, but to each other.

At the same time Alexandrian cosmopolitanism was subject to a kind of curious overlapping that could lead to the possession of several identities at one time. A family from Thessalonica installed in Alexandria for generations could have a mixed pedigree – they might be Greek, but they could simultaneously be Jewish and Egyptian as well, and all the while hold French passports. A composite make-up like this was not a drawback, but just the opposite. Like card-players with stacked decks, Alexandrians could play whichever suite served them best at a given moment. In the end an Alexandrian was just that, an Alexandrian – a world citizen, a possessor of numerous identities, who belonged above all else to the city. For decade after decade the metropolis was a sort of never-never land, a refuge suspended in time and place, seemingly immune from the changes occurring all around it.

In the end, of course, the system foundered. Ottoman influence in Egypt waned and at last died, as it did all around the eastern Mediterranean. Nationalism took its place. In Syria, Lebanon and Palestine colonial protectorates were drawn up by English and French authorities, then taken over by today's independent national states. Borders were closed, barriers to trade and movement thrown up, and the free exchange on which cosmopolitanism thrived vanished.

But multicultural Alexandria also disappeared for another reason – its cosmopolitanism did not go far enough. A small Egyptian elite did develop at the highest levels of Alexandrian society. The gap between it and the huge mass of ordinary Egyptians, though, only widened. From the 1920s Egyptian nationalism, supported by an emerging middle class in its justified demands for a greater share of the wealth, grew stronger by the year.

And as it did that subtle, identity-juggling legerdemain that was Alexandrian cosmopolitanism became ever more difficult to perform. During the First World War E M Forster had still been able to believe in cosmopolitanism. In the city guidebook he wrote he looked at Alexandria not through the eyes of a Briton in an Arab land; his vision of the modern city was shaped instead by the universal, Hellenistic values of Alexandria's past. But by the Second World War, when Lawrence Durrell pitched up following his escape from Nazi-occupied Greece, the writing was on the wall. In reality the febrile place portrayed in his *Alexandria Quartet* was not so much lush and sensually over-ripe as so brittle as to be close to snapping – this was a fragile society grasping desperately at life in the knowledge of its own clearly foreseen end.

What would old cosmopolitans like Forster or Durrell make of the present scene, I wondered? For at last something was happening outside the Brazilian Coffee Stores. The two men who had led and tended to the cows, stroking them affectionately and patting their heads, were replaced by set of brisk and businesslike men in white cotton smocks. They weren't nearly so affectionate. They hauled one cow away around the corner. First they tied the other cow's rear legs together, then its front legs.

I looked at the man beside me for explanation.

'It is in the Koran, and in the Bible and the Torah, too,' he said. 'Abraham was a holy man who loved God. He loved God so much that he was ready to sacrifice his son Ishmael to him. God was pleased by Abraham's love, but he said that such a big sacrifice wasn't necessary – a little sacrifice would be enough.' He smiled at God's compassion and understanding. 'So Abraham killed a goat instead. This is how on the last day of Id al-Kabir we celebrate God's mercy and Abraham's great love for him.'

The purpose of the exercise had finally sunk in. My second croissant arrived. I ignored it. I wasn't ready for both breakfast and a blood sacrifice.

'But that's not a goat,' I said vapidly to my fellow coffee-drinker as we watched the animal being pushed over onto the sidewalk.

'No,' he agreed. 'It is a cow.'

Now there was a long thin knife in one of the smocked men's hands, and my companion grew voluble. 'It cannot be a goat. A goat is too small to feed all the poor people in this area. Even a cow is too small. Every year the Brazilian Coffee Stores buys not one cow, but two! They are very generous. The cows are for the community. After they are sacrificed the meat will be divided and distributed. It is a feast day for even the poorest family. It is a time of joy for everyone.'

Obviously the cow hadn't been consulted on the joyousness of the occasion. Bible, Koran or Torah, it didn't matter – whenever religion sets out to prove its love there is always a price to pay. The struggling sacrificial victim now had half a dozen men holding it down. When it was finally still its throat was cut. Bright red blood spurted onto the white jackets of the men at its head, then flowed in copious streams over the sidewalk and into the gutter. Twice the beast struggled to its knees, its throat bubbling, before it slipped in its blood and fell over again. Accompanied by goggle-eyed children tightly holding their parents' hands, the crowd was now gathered in a deep circle around the prostrate animal. They were no doubt thinking not only of Abraham's great love for God but also, thanks to the generosity of the Brazilian Coffee Stores, about dinner.

Not only had my appetite gone; my hangover seemed to have returned as well. As one sacrificial creature was dismembered and the sidewalk hosed down in preparation for the next I left the café. I walked back to the hotel thinking about communities and their ceremonies. This was only another kind of social ritual, I told myself, another way of showing community cohesion, and I should be more accepting of religious customs.

But that didn't prevent me from feeling queasy. As social rituals go, coffee, croissants and other small pleasures seemed so much easier. Especially after a night out on Omar Khayyam. It probably served me right. But not even queasiness, though, could stop me wondering about the city's old *millet*-based cosmopolitanism. The world had changed. But was there no use for such arrangements any more?

Ten

It was late February – more than a month had gone by and suddenly I realised I had barely strayed from the centre of Alexandria. Enough, I decided on a warm day that held a hint of coming spring; I would take the train out to Aboukir Bay. I didn't think I'd see any traces of one of Nelson's greatest victories there – most of the French fleet he'd attacked had gone straight to the bottom. But the fish restaurants were supposed to be good.

The train carriage I climbed aboard at the Alexandria station for the one-hour trip had seen some hard riding. The sliding doors were stuck open, some of the windows were broken, and the floor was dusty and littered with sunflower-seed shells and used tickets. But it was mid-morning, too late for the daily commuter crush, and I managed to get a seat before the carriage was invaded by a crowd of noisy schoolboys.

The train swayed out of the station, out of the old European centre of the city, and on into a desperate Alexandrian future. There was nothing especially frightening or horrifying about the dense urban build-up that stretched more than fifteen miles along the coast to Aboukir – it was simply the relentlessness of it all, the unrelieved press of too many people squeezed into too small a space without a margin of comfort or any hope of improvement. As far as most suburban Alexandrians were concerned, this *was* improvement.

The high-rises that climbed into the air on both sides of the track were gimcrack and shoddy. You couldn't tell if they were still being built, had already been completed, or were now in the process of being pulled down. Built on tiny plots of land by get-rich-quick developers, they towered, thin and spindly, up to twenty stories high. Many had no exterior finishing. Revealing thin skeletons of breeze-block and rough red brick, they looked ready to topple at any minute.

They were suburban only in principle – they'd been turned into vertical villages by the rural migrants who inhabited them. Balconies were hung with laundry, with bicycles, with strings of drying onions and garlic. Satellite dishes were the only signs of modernity. In the streets outside the high-rises there were donkeys pulling carts and geese enclosed in sidewalk pens. On the right-of-way beside the track – the one area in this urban wasteland where concrete gave way to soil – cabbages grew in rows. And everywhere there were people, hundreds of thousands to the square mile, the thronged inhabitants of an overstretched world. Every large city on the globe has an apocalyptic vision of its future, but Alexandria's seemed closer than most.

Mile after mile, the train screeched to a halt at succeeding stations. A balloon seller sat down next to me. His place was taken by a Koran reader, then by a tired bureaucrat with a plastic briefcase and different-coloured pens stuck in his shirt pocket. The schoolboys got off. Head-scarved housewives returning from shopping got on. The densely packed city slipped past my window until we reached the end of the line.

Aboukir is part of larger Alexandria today, and if its crescent-shaped beach once housed a simple fishing village it is now fronted by the same gawky high-rises found everywhere else. I was disappointed. The waterfront was strewn with garbage and the beach cafés amounted to little more than rickety tables and faded umbrellas set in dirty sand. Not even the Zephyrion, an old and celebrated Greek fish restaurant sitting over the water, looked terribly appealing. A fresh coat of white paint more or less hid its weeping rust stains and a new sunshade of blue canvas was stretched over its terrace. But beneath it the restaurant's chairs and tables were empty. I watched a wet-suited diver emerge from the waves with a fish, sparkling silver in the sun, impaled on the tip of his spear-gun. Only the sea seemed fresh and clean. Then I headed back to the station.

I had questions and I knew where I might get some answers. In a corner of the Alexandria Library I had noticed a sign with an arrow indicating the 'Alexandria and Mediterranean Research Centre'. I made an appointment and the next morning was sitting in front of its director, Dr. Mohammed Awad.

I was lucky to see him. Mimi, as he was called by everyone in Alexandria, was a whirlwind. A dapper dresser with salt-and-pepper hair, he looked owlish when he gazed at blueprints through the circular lenses of his heavy-framed reading glasses. Without them he looked more like a high-spirited schoolboy with an irresistible urge to stir things up. His face was often creased in a broad, spontaneous smile. He was lively, informal, sociable, and always on the point of leaving for somewhere else – he seemed forever to be giving urgent, last-minute instructions to various assistants and secretaries as he swept off to his next appointment across town. For all that he never turned down an opportunity to engage with anyone. He was on half the committees in town, and locked in mortal combat with the other half. When it came to his passion, Alexandria, Mimi Awad was a man of infinitely expanding energy.

The city and its resurrection was the constant leitmotif of all his conversation. He was an architect by profession, head of one of the city's most successful architectural firms. He owned a construction company, and frequently built the houses he designed. He owned workshops, and had local artisans manufacture the metal, glass and wooden elements that went into his houses. He taught a course on the aesthetics of architecture at the city's university. Much of his energy at the research centre, too, went into Alexandrian architecture and its rich history. Yet by the end of our meeting I understood that the city's well-being was for Mimi more than just a professional question. It was an obsession. It wasn't until later that I understood why, but so passionate was he about the fate of the city that I couldn't help feeling his own personal fate depended on it as well.

I described my train trip to Aboukir. Were Alexandria's future prospects, I asked, quite as bad as they looked?

Mimi Awad took the longer view of things. The spectre of urban dysfunction, he told me, hadn't loomed up out of nothing – to see the future you had to look fifty years back into the past, to Nasser's coup and social revolution. With the nationalisation of the Suez Canal and European attempts to wrest it back, Alexandria had become a focus of resentment. The banishment of its foreign communities drained the city's lifeblood. Private capital had fled. Municipal institutions were national-ised, decisions referred to a governor appointed from Cairo. Alexandrian businesses had relocated to the capital. Their city emasculated, many Alexandrian intellectuals, too, had left. Such moves hadn't slowed the influx of migrants to the city, but they had put a brake on most innovative attempts to cope with it.

'There is a logic here that argues for the destruction of the old and the growth of the new,' Mimi sighed. 'It has become almost uncontrollable.'

For Nasser's revolution affected not just populations, but the places where they'd lived. Confiscated by the state, buildings owned by foreign-ers and Egypt's former elite became schools and administrative centres. Under-financed, barely maintained, they quickly became run down. Old buildings kept on in private hands had suffered even more. So low were rents fixed by the government that their owners' running-costs became greater than their income – any renovations by proprietors meant they were subsidising their tenants. For some owners the solution was simple. They would deliberately neglect or even abuse their buildings until, once they were beyond all possibility of repair, state permission was granted for their sale to property developers.

The result was the inexorable disappearance of Alexandria's past. The Italian villa I'd seen near the railway station was just one example – much of 19th and 20th-century Alexandria was slowly crumbling to pieces. Alarmed at the extent of the decline, Mimi had founded a conservation body ten years before – the Alexandria Preservation Trust had now listed more than 1,500 buildings of outstanding architectural value as being at risk.

Of course there was an alternative, said Mimi – even now there was still time to rescue a disintegrating past. 'Alexandria could be turned back into the sophisticated city it once was. But change has to come at the base – prestige projects alone are not enough.

'Nothing exists in isolation. How can the new Library achieve its aims unless the city around it is revived and functioning as it should? Alexandria's problems are political problems. We need long-term vision – we need planning, consultation, management, impact assessment, financial control. We need to get rid of corruption. Right now there is not much incentive for that kind of change.'

Reconverting a shabby and provincial backwater into a world-class city seemed a tall order, but Mimi had no interest in any lesser challenge. He was barely into his stride when an anxious secretary reminded him he was already forty minutes late for his next meeting. But Mimi wasn't finished. He'd been surprised to discover I had been out to Aboukir the day before; it was the very place he was joining a dinner party that evening. Why didn't I come along? he asked.

It was dark when I met Mimi at his downtown architectural office. But not so dark that as we drove along the Corniche towards Aboukir he didn't keep his gaze roving over the details of passing buildings. These were hardly the poor quarters backing onto the railway line running some distance inland; a good deal of Gulf investment capital had gone into the new residential areas stretching along these prime waterfront locations. In Mimi's eyes, nonetheless, most were abominations.

'We have a wonderful architecture that is rooted in traditional Egyptian culture,' he told me, 'We could use a vernacular style and local materials. But when we build today we think what's best is what's foreign. We've seen it all on television and we don't care where it comes from. We take a bit of everything. We end up with kitsch, a mish-mash of California ranch-bungalow grafted to Côte d'Azur villa with a few Greek columns thrown in for free. It is truly awful.'

The conversation lightened when we parked outside the Zephyrion. With the surrounding shambles now invisible in the night, with the sound of the waves on the beach echoing the rise and fall of lively conversation at the tables, it seemed a different place. And even a different time. For

Mimi Awad's dining companions were not everyday city residents – they came from that small and shrinking band, the last of the cosmopolitans of Alexandria.

They sat at a long table, ten or twelve individuals, all of whom spoke English, French and Arabic equally well – they would switch from one language to another without hesitation, sometimes in midsentence. I sat between Ibrahim, a Coptic Christian professor of law, and Josette, a Gallicised Lebanese-Alexandrian just returned from a semester's lecturing in Montreal. Opposite was Omar, a Muslim antique dealer. Further down the table were Greco-Alexandrians, Franco-Alexandrians, and foreign-dwelling Alexandrians who, never having settled happily into exile, spent their lives in a limbo of travel between their adopted cities and home.

They all ate with the pleasure and extravagance of true Mediterraneans. Waiters delivered an endless stream of food and drink to the table. There were plates of hummus and baba ganuj; bowls of tahini and different kinds of dips and salads; dishes of fried calamari and giant red prawns the size of your finger; platters of grilled dorado, fillets of sole, servings of small, bright red rouget. Toasts were made over glasses of raki, and the bottles of cold beer kept on coming. No sooner was a space on the table made by the removal of an empty dish than it was filled again by the arrival of a full one.

The conversation never stopped and the pleasure of the diners grew as the meal progressed. The air became warm and heavy in the room, the faces flushed. Was this what Durrell's Alexandria, that comfortable, self-satisfied mercantile community, was like, I wondered? A waiter opened a window; fresh air wafted in, and over the aromas of food I smelled the sea nearby. It was cool and sensual. For a moment I could imagine myself settling down to the insouciant, bourgeois life of a Levantine *commerçant*. Sea and sun, friends and family, money – all in all, it might have been a secure and happy life. But in the end, of course, it wasn't. If these friends were gathered here now it was in commiseration, their present temporarily blotted out by a willed return to the past.

Mimi had led the conversation all evening, and towards eleven o'clock proposed we all drive off to his favourite ice-cream shop for dessert. No sooner had everyone agreed than he and Paul, the friend who was also his doctor, both pulled out hypodermic syringes. Together, with much cheering and applause from the table, they both plunged the needles through their shirt-fronts and into their stomachs.

Mimi caught my horrified look. 'We're not drug addicts, you know,' he said with a big shrug and a grin. 'We're diabetics. We always do this before we go for ice-cream. Then we don't have to worry so much. I like to order double vanilla.'

It was done lightly, but there was something else in their bravado as well. When you are a certain kind of Alexandrian you are living on borrowed time anyway; when confronting fate in such a case it can do no harm to put your thumb to the end of your nose and gently waggle your fingers at it.

Our little convoy of four or five cars made its way back towards town along still busy streets, and parked near some brightly lit take-out shops. The area was changing fast, said Mimi – half a dozen expensive apartment buildings had popped up across the road. But it was only after he was standing by the cars with his friends, ice cream in hand, that he noticed a new sculpture on the roundabout in front of the apartment complex.

As civic sculpture goes it was an odd object. Some of its parts were identifiable but the meaning of the whole was a mystery. A sort of amphora, eight or ten feet high and composed of garishly coloured mosaics, it sat on a concrete base covered with hieroglyphics. Surmounting it was an illuminated globe, which may or may not have represented the world.

Mimi was appalled. 'What is it?' he asked his friends. 'Do you know what it's supposed to be?' There was unfeigned despair in his voice. Whatever it was, it was awkward, tasteless and supremely ugly. Nobody had any answers. His ice cream still in his hand but forgotten, Mimi asked the same question to strangers lined up at the ice cream counter. 'What is it? Have you any idea at all what it is?'

There were no suggestions there, either. Mimi ran across three lanes of honking traffic to the roundabout, looking up at the structure as he slowly circled it. He even asked the night-shift worker sweeping the street there the same question: What is it? I could see the overalled man shaking his head and looking at Mimi as if he were slightly demented.

Mimi returned to his car shaking his own head.

'Of course nobody knows what that ... that *thing* is,' he said in an anguished tone. 'Not even its maker does.'

However garish it was, I had never before seen anyone quite as upset over a piece of street-décor. But for Mimi Awad it was something else. He knew perfectly well what it was. It was one of the gaudier signposts on the road to Alexandria's dissolution.

Eleven

Moroccans and Spaniards, Italians and Tunisians, Greeks and Egyptians – all have the same outlook on the Mediterranean. In one way, though, they take a very different view of it. If you are facing the Mediterranean on the European side of the sea, you have a southern exposure – you get the sun all day long. But if you sit facing the Mediterranean on the African coast you are facing north. This may not sound too terribly disturbing, and generally it isn't, unless you spend the winter months in an unheated building facing the seafront. Not a single warming ray of sunshine ever entered my room at the Union Hotel, and I was always cold.

The view made it worthwhile. But sometime toward the end of February the Mediterranean, in one of its last, capricious winter moods, decided to send a great storm down on the city. The temperature dropped, black clouds came rolling southwards over the horizon, and it rained for three days. It was no ordinary rain, for it was carried on high, violent winds. It didn't so much fall as fly in horizontally from the sea. The Union Hotel took it full in the face.

The wind and rain not only moaned about my balcony; it howled and whistled its way right into the room, for the sliding glass doors did not meet evenly. The ceiling's acoustic tiles didn't like it – they thumped all night long as the wind lifted them up and banged them down. The floor liked it even less. By the end of the third day so much rain had invaded the room that the carpet was soaked through.

A strange, sour smell, an organic odour of rot and fermented fibre, took hold of the room; it continued to grow in strength and potency even after the storm had subsided. Eventually the air in the room grew unbreathable. It gave me some regret, but I knew the time had come to abandon the Union Hotel.

I described the flood in my room to Mimi Awad, for I had grown into the habit of dropping by his office towards the end of the day. He solved my problem immediately. He had a large house out in Rushdi, a suburb some three or four miles away, he told me, and even in the evening was rarely at home. I was welcome to move over there.

And so began another cosmopolitan phase in Alexandria – my own. It lasted only a couple of weeks, but it changed my view of the city. Constantly lively and entertaining, it was at the same time steeped in a kind of twilight melancholy. It is a mood that takes me still when I think of Alexandria.

Mimi was right. He was so busy that his house felt barely lived in. It was well furnished and decorated. It was vigorously cleaned and dusted every day. Its tall vases of fresh-cut flowers were regularly replaced. But still the place felt uncared for. On exhibition in a gallery in the Library was part of Mimi's treasure of photos of old Alexandria, a personal collection so vast and valuable the Smithsonian Institute had offered to buy it and been refused. But in his house in Rushdi there were a dozen silver portrait-frames, the kind used for family photos, scatted about on shelves and tables – only three had any photos in them at all. The others were empty. Mimi seemed to have given so much of himself to the rest of city there wasn't much left for his own small piece of it.

The real residents of the house were Naguib and Max. Naguib was Mimi's major-domo, a tall, elegant Egyptian who had previously practised his profession in Athens and Beirut. He was conscientious, dedicated and thorough. But the boss of the house was Max. Max was a Doberman Pinscher, a sleek and powerful beast with plenty of male attitude. Given Mimi's near-total absence in the house, it was on Max that Naguib lavished all his attention. Max had biscuits and shortbread for breakfast, half a chicken with rice for lunch, and fruitcake at tea. If there was a bitch in heat anywhere in the quarter, Naguib made sure that she and Max got more than friendly in the course of their afternoon walk. Naguib called Max 'Habibi'. He was thoroughly gaga about the dog.

He often grew quite irritated, on the other hand, with Mimi. I can't say that from his point of view I blamed him. Mimi kept the oddest of hours. He generally got up at ten o'clock, had lunch at six in the evening, finished work four or five hours later, and only then began socialising. He got to bed by three or four o'clock in the morning. But that could change at any time according to Mimi's frenzied work-rounds. Naguib would end up giving Mimi's carefully cooked lunch to Max day after day when he failed to show up, then might be called upon to prepare dinner for half a dozen guests at midnight. Mimi drove Naguib half mad.

And what was it all for, this driven, slightly manic life? It was for Alexandria. Sometimes I accompanied Mimi as he shuttled between Library, university, office and building site. It was nothing for him to jump out of his car in the middle of daytime traffic to question a construction crew on its stylistically doubtful restoration of an Ottoman mosque. It was nothing for him, either, to receive an urgent call in the middle of the night and disappear, video camera in hand. He would return hours later, having gathered evidence of illegal building excavation conducted under the cover of darkness to get around an archaeological conservation order.

But the most curious of all times were the cocktails, dinner parties and social soirées where the remnants of old Alexandrian society met. There was some rendezvous or other almost every night, and I usually tagged along with Mimi.

I spent evenings in gloomy palazzi so vast and draughty their owners confined themselves to a couple of heated rooms. I met trembling, quavery-voiced men who took great pleasure in recounting the sexual peccadilloes of their youth. I chatted with fragile, china-doll-like women, papery-skinned and heavily made up, who still behaved like young coquettes. It was like rooting around in the leftovers of *The Alexandria Quartet*, stirring up the settled dregs of once lavish and decadent lives. But before long I started feeling like a cosmopolite myself. What held true in the past holds true today – anyone can become an Alexandrian.

One evening we were invited to dine with a Levantine friend of Mimi's in the old centre of town. Mimi was silent as we drove there – he'd just learned of the death of one of the members of the aged and dwindling Greek community. Passing the once great villas that lined either side of the rue Fouad, I asked him if he really thought that his was the last generation of multicultural Mediterraneans to inhabit the city.

For the longer one spends in Alexandria, the more one feels that what lies at the heart of the city's deepest nature is regret. So inconsolable were Anthony and Cleopatra on being deprived of the Alexandria they loved that they killed themselves. Not much had changed since – twenty centuries later the Greek Alexandrian poet C P Cavafy was still celebrating the sense of divestment and loss that inhabits the city's soul. No matter what the age, one suspects, all Alexandrians gaze behind themselves in longing.

But Mimi had little doubt – this was the end of it.

'How can it be otherwise?' he asked. 'One by one we are dying out. We are the last, and it is a role we must accept. Alexandria will change again and again, as it always has. But soon the last generation of old cosmopolitans will be gone.'

Twenty guests turned up that evening in an old apartment richly furnished with the ornate taste of an earlier age – Persian carpets, heavy damask hangings, ormolu clocks and the dark, solid furniture of the French bourgeoisie. The party was the same mixed racial salad I'd encountered at the Zephyrion, but some of the guests were new to me. To my left at the table sat Daoud, who claimed a warrior's mixture of Bedouin, Chechen and Scots blood; to my right sat Princess Lucie, a Syrian Christian so nicknamed because in her distant youth her father been granted a title of noblesse by the Pope.

There were drinks first, then a candle-lit dinner officiated by servants in white jackets. The curried chicken was good, but what impressed me most at the table was the conversation – there was barely a word that didn't have to do with the much-regretted city. It didn't matter if the event discussed was fifty or five hundred years old – as far as these Alexandrians were concerned it was as vital, as necessary to their continued existence, as if it had happened the day before. Over the course of dinner we discussed the state's disposal of various pieces of expatriate property; episcopal relations between Alexandria and Byzantium in the early Christian era; the fate of the statue of the Khedive Isma'il long ago removed from a public square; the fate of Alexandrians who had equally long ago removed themselves to Athens; school days at Victoria College, the elite Anglo-Alexandrian institution that Mimi and half the men in the room had attended; Venetian Renaissance trade routes in the eastern Mediterranean; and the precise etymology of '*Aegyptogus*', that ancient word meaning Greek born in Egypt.

It seemed to me that all these subjects must have been debated before. Not even the question, 'Is one Greek, Egyptian or Alexandrian?' – surely discussed around a thousand tables in the past – discouraged the enthusiastic flow of words. The inevitable consensus, of course, was that one was, above all, Alexandrian. I could only come to the conclusion that the entire proceedings were nine-tenths ritual – if these Alexandrians lived their city and its past this feverishly, it was because without it they were nothing. Their allegiance was a kind of disease deep in their bones, inescapable and fatal. This talk of old Alexandria was not a sign of vitality, but a last rally, the flaring of a guttered candle before its final extinction.

It was late when we broke up. But even as the party walked back to parked cars the old houses on either side of deserted streets continued to evoke memory. Outside one dark and crumbling place we stopped for a full ten minutes to argue vociferously over which branch of which old family it had once belonged to.

For me it was all too much emotion over something that had happened all too long ago. Despite the myth, I remarked to Mimi on our drive home, I sometimes found it hard to imagine that Alexandria had been so very different from other international cities.

Shanghai and Tangier came to mind – they hadn't been shaped by love or a warm commitment to community, I said. They'd been shaped by an ardent desire to make money.

Mimi agreed. 'Where is any city shaped by love?' he asked. But then, perhaps still moved by the evening's stories, he went on to tell me another story – his own.

Mimi was half Greek, half Egyptian. Both his grandmothers had come from Greece, and both had met and married Egyptians in Alexandria. He'd been particularly close to his paternal grandmother, a woman of uncommon and resolute character. It was she who looked out from the silver-framed photos in the house in Rushdi.

She had been born on the island of Limnos, the daughter of prosperous farmers who'd had no need at all to emigrate. But when she was nine the family was visited by her uncle, who owned a café in Alexandria. He regaled her with stories and romances of the city; she was so impressed she decided it was the only place she wanted to live. A precocious and strong-willed child, her mind was so set that she prevailed against her parents' opposition. It was finally agreed she would spend two years in Alexandria with her uncle and aunt, who had no children of their own.

The twenty-four months had almost passed when her uncle drowned in a swimming accident. But despite the tragedy Mimi's grandmother sent news that she refused to come home. Regardless of her parents' distress, she decided to stay on with her widowed aunt, convinced more than ever she belonged to Alexandria. She was eleven years old.

Four years later she met a young Egyptian labourer working for a builder at her aunt's house and fell in love. Her aunt was aghast. The Greek priest at her church was aghast, too. Even the young man's family was aghast. Alexandria might have been a sophisticated place, but it was not a place where Greek Orthodox Christian girls married penniless Egyptian Muslim labourers. But nothing, not even threats of excommunication, would dissuade her – the couple were married and the young woman did not set foot inside a church for another twenty-five years.

'My grandfather was hard-working as well as handsome, but it was my grandmother who had the determination,' Mimi smiled as we drove beside dark water on a near-empty Corniche. 'They were very poor at first and she had just one dress. She would wash it at night and expect it to be dry by the morning. When it wasn't she'd wear it anyway. She caught pneumonia several times. But she never gave up – it was she who pushed my grandfather to set up his own construction business. It took decades, but he was successful. By the 1920s and '30s he was attracting wealthy clients and big projects – some of Alexandria's later European buildings were built by my grandfather.'

So who said that Alexandria was solely a city of commerce and naked greed? I remained quiet for the last couple of miles home. Not only did Mimi's story refute the very notion; it also suggested something about the man himself. For the first time I began to understand why Mimi persisted in struggling so hard against such odds. No past could be more cosmopolitan than his. In attempting to save cosmopolitan Alexandria he was, of course, attempting to save himself too.

Twelve

Suddenly it was March and spring had come to the eastern Mediterranean. The air grew balmier, buds opened on trees in the city's plushier quarters, and while the rain still came and went there was none of winter's sting left in it. It was time, I knew, to be moving on. Good travelling weather had arrived and the way ahead was long.

But there was one short trip I wanted to make before I left Alexandria. Apart from the half-hour we'd sat on a café terrace on the Corniche, Mamdouh and I had never spent any time outside Petros. A short excursion was the excuse he needed not to go on his detested rounds of restaurant inspection – he would phone in sick, he said, and we could spend the day together.

I'd long had a visit in mind – the town of Rashid, a forty-minute bus-ride away. Once I'd stood by the White Nile at Lake Victoria, close to its source, and imagined the river's 4,000-mile trip to the sea. But Rashid was not simply the point where the Nile met the Mediterranean. Known as Rosetta in earlier times, it was also the place where French soldiers discovered a basalt slab inscribed with the same text in Greek, demotic Egyptian and hieroglyphics – in the hands of the archaeologist Champollion the Rosetta Stone became the key that opened a thousand secrets written on the walls of Pharaonic tombs. Once an Ottoman stronghold, Egyptian tourist literature also touted the town as a treasure-trove of 18th-century merchant-trader's mansions.

The trip to Rashid was pleasant enough. We sat chatting to other passengers as our minibus ran eastwards along a flat, sandy coast through sugar-cane fields and groves of date palm. I was feeling good and Mamdouh was delighted with a rare change of scenery – he'd been to Rashid just once on a school outing thirty years before, and barely remembered it. We were both looking forward to the good fish lunch we had promised ourselves there.

But Rashid was a letdown from the moment the bus halted on the edge of town. Had I been living the big-city life too long? The marketplace we got down in was poor, its aisles muddy and unpaved, its rickety fish stalls smelly and swarming with flies. Mean little houses, not much more than cubes of concrete with metal doors and shutters, lined the narrow lanes that led into town. Soon the streets would open up, I thought, and the houses become more imposing. But they didn't; the town centre was as dull and monotonous as its periphery.

Even the Nile was a letdown. It ran by the town, broad and green, and with the big, bright seagoing fishing boats that were moored to its sides it might have been attractive. But the closer one got the less attractive it became – so much garbage had been dumped in and along the river that in some places its banks were made of refuse many feet thick. There were a few scurfy-looking garden cafès amidst the mess, but of fish restaurants not a sign. Rashid was a hole.

On a square not far from the river we found the city's museum. Large iron cannons lay flat in the mud outside locked gates, and the place seemed to have been closed for some time. But the policeman standing outside didn't like Mamdouh asking questions about it – he had a bossy, overbearing face and a small-town cop's suspicion of strangers. He liked it even less when he discovered I was with Mamdouh. European tourists had to be with official guides, he said. In no time there were three policemen and a crowd of bystanders surrounding us, and Mamdouh was answering a battery of questions.

It was all taken down in little black books, and I could see that if Mamdouh was angry with the stupidity of this behaviour he was even more afraid of it. Bored, petty and vindictive it may be, but the power of local Egyptian officialdom is absolute. 'They are making me feel like a criminal,' Mamdouh said hotly. It was only after much suitably servile explanation that we were finally let go. But not let alone; a police department flunky in a stained and threadbare suit was dispatched to accompany us.

Perhaps he was too low down the pole to be anything but self-abasing himself; he was inoffensive enough, and showed us around from one Ottoman 'mansion' to another. Empty shells of buildings, they were few and scattered widely about town, and only mildly interesting. After his recent humiliation Mamdouh was even less fascinated than I was.

Only at an old mill-house did he come to life. Each of these places was locked and in the charge of a young female guide from the neighbourhood – headscarfed and earnest, they were summoned in turn and duly gave a short tour in almost unintelligible English. In recent months Mamdouh, approaching forty, had been thinking it was time to find a wife and settle down to married life – even if he hadn't had a lot of contact with women he'd had them much on his mind. Now he literally started back in surprise as he followed the mill-house guide up a steep flight of stairs. I saw the reason for his consternation when we arrived at the first floor. A short, stocky woman in a calf-length skirt, her unshaven legs were covered in thick, spiky black hairs. It was too much for fastidious Mamdouh – in Egyptian society even vaguely civilised women pluck their bodies hairless. '*Peasants!*' he hissed to me, shaking his head. 'These people are *peasants.*'

The last straw came when we took a horse carriage out of town to the old stone fort that guards the river's entrance. This was where the Rosetta Stone had been unearthed. From high on battlements successively occupied over the centuries by Byzantine, Mameluke, Arab and French soldiers I could look downstream and see a line of surf breaking over a sandbank at Nile's mouth. Mamdouh, however, had eyes only for the plain-clothed policeman waiting for him on the ground below.

This was more serious than the nosiness of mere city police. The man flashed some sort of internal state security ID card at us. Did we know, he asked Mamdouh, that it was illegal for an unauthorised Egyptian to conduct a foreigner around a strategic military site on a national frontier? It was all a show of bombast and self-importance, of course, but the man called in Mamdouh's details on his walkie-talkie and appeared to be ready to haul him in. It was only after I spent a quarter of a hour with the man protesting my good faith – and willingness to part with a bribe – that he agreed to let us go.

Mamdouh was spitting angry as we rode in a carriage back to town. 'Thieves! Liars! Ignorant, dirty people!' he muttered over the clopping of the horse's hooves on the tarmac road. I had never seen Mamdouh even vaguely upset, but his pride as a host had been shattered. He was dishonoured by Rashid and its people.

He calmed down over a glass of tea as we sat waiting for the minibus home. I tried to make a joke of it all. I asked him if, given possession of an Ottoman merchant's fine house and business, he would condescend to live in Rashid.

'Never!' he said. 'I could never live anywhere but Alexandria. When the wind blows there it smells good. When it blows here it stinks. The worst thing is the people. Just look at them. They are foolish – there is nothing in their faces. All they think about is food and money. Let us go home.'

In the bus on the way back Mamdouh was silent and I was left alone with my thoughts. Alexandria may have become a backwater abandoned by its sophisticates. But here, I reflected, was a traditional Muslim with a state-school education, a lousy job and no prospects for the future. And still the city had given him a certain kind of attitude. Mamdouh, with no cosmopolitan background, was a cosmopolitan nonetheless. At Aboukir I pulled him out of the bus. We spent the rest of the afternoon celebrating our escape from Rashid with lunch – there was no better place for it – at the Zephyrion.

Thirteen

I had my last dinner at Petros a few nights later, said goodbye to Mamdouh, and went to pack my bags. Mimi Awad, unusually, had nothing scheduled. So full of life and enthusiastic in front of any social evening, in inactivity he suddenly looked tired and worn. I was feeling restless, unsettled by my impending journey. Finally we went out for a last farewell drive through Alexandria.

We headed downtown along rue Fouad, the old Canopic Way. Somewhere close to where the Gate of the Sun, the entrance to old Alexandria, must have stood, Mimi pulled over. On a broad median strip in middle of the road was a ceremonial square and, at one end of it, an equestrian statue. I'd barely noticed it before in the rush and snarl of traffic. Now I asked Mimi what it was.

'It's Alexander,' he replied. 'He's marching in triumph into his new city. Do you see the little winged deity he's holding in his hand? It is Nike, the goddess of victory. I designed the square and its little garden, but the statue almost didn't go up. For me it's a symbol of cosmopolitanism. But for Arab nationalists, Egyptian militarists and Muslim fundamentalists it's a humiliation – for six months there was a ferocious campaign against raising the statue. With time the city becomes more, not less, conservative.'

He pointed to the diminutive Nike again. 'In the end this was her victory, but a narrow one.'

Mimi seemed melancholy and vulnerable to the past this evening. Usually he pursued it; tonight it seemed to be pursuing him. We left the statue of Alexander and, skirting the high walls of Terra Sancta and the foreign cemeteries, continued on down rue Fouad.

'Sursock Palace,' he said under his breath, as much to himself as to me, as we passed a great neo-renaissance pile rising from the shadows by the side of the road.

'The Benaki Villa,' he said a moment later. Then, 'Menasce House', 'The Villa Senegalia', 'The Palazzini Aghion', 'The Mohammed Ali Club'. One after another tall palaces materialised before us, filed solemnly by, and disappeared again into the night. These were old friends. Mimi knew every one of them intimately, their make-up and character, their precarious state of health, their improbable history, their likely fate.

We turned down Sherif Street into the old financial district. Here, too, were great dinosaurs of buildings, their formal classical facades promising a durability that had proved illusory. Once again the soft litany, slow and measured, began. 'The Banco di Roma.' 'The Bank of Athens.' 'Lloyd's Bank.' 'The Anglo-Egyptian Bank.'

We circled the city centre, passed in front of the railway station, then headed towards the old Jewish area of Moharrem Bey. Left and right we turned, Mimi worming his way past crumbling hulks into the heart of the quarter. Finally he pulled up in front of a set of rusty iron gates and cut the engine.

Kicking aside the broken boxes and rotting vegetables of a street market that sheltered there in the daytime, we climbed out of the car. In the dim light of the street lamps we looked at the house that lay beyond the gates. Abandoned for years and covered with grime, it stood in gaunt ruin. A wide flight of broken marble stairs rose to a terraced entranceway. Wild vines grew up through cracked and broken balustrades. Windows were smashed and peeling shutters hung at crazy angles. A sudden gust of wind stirred a noisy little whirl of dead leaves on the terrace and then died.

Once again I was reminded of the ruin I'd run across on my first day in Alexandria. But this one was different. No one would ever live here again. Once the house had given on to a large garden. In its place, just feet away, now rose a new apartment block in the last stages of construction. All that remained was the house's final demolition.

'What is this place?' I asked Mimi.

'The villa Lawrence Durrell lived in,' he answered. He did not have a lot more to say – the house spoke for itself. 'For many years we tried to save it. Now it's too late.' He stood there quietly for a moment, then shrugged.

'Why didn't it work? Why didn't Alexandria work?' was all he could whisper.

He needed air and a breeze to clear old cobwebs from his head. Without another word Mimi got back into the car and we headed for the sea. At the end of Ras el-Tin, the Headland of Figs, we stopped once again beneath the walls of Qait Bey and got out.

The fortress was deserted at this hour and the water beautiful. On this early spring night it looked like liquid black silk. We stood for some time gazing back across the harbour. From here, bathed in lights and reflected in the water, Alexandria looked as great a city as it had ever been.

And was it? Of course it wasn't. Long ago Alexandria had been the most splendid metropolis on the planet. It had been a city where a universalist ideal had made it a hinge of three continents, a place where the intellectual achievements of the entire world had turned on each other. Even half a century ago something of that ideal had lived on in the city's cosmopolitan life, in its plural attitude and multicultural makeup. And now its material vestiges were crumbling. What remained was memory, and even that was fast fading.

I felt the stirring of a breeze. I turned around to the dark sea and took a deep breath of air. Where, I wondered, had this wind last passed over dry land? The plains of Syria? The Dardanelles straits? The islands off Asia Minor? I was ready to leave Alexandria, anxious to see them all. Perhaps somewhere out there in the dark lay other clues to an old Mediterranean globalization, other port-cities where even now the human exchanges that created the liquid continent lingered on.

We got back into the car and Mimi rolled down his window. The breeze was bringing to Alexandria what it had always brought, the promise of the thousand possibilities that lay across the water. It lifted my spirits. It seemed to lift Mimi's spirits, too.

'Do you think it's time for ice cream?' he asked.

Fourteen

I shifted my backside on the cold, hard bench of a Cairo bus station. There were times when I wished I'd done my travelling a century or more before. 1872 would have suited me fine. In that year Monsieur J Frugoli, Principal Agent of the Messageries Maritimes steamline company at Alexandria, posted the following tariffs for its Syrian Service, departing fortnightly on Saturdays:

From Alexandria to:	*1st Class*	*2nd Class*	*3rd Class*
(in French Francs)			
Port Said	45	32	19
Jaffa	78	59	30
Beirut	110	82	40
Tripoli	135	101	50
Latakia	155	117	60
Alexandretta	182	138	69
Mersin	207	157	77
Rhodes	306	231	118
Smyrna	377	284	148
Mitilini	407	308	155
Dardanelles	428	323	166
Gallipoli	436	329	168
Constantinople	469	354	182

It was a dream voyage. It wasn't so much the idea of first-class comforts that made me envious, although I was sure that even a third-class ticket with Messageries Maritimes would have brought more comfort than the bus I was about to board. What seemed almost miraculous were the destinations on offer. I would have gladly travelled deck-class on bread and water to sail into these Levantine ports one after the other. Never mind the leaps in transport technology that lay far in the future – in Monsieur Frugoli's time it was much easier getting around the eastern Mediterranean than it is today.

If a Saturday departure didn't suit, the French maritime company wasn't the only one to stop at the harbours dotting the great curved arc of the sea. The Khedival Mail Line, Lloyd's Austrian and the Russian Steam Navigation and Commercial Company were among others offering similar services along these coasts. But where were they all now? I had checked and re-checked. There was a summer ferry-service to Brindisi and Venice, but that was months away. Short of smuggling myself aboard a freighter, it was impossible to get out of Alexandria by sea. In the end I had bought a ticket from the East Delta Bus Lines – hardly a name with the same kind of romantic resonance – and was headed to a seaport not even on the Mediterranean.

Such were the kinds of choices left to travellers in a politically-fraught Middle East – for anyone who had drawn the line at flying there weren't many options available. Then again, there probably weren't all that many people these days who actually wanted to see a succession of old port-cities in the eastern Mediterranean.

But I did. With appetite whetted and long, warm spring days stretching ahead, I felt the entire coastline beckoning. Already, though, I knew that the dozen places listed by Monsieur Frugoli posed a dozen different logistical problems. Long ago I'd acknowledged I wasn't going to see Jaffa, Haifa or any other port in Israel. Twitchy travel relations between Arabs and Israelis – matters of visas, passport stamps and closed borders – simply made it too complicated. In fact, just getting to the Mediterranean coast north of Israel was difficult enough.

You could cross the Sinai Peninsula by road, but once on the other side you couldn't get over the top of the Gulf of Aqaba to Jordan – the port of Elat and a five-mile coastal stretch of Israeli territory barred the way. Instead, you had to drive south down the coast of the Gulf, and halfway to the Red Sea catch a boat north again at Nuweiba; once back up the Gulf, it deposited its passengers on the far side of Israeli territory in the Jordanian city of Aqaba.

I wasn't actually looking forward to an all-night bus ride, or even to this leg of the trip as a whole. It seemed an awfully roundabout way to go, and the journey was known to be tough and full of delays – getting from Cairo to Aqaba, less than 250 miles as the crow flies, often took twenty-four hours or more. That came to an average of just ten miles an hour.

It was a speed considerably slower, I calculated, than that of the standard military camel charge. In the Arab uprising of the First World War Lawrence of Arabia had once thundered into Aqaba at the head of hundreds of mounted and determined tribesmen. They were in a hurry, hurtling towards the post-Ottoman independence that Lawrence had promised them. In the end his efforts failed. But something at least could be said for that thundering charge – a direct and lightening-fast advance on the city had to have been a good deal more satisfying than this back-and-forth trundling about. I boarded the East Delta bus wishing that Lawrence – or even better, Monsieur Frugoli – were still in charge of things.

We left Cairo at eleven o'clock in the evening, a spaghetti of suburban motorways finally leading to a straight, two-lane highway that was almost deserted. Outside there was nothing but a quarter-moon and dimly lit roadside scrub. Occasionally we pulled over, waiting for no discernible reason before rumbling back onto the highway. Once we dropped down into a long, brightly lit concrete tunnel, a passage which I assumed ran beneath the Suez Canal. The only remarkable thing was the desert cold. The bus was unheated, and by two o'clock it wasn't far from freezing outside. Inside, passengers huddled into the folds of their long *galabiyas,* wrapped lengths of cloth around their heads, and fell asleep. Mouths gaped, limbs protruded into aisles in prolonged poses of rigor mortis. In the sickly yellow glimmer of the bus's ceiling lights we looked like zombies from *Night of the Living Dead*.

We stopped at Taba, the border crossing just a couple of miles from the Israeli town of Elat. A few passengers got down, an Egyptian policeman checked passports, and we turned south to drive alongside the Gulf of Aqaba.

In the distance across the head of the gulf we could see two twinkling masses – the city lights of Elat and Aqaba. At the same time daylight was beginning to swell in the east. It revealed the road we were travelling, a winding strip of tarmac squeezed between water and bone-dry hills of bare rock. On the far side of the gulf, too, the desert ranges of Saudi Arabia climbed sharply away from the shore. But not even this deep, narrow fold in the earth could hide away from day forever. Just outside Nuweiba the sun's rim appeared over the mountains and the whole world – sea, sky and rock – was suffused with light. For a few moments even the craggiest headland glowed a soft and delicate *bonbon* pink.

Nuweiba straggled alongside the sea, a town of low, white concrete buildings and sand-blown streets just a couple of blocks deep. The bus came to a halt by the harbourside. The zombie passengers abruptly awoke, hustled themselves off the bus and disappeared. Where to, I have no idea; perhaps they knew a good place to remain comatose for the six hours that remained before the sailing to Aqaba. That left just the foreigners. With our bags slung from our shoulders we wandered into a waterfront café – in reality no more than bits of ragged canvas hung over a wooden frame – and ordered tea.

There were four of us. We were all from different places, but in the way of travellers come together by chance in strange places we immediately formed a group.

Lotfi, confident and outgoing, immediately became our leader. He spoke little English but excellent French. He had a pleasing, cheerful manner and didn't hesitate to use it – he could charm anyone to pieces in five minutes. Conscious or not, it was a trick that came in useful. Lotfi was Tunisian, a buyer and a seller. When pressed as to exactly what it was that he bought and sold he was evasive. But his business took him all around the shores of the Muslim Mediterranean. This was his fourth trip to Damascus.

Lotfi travelled light. Apart from a small holdall he didn't have much more than the leather jacket and the clothes he stood up in. The rest of us were bleary-eyed and tired. Lotfi, who was thirty-five but looked ten years younger, was clear-eyed and fresh. He was now five days out of Tunis and moving fast. In order to cut down on expenses and avoid hotel costs he travelled day and night, and hoped to be in Damascus in the next thirty-six hours. Apart from ten-minute catnaps, he claimed he hadn't slept on this trip at all, and I believed him. He was a natural-born traveller and trader, deft and self-assured in his life on the road, and it pleased him in a way that no sedentary occupation could. I doubt that what Lotfi did was entirely legal, but it didn't stop me liking him.

I liked him even more when I saw the way he looked out for Jimmy. Jimmy was a tall, gangly twenty-year-old Iraqi with a wispy bit of beard on his chin and a prominent Adam's apple. When he spoke he surprised you because he had a reedy, falsetto voice that was pitched higher than most girls'. He was a Christian Arab – Maronite or Syrian Orthodox, I cannot remember which, but at any rate had been brought up in one of those isolated churches that has persisted and survived in the Middle East for centuries. He was goofy about God, and had a touching belief that anyone nominally Christian was automatically a good and trustworthy person. It made you fear for him.

The fact that he felt he had some sort of divine backup only put him at risk, for he was setting off down a murderous road. Through an evangelist Christian connection Jimmy's father was working in a supermarket in Tennessee. But Jimmy, who until now had avoided the Iraq war by staying with his uncle in Cairo, was on his way home to his mother in Baghdad. Lotfi promised Jimmy he would get him as far as Amman, but when he turned east he would be on his own. He had a stack of documents, every necessary paper neatly wrapped in a plastic bag with elastic bands, but he was very nervous.

I sometimes wake up at night and wonder if Jimmy made out all right.

As soon as he discovered I was from what he called a 'Christian nation' he dived into the inside breast pocket of his jacket to present me with a card – there was a calendar on one side and a blurry three-colour print of Jesus, hands outstretched in welcome, on the other. But it was Jimmy's physical gesture that concerned me. It was too abrupt, and I hoped he never tried that particular ice-breaker with a nervous American soldier at a roadblock. If he did, the world would be one Christian short.

The fourth member of our little band also presented me with a card as we sat sipping tea in Nuweiba's rosy morning light. I looked at the picture on it, compared it to the man in front of me, and looked at the picture again. It showed a pale face with lustrous black curly hair, an enormous moustache and a sort of Sergeant Pepper uniform – a silver ceremonial sword and big red pasteboard epaulettes with lots of braid, medals and ribbons. It made me want to laugh out loud, but I didn't, for there was no doubt about it – it was a picture of the man in front of me.

'Alsheik Adam Mohammed Amin', I read the name under the photo, and he smiled and nodded. 'Da!' he said enthusiastically, pointing at his chest. And that is as far as we got, for Amin spoke Chechen and Russian, and shared no other language with any of us.

He was a neat little man barely five and a half feet tall, and for this journey he was in civilian dress – a beautiful sheepskin coat with the wool turned inside and a curious brimless cap of the same stuff. But there was no doubting his martial manner. He sat ramrod straight and bore himself with a dignity that, unlike his photo, demanded respect.

Who was he? None of us could figure it out. Was he a Chechen rebel, on his way home from some fund-raising mission to a Muslim fundamentalist group? Was he a pro-Russian Chechen returning from a secret peace-making conference? Everything we found out was communicated by means of mime, and Adam Mohammed Amin was a showman. He did a very good Grozny, graphically displaying its ruined flatness by chopping down imaginary buildings with a sideways motion of his hands. He even shot himself up with a make-believe machine gun, hanging his head and lolling his tongue out the side of his mouth. But as to whose side the

General, as I began thinking of him, was actually on remained a mystery. No doubt it always will.

But not even sweet tea and a Chechen mime-show could halt the onset of fatigue. I had to get some sleep. I tried lying down for a while, my head on my bag, at the back of the café. But there were rats running along a wooden cross-pole above me, and I was afraid one of them might fall. Finally I stumbled outside, telling my friends I would find them later, and plodded my way down to the water.

Once a sandy beach had stretched away from the harbour. Now it was covered in a thick layer of garbage and so filthy that the water beyond looked shockingly clean by comparison. I had never seen a sea as clear and limpid. But I cared nothing for any of it. I found a little depression in the sand that was out of the wind, laid my head on my bag again, and was instantly asleep.

I woke up hours later, hot and muzzy-headed. The sun was now well up in the sky and without moving I could tell that one side of my face had been burned bright red. My eyelids were stuck together. There were plastic bags and grease-stained chunks of styrofoam inches from my gaze when I finally opened them. I was grimy. I felt like a vagrant. Was this what the travelling life had come to – waking up sunburned on a filth-strewn beach in the middle of nowhere?

Suddenly I remembered the ferry. I sat up and looked at the harbour. A long line of transport trucks, their exhaust-stacks roaring, now waited before the harbour gates. Behind a concrete wall protecting warehouses and loading gantries I could see a ship with its own stacks pushing out heat. I scrambled to my feet. I was not going to be left as a cast-off beach-comber in this sorry place.

There was no one in the café. At the port's passenger gates hundreds of Egyptians were waiting in a queue that went far down the street and around the corner. I was about to head to the back of the line when I was grabbed by the arm.

It was Lotfi. 'Are you crazy?' he said in French, pulling me towards the front of the line. 'Come on. I've been looking all over for you.'

I objected, not wanting to jump ahead of passengers who'd been waiting patiently for hours.

Lotfi smiled and shook his head. 'These people are peasants. Believe me, it's not for you. You'll see.'

And I did see. Lotfi leading, we pushed our way through the gate and followed a single file of men that snaked its way between warehouses and into a vast, hangar-like building.

There were crowds of Egyptians already in there, divided into half a dozen lines inching towards glass-fronted immigration booths. At first I thought it was prayer-time; everyone was down on his knees. Then I saw that this was merely a crude form of crowd control – uniformed policemen stood beside the kneeling queues moving the men forward.

The immigration officers in the booths might have been processing cattle. They stamped documents and tossed them down with bored disdain. When a visa or work permit proved deficient wayfarers were sent off like bothersome flies, with a flick of the wrist. If they tried to argue their case they were hustled away by police and the next applicant called for. A holiday cruise this was not. But no one showed any upset at this treatment. It was the way things were done.

We cut in at the head of the line. There wasn't a squeak of protest behind us as we were stamped and waved through. 'Who are these people?' I asked Lotfi. 'Where are they going?' On the far side of a security barrier we found Jimmy and the General installed and waiting for us.

'I told you. They are nothing,' Lotfi shrugged as we sat down beside them on a bench in a crowded waiting area. 'They're migrant workers. They've been home visiting their villages in Egypt. Now they are returning to jobs in Jordan, Syria, the Emirates, Saudi Arabia. They are paid slave wages. But they are happy. At home they are paid nothing at all.'

The Egyptians spread themselves out on benches and floors, surrounded by mountains of baggage and hungry cats patrolling for handouts. In travelstained *galabiyas* and head-cloths they were large, imposing men with work-thickened fingers and noses like large, blunt rudders. Their manners were rough. They stuffed their mouths with flat-bread and boiled eggs and raw onions. They wiped their moustaches on their greasy sleeves. They smoked endless cigarettes. They spat, chatted, laughed and guffawed. Were they happy, as Lotfi insisted they were? I had no idea, but not one of them showed the slightest impatience as, hours after its advertised sailing time, we continued to wait for our ferry.

When the time did come there was an almighty rush, hundreds of men all trying to pile up gangways at the same time. They swarmed over the boat, loud and anxious in their claims for this place or that. Our party of four found an awning-covered bench near the stern. But it did no good, for once everyone had settled down we waited another two hours moored fast to the quayside.

I couldn't say I minded staying close to dry land. The decks of the ferry seemed dangerously packed. The vessel appeared to have developed a pronounced list to starboard. 'Aqaba Ferry Disaster; Hundreds Drown' – it was the kind of bottom-of-the-inside-page headline you see all the time. But once we got underway I forgot all about danger. I had never seen a sea like this.

It was wholly different from that other sea lying only 150 miles away. The Mediterranean is just what it says it is, a middle sea. At certain times and places it can seem the loveliest thing on earth, but its beauty is the beauty of moderation, of balance and harmonious proportion. It is a sea built to the measure of man. The Gulf of Aqaba was nothing of the sort. It was a wholly immoderate thing. Never mind 'azure', 'cerulean', 'lapis' or any other brave attempt at hyperbole – its waters were impossibly blue. So were its mountains impossibly red, its air impossibly clear. So stark and alien was its splendour it hardly seemed to have a place for humanity at all.

Was that why the men aboard treated it with such contempt? They ignored the sea. Without the slightest glance at their surroundings they settled down once again to talk and smoking and food. Soon the decks were littered with eggshells and pumpkin seeds, banana skins and cigarette stubs. And when they finished they slung the remains of their meals overboard. For as far back as I could see we left in our wake a soggy record of our passage, plastic bags and floating bottles, bobbing soft-drink cans and empty Cleopatra packets. All were dispatched into this cleanest of seas with the blithest indifference.

And yet, for all that, there was a likable sociability about these travellers. They were a rag-tag tribe, but a tribe nonetheless. A few hours before, most of these men were strangers to each other. Now, crosslegged or stretched out on the deck together like old friends, they owned the boat. Their gregariousness, loud, emotional and excitable, took it over.

It was almost sunset when a thousand passports, collected on boarding, were redistributed with Jordanian entry stamps in them. A ship's officer stood on the poop deck as a stiff wind whipped the men's robes and the green, scimitar-emblazoned Saudi flag that flew from the stern. He shouted out names. The throng pressed in close to hear.

'Mohammed Badri Sulieman!' screamed the officer against the wind. There was a muffled response from somewhere in the rear of the crowd and a passport was passed overhead, from one hand to the next, until it reached its destination.

'Abdullah Ahmed Latif!'

'Mohammed El Shafi Mohammed!'

'Ali Zulficar Rafat!'

One after another the names were recited until all the passports were with their owners. By this point the sun was down over the Sinai desert and the wind had turned bitterly cold. Ahead we could see the lights of Aqaba. We'd be ashore in an hour, I told Lotfi. He nodded, but tentatively – no one, the gesture said, could predict rhyme or reason in the ferry's progress. Soon after the vessel slowed, and it was two more hours before we even entered port. Once docked, we spent another hour crushed in a corridor leading to the gangway.

I lost Lotfi, Jimmy and the General in the frantic rush that swept the boat when the doors were finally opened; although I waited some time in the Jordanian customs shed I never saw them again. I caught a taxi downtown and rented a $14 room in the Hotel Dweikh. Hungry for a bit of pampering, I took a lift to the eighth-floor bar of the Aquamarina, a plush

106

resort-hotel overlooking the water. The beer was cold, the conversation restrained, and nobody spat peanut shells on the floor.

But for all the Saudi millionaires and well-heeled Westerners who frequented Aqaba in the tourist season I had the feeling the city was rather a dull place. It seemed too clean and empty after Alexandria, too well run and predictable after the ferry. The Hotel Dweikh, though, had a surprise reserved for me. Fast asleep an hour after turning in, I crashed to the floor when the box-frame on which the mattress and springs of my bed was resting gave way.

I didn't move, but stayed there on the floor until the next morning. I was too tired to bother trying to fix anything. Besides, even the floor was a lot more comfortable and reassuring than the place I'd been dreaming about. In my sleep I was still lying in the burning sun on a flotsam-covered beach somewhere on the Gulf of Aqaba. Happily, the travelling life hadn't come to that yet.

Fifteen

Does the Mediterranean Sea, as so many of its admirers claim, really have a beneficent and spirit-raising effect on its inhabitants? Does it moderate the temper, soothe the troubled soul and provide *allégresse*, that little bit of lift which makes all the difference in life? A couple of days later I was inclined to believe that it does. After months spent in the company of lively Alexandrians, Damascus seemed a dour and unyielding sort of place.

The bus connections had been good and I arrived in the Syrian capital just eight hours after leaving Aqaba. Not even the border crossing from Jordan, often a lengthy ordeal, had taken much time. Syrian customs officers had begun a thorough search of the bus. I supposed they were looking for arms or drugs. They seemed particularly interested in a small refrigerator, a piece of equipment much valued by thirsty travellers in the Syrian summer heat, bolted over the bus's right rear wheel well. Having detached it from its base to see what might lie below, they spent most of their time lying prone on the floor, cursing and trying to locate the screws they'd lost somewhere down inside the bus's innards. By the time they'd got the thing more or less reattached they were so fed up that the rest of the procedure was perfunctory and we were soon on our way. There might have been five kilos of heroin and a dozen assault rifles sitting on the racks above our heads. It was reassuring to see that Syrian officialdom, with such a reputation for repressive efficiency, could be just as inept as any other officialdom.

In Damascus I inspected half a dozen small hotels. Without the world knocking at its door Damascus didn't have a vast range of choice in accommodation. It was either one of a couple of luxury hotels – against my principles on this non-touristic tour of the Mediterranean – or any of a large number of cheapies.

If the hot-water supply at the Candles Hotel was limited to a couple of hours a day the sheets were at least laundered and the blankets unstained. Nor were there any of those flimsy plastic bathroom slippers that the really squalid places laid on in lieu of occasionally cleaning the floor. I think it was the absence of the slippers, plus the nearby presence of the Hijaz railway station, that tipped the scales in favour of the Candles.

The station lay just across Hijaz Square, and compared with the grey, grim, poured-concrete constructions that made up much of modern Damascus it was a handsome building. But it wasn't just the look of the place. The truth is that for most of my life I've been a sucker for Lawrence of Arabia. As a twelve-year-old I'd tried Lawrence's *Seven Pillars of Wisdom* and found it an obscure and baffling read. I still do. But sitting in a darkened cinema a few years later I watched Peter O'Toole gliding about the desert in flowing white robes, his burning blue eyes half-mad. At the time I couldn't imagine Hollywood getting any better, and I still can't.

As Lawrenciana goes, the Hijaz railway is vital. Begun by the Ottomans in 1907, it was built ostensibly to ferry Muslim pilgrims on their way to Mecca down the Arabian Peninsula to the city of Medina. Its strategic military value became apparent in 1917, however, when Lawrence began blowing up trains to disrupt Turkish troop movements. As a rail terminus today the station is anything but vital – beneath its decorated ceiling and upper-floor gallery I gazed at architects' scale-models, plans for yet one more modern concrete complex into which the disused station was to be incorporated. But it made no difference – every time I passed the antique steam locomotive that stood on the square near the station doors I half expected to find it lying wrecked and smoking in the wake of a daring daylight raid.

Perhaps I didn't have to look very much further than the Hijaz station to trace the source of Damascene gloominess. Lawrence was not the first to have marched into the city at the head of triumphant warriors. Damascus lies only fifty miles from the Mediterranean, but it is blocked from the sea by the 6,000-foot-high Anti-Lebanon mountains. Sea trade has never been the city's *raison d'être*; instead it has traditionally straddled the inland routes leading from the Asian interior, and grown rich by controlling them. Sitting out on a broad, inhospitable plain, it has also been the target of enemies seeking the same kind of control. The longest continuously inhabited city in the world, it has been rolled over by foreign armies countless times in the last 6,000 years.

Not entirely countless. As I sat on my bed one evening waiting for nine o'clock – an odd hour for the hot water to come on, but better than nothing – I took my guidebook and made a quick tally of the various invaders and occupiers of Syria. My list was partial, for I only began in the year 2334 BC. But it read like this – at various times Damascus had been taken over by: 1) the Mesopotamian Akkadians; 2) the Egyptians under Thutmose I; 3) the Mitanni Empire; 4) the Hittites; 5) the Phoenicians; 6) the Philistines; 7) the Aramaeans; 8) the Judeans; 9) the Assyrians under Sargon II; 10) the Babylonians under Nebuchadnezzar; 11) the Achaemenids; 12) the Greeks under Alexander the Great; 13) the Seleucids; 14) the Romans under Pompey; 15) the Persian Sassanids; 16) the Arabs; 17) the Cairene Fatamid dynasty; 18) the Crusaders; 19) the Mongols; 20) the Ottoman Turks; 21) the Egyptians, again, under a son of Mohammed Ali; 22) the Hashemite ruler Faisal, aided by Lawrence; 23) the French under League of Nations mandate; 24) the Egyptians for a fourth time, as senior partner in a short-lived United Arab Republic.

Well there you go, I thought as I heard the hot-water pipes finally rumble and gush – if you'd been knocked around by various foreigners a couple of dozen times even before the local Ba'ath party installed its less-than-benevolent regime, you too might just be the slightest bit hesitant in the *joie-de-vivre* department.

But there could be no doubt that Damascus, despite the torchings, razings and regime-changes, had over time continued to maintain control of the trade and caravan routes. It is a city of old-fashioned merchants and traders still. Not far past the Hijaz station new Damascus suddenly vanished and motorised traffic disappeared. On the far side of a high surrounding ring of stone walls lay old Damascus. In its warren of streets, change, if it is takes place at all, is measured in centuries.

I hesitated on the morning I stood before its main gate and the high, vaulted arcade of the Souq-al-Hamidiyya. Having taken a great dog-leg around Israel, I was anxious to get back to where, on this trip anyway, I belonged – the coast. My next stop was Latakia, Syria's biggest seaport. But I found it hard to side-step an ancient capital where so much of the eastern Mediterranean's fate was decided, and where so many of its actors now lie buried. This was the kind of place that could hold you back for days.

I plunged on in. The souq was cavernous, a long, busy, stone-flagged market dimly lit by shafts of sunlight penetrating the iron-roofed vault above. It was as I feared – behind the walls of Damascus sat an entire medieval Islamic world, much of it still intact and alive.

I wandered in the vast white marble courtyard of the Umayyad mosque, in the 8th century the very centre of the Islamic world. I visited the tomb of Saladin, the warrior whose capture of Jerusalem in the 12th century brought down the wrath of the Third Crusade. I watched an old woman on her knees, weeping in adoration before the mausoleum of another famous warrior, the Mamluke Sultan Beybars – he'd swept Christians from Antioch, burning it and them to the ground in the process. One sepulchre I stood in front of was said to hold the head of John the Baptist, a prophet to Islam as well as to Christianity. A second was purported to hold an even more celebrated head, that of Hussein, the assassinated grandson of Mohammed and the founder of Shi'ism. What happened centuries ago might have happened yesterday. Wherever I went in the old city I came across the same thing, people prostrated before the tombs of long-gone saints and warriors, kissing framed portraits and rubbing silver grillwork as if touch alone would bestow the departed one's blessing.

Growing weary of medieval martyrs I took myself off to Bakdash, a venerable, century-old pudding shop. But here, too, the citizens of

Damascus maintained their sombre alliance with the past. Bakdash made and served 3,000 bowls of pudding a day, but it would have no truck with modern efficiencies of any kind. I watched mesmerised as a cook poured milky-white custard from a large, spouted pail into endless rows of bowls. They filled at the precise rate of one bowl every second and a half.

'No machine can do better,' the man behind the cash register told me soberly as I spooned up my own pistachio-sprinkled pudding. 'He hasn't spilled a drop in thirteen years. Not one drop.'

There was something of this same methodical and unchanging traditionalism in every shop in the old city. It didn't matter if it was a boy turning chess pieces on a pedal-driven lathe, a tailor sewing sequins on a belly dancer's dress, or a brassmith working the bellows of his charcoal furnace. It wasn't just a matter of doing things in the old way. Damascenes appeared constrained, prevented from the possibility of doing new things in new ways. They seemed stuck in the past, cut off from the rest of the world's modernity.

Even their cars were outdated. Sometimes a shiny big Mercedes with Lebanese plates – new money from a revived Beirut – would come nosing slowly through the narrow streets. But more often it was fins and torpedo-bumpers, the dinosaur appendages of Lincolns and Chevys carefully conserved from another age.

What was holding the place back? What made its people so buttoned up, so lacking in ease and facility? It was a question I asked myself all afternoon.

It was after dark when I finally emerged from the old city through its Christian quarter. Behind me lay biblical Damascus – the 'Street called Straight' and the window where a fleeing Saint Paul had been lowered from the city walls in a basket. Every alley in the quarter had been decorated with Christian symbols – religious images hung on outdoor walls and small statues were affixed above doorways and in wall niches. Now, back in the new city again, the street hagiography changed. Instead of Christ figures and Virgin Marys, the icons paid homage to Syria's secular deities, the Assads.

They were everywhere. The country's leading family were sanctified in statuary, hoardings, banners, murals, framed photos, posters and paste-on transfers on the rear windows of family cars. Just as common as Bashar al-Assad was his dead father Hafez, the man from whom he'd inherited the presidency. Also in evidence was Bashar's elder brother, Basil. Groomed for the top post but killed in a road accident before he could take over, the favourite son looked positively sinister in his signature three-day beard and aviator's sunglasses. Perhaps it wasn't just the dark clouds of the past that lingered over the Syrian plain, I thought. The self-perpetuating Assads appeared to cast a long shadow across it, too.

That evening I wandered around cold, windblown streets looking for somewhere to eat. The city centre was deserted and, like the capital's hotels, there wasn't a great range of restaurants. They were either formal and overly elaborate or little more than take-out stands. But finally I stumbled across an establishment that looked cosy enough.

'Al-Rayees Restaurant (Ex Normandie)', said the sign outside. Inside there was a vague remnant of French provincial atmosphere left behind from the days of the Mandate. It was all a little shopworn. There were chandeliers hanging from a high, dim ceiling. Floral wallpaper, yellowed and curling at the edges, covered the walls. On one side of the room hung a framed print of Millet's 'Les Faucheurs'; from the other glowed the enigmatic smile of La Joconde. Had the Normandie been aiming to create the fresh and carefree mood of an outdoor *ginguette*? In one corner artificial vines ran up and over a white wooden trellis. It was a contrivance that failed miserably in the restaurant's thick, stale fug of tobacco smoke.

But it wasn't the décor of the restaurant that really interested me. It was the clients. The room was crowded with diners, all of them men, and as far as I could see not one of them belonging to the present era.

If I had shown up at a 1950s convention of intellectuals, artists and academics I couldn't have felt more of an anachronism. Everyone was dressed in Western fashion, but they were the dated styles of half a century ago. There were men with trim moustaches, tweedy jackets and thick, horn-rimmed spectacles. There were men in baggy flannel suits. There was one man with pointed, waxed moustaches, a black Astrakhan hat and a cape thrown over his shoulders. Even the staff came from another age – they dressed in black suits and bow-ties, and looked more like diplomats than waiters. No one was under sixty.

And no one was less than half-sloshed. Although the tables were covered with plates of food, most of it was *mezze*, a side-show. The main events here were drink and conversation, and everyone was hard at it. When the patrons of the Al-Rayees (Ex Normandie) stopped talking to pour raki, there was barely room left in the glass to cloud it with ice and water.

I was shown to a table covered with a fresh white tablecloth and given an English menu. The prices were ridiculously cheap and the spelling approximate – items ranged in cost from a box of 'Papper Klinex' (20 cents) to a steak 'Chateau Brillaund'(less than $3). As I studied the menu I also studied the dozen or so Syrians sitting at a long table in front of me.

One of them caught my glance and lifted a glass; with a beckoning hand he invited me over. His name was Fateh Ayub, he told me in English, and he always met his friends here. Would I join them? He wouldn't take no for an answer. In a minute I was picking at *mezze* and knocking back raki with the rest of them.

'And what do you think of our restaurant?' Fateh asked me, waving at the smoky room as he refilled my glass. I replied that I liked it.

'I have lived in many countries in my life, and travelled all over the world,' he said. 'But this is still my favourite place. Of course it's unfashionable – that's why we come. The same group of people – painters and writers and bohemians – have been drinking here for thirty years. It's our retreat. Listen to the music. That's not a pop-song; it's classical – the Arab *oud*.'

I liked Fateh Ayub right away. He was the first Syrian I'd met, and not what I'd expected. He was friendly, generous, hospitable and, in a country out of touch with the rest of the world, pleased to meet a foreigner.

I told Fateh I was heading for Latakia, and then on around the Mediterranean coast. Latakia is not a town of any great tourist value, but Fateh surprised me by approving of my destination and telling me what I'd been telling myself for weeks. In a fragmented world, he said, the Mediterranean has always been a place of contact and exchange – it has a lot of old lessons to teach.

Fateh was a painter and loved the traditional Arab arts. But nothing excited him more now than the creative possibilities of cyberspace. For it, too, was a place of contact and exchange. 'Imagine,' he said with delight, 'communicating your ideas to anyone you like, anywhere in the world, instantly. Is there anything as fantastic?'

We talked for a long time and drank more raki than we should have. But no matter how relaxed we became, I noticed, Fateh never came even close to mentioning politics, the Assads or the regime they directed. There was little mention of public life at all. It shouldn't have surprised me. There are at least eight internal security services in Syria, each with its own network of secret policemen. In such a state some subjects are simply taboo. Our table finally broke up around midnight. As I gazed around a roomful of inebriated men preparing to go home, I began to appreciate Fateh's views of the digital world. For most of us the Internet has lost its lustre and become just another tool. But for people like these – men who in a different place and time would be deep in the debates of public life – there weren't a great number of consolations. Drink and the Internet were two of them.

I had a sore head the next morning but there was no time even for coffee at the Damascus bus station. Two soldiers were searching passengers' baggage at a barrier at the station entrance. On the other side a tout took charge of me. Less than two minutes later I was in a departing bus and on my way to Latakia.

At the very back I found the last available seat and squeezed myself down beside a young man. He was large, strongly built and wore black. His hair was close-cropped, his nose prominent, and on his forehead was a fixed scowl. We said nothing for the first ten minutes. Then, as the city gave way to bleak, stony expanses of open country, he spoke.

'Have you telephone?' he asked without preamble, the accent thick and the words coming slowly.

'Yes, I have a telephone at home,' I answered.

'Have you ... car?' he said with the same pained deliberation.

'Yes, I have a car.'

'Have you ... house?'

'I have a house, too'

'Have you ... woman?'

The have-you questions continued in this same slow, uninterrupted fashion for some time. It began to dawn on me that my questioner wasn't in the least bit interested if I had a telephone or a woman or anything else. He was more interested in talking. He was practising his English.

The exercise became tedious and to stop it I began asking questions of my own. My travelling companion's name was Samir. He was twenty-four years old. He'd been studying English for six months. He tried to watch movies in English – 'I like Jean-Claude van Damme; you like Jean-Claude van Damme?' – but they were difficult to understand. Talking to foreigners was better, but they were hard to find.

'My English very, very good, no?' Samir would ask me every couple of sentences. Yes, I would say, very good. But it wasn't. It was bloody awful, and I was beginning to resent the man's blunt insistence. Not only was he slow and plodding; he didn't seem to have the sense or manners to know when to let up. As I gazed out at a cold grey sky and the remains of winter snow capping the hills above the plain he launched into another exercise taken from his grammar classes. Have-you-been. Have-you-seen. He was no good at it, but was becoming demanding and dictatorial. He was asking questions and he wanted answers. Not even my turning my head away put him off.

Fifteen minutes later we were back to the original subject, telephones. Samir was showing me his new Nokia mobile, and on its screen was flipping through the pictures he'd taken with it.

'This my brother ... this my father house ... ' I was barely watching, by now thoroughly fed up. But then he said, 'This me,' and there was Samir posing, a uniformed thug with a pistol in his hand and Basil-style shades on his face, the scowl stronger than ever.

Samir was pleased to see he had my attention. He was a member of the presidential bodyguard, he told me, and served in Bashar Assad's official residence in Damascus. There was no fear of politics in this man, I could see. In no time Samir had launched himself into fulsome praise of the President and made ringing paeans to the greatness of the Syrian state and army. The more he talked the more swaggering he became. Samir hated the Yahoudis (the Jews). They had stolen the Golan from Syria. They had built a wall around al-Quds (Jerusalem). They killed babies in Falisteen (Palestine). Syria had many enemies. But he, Samir, was there to protect it. He may only have been a 24-year-old punk hoping a tough-guy demeanour would impress me. But it worked. I was impressed. Samir made me nervous.

On the other side of the city of Homs the bus pulled over in front of a highway restaurant.

'Come,' said Samir. I said I would stay on the bus.

'Come,' said Samir again, beckoning at me. 'It is not your decide. You are my country guest.'

Inside he told me to sit. I sat. He ordered kababs and salad for me, and after, coffee for both of us. 'Eat,' he said. In the middle of the meal he got up and paid for everything. This was bad. It put me under an obligation – I would have to go through more mindless talk in more execrable English. Samir had me, a captive conversationalist, and he knew it.

Not far past Homs we began a descent coastward through the stony hills of the Jebel Ansariyya. Very quickly the country changed. As we headed down the sky cleared and the air warmed, and suddenly I knew I was close to the Mediterranean again. There were trees in red blossom and yellow wildflowers on the grassy slopes. Lower down on a broad coastal strip there were fields already high with grain and long rows of plastic-covered hothouses growing tomatoes. Small coastal villages began appearing, the walls of their simple, cube-like houses glowing pink and ochre in the bright sun. Women and girls stood by the roadside, selling bright piles of citrus fruit – oranges, lemons and the largest grapefruits I had ever seen.

It was a happier landscape than the one we'd left behind. Even the people in it looked happier. Through the bus window I could see villagers relaxing in the spring sunshine, laughing, sharing stories as they walked by the road. There were buoyant spirits here. There was *allégresse* in abundance. My only trouble was that I wasn't all that happy myself.

As we rolled along Samir had been talking on his mobile phone. Now he turned to me. 'My sister,' he said. 'In Latakia. First I show you everything. And tonight big dinner. We eat her house.'

I saw catastrophe yawning before me. I was being turned into a pet foreigner. I'd known Samir was going to spend a few days off work with his sister and her family. Now he was going to show me off like a trophy. There would be a lengthy, ceremonial meal, more tough-guy posing, more mangled English exercises. I couldn't do it.

'Samir,' I said, 'it's not possible. I've travelled all the way from Cairo. I'm tired. I need sleep.' On and on I went, but Samir wasn't having it. He refused my refusal. His face went red. 'You will come,' he said, 'No questions.' He began bullying, his voice growing louder. Did I want him to lose face in front of his sister and her family? Was I rejecting Syrian hospitality? He left me in no doubt that I was doing him a grave dishonour.

The more Samir barked at me the more I was determined to resist him. And finally he gave up, sitting sullen and wounded. He wouldn't say another word. The passengers around us looked away, embarrassed.

When the bus arrived at the station on the outskirts of Latakia Samir stomped off, head down, without a word. I stood with my bag on the platform, undecided. Latakia was not a big place. What if I bumped into Samir in the next couple of days? By then he might have recovered his cool and press his invitation even harder. Worse, he might have decided I had insulted him unforgivably. Was I being paranoid, or was he the vengeful type, someone capable of getting me into some kind of trouble? I mulled it over. Five minutes later I jumped on the next bus to Aleppo, miles from the sea on the far side of the mountains. I was there by sunset.

Sixteen

I skulked around the souqs of Aleppo for the next three or four days, not feeling very proud of myself. It wasn't just that I had run away from a bully. I was also missing out on Syria's largest, busiest port. More than that, just fifteen minutes up the coast from Latakia lay the dead city of Ugarit, the oldest maritime trading centre in the world. But the thought of that scowling, resentful young thug, elite member of the *Sirayat ad-Difa' 'an-ath-Thawra* – the Brigades for the Defence of the Revolution – was enough to keep me a safe distance away.

There were a couple of compensations. One was old Aleppo, still intact and, if anything, an even more magnificent medieval city than Damascus. The other, next to the tyre bazaar in the new city, was the Backpackers' Hostel.

It had everything – satellite television news, an Internet café, a library, music, cold beer, full guiding services and a terrace dormitory for $2 a night. The place was packed – the clientele were the kind of young, adventurous travellers who end up in destinations that regular tourists wouldn't dream of setting their big toes in.

I met Charlotte Holloway watching BBC World on the hostel's covered rooftop. Together we contemplated the latest rounds of violence in Gaza, Iraq, Lebanon and Afghanistan. When the news was over and someone flipped channels to a re-run of *Friends* we went out to a pastry shop.

Charlotte ordered in what sounded like fluent Arabic. I was suitably impressed, until two gigantic servings of baklava smothered in nuts and dripping syrup arrived.

'Oops,' she said. 'That happens. A quarter-kilo is the only measurement I know in Arabic, so I do tend to over-order. And that's two portions I asked for. It is quite a lot, isn't it? Sorry.'

Charlotte was not an Arabist at all. Neither was she an over-eater; she was tall and slim and could eat as much as she liked. And so we set to work on a pound of sticky pastry, and as we did so she told me about her archaeology studies at Cambridge. Operating on a shoe-string budget, she was in the middle of researching a thesis – her specialisation was in pre-classical contacts between Greece and the rest of the ancient world. She had also done work in Egypt and Albania, and would be flying on to Greece in the next couple of days.

Her obvious passion for her subject intrigued me – she'd soon pushed her baklava away and was detailing the intricacies of research that bordered on the edges of pre-history. I told her about my own non-academic interest in the Mediterranean as a place of human exchange, and of some of the things I'd come across in Alexandria. She listened carefully, sometimes nodding. At others she shook her head in disagreement.

'You're too European in your ideas,' she told me. 'Of course connective ties have always held the Mediterranean together. But why should it have been just the Mediterranean? They may have been concentrated there, but the same kind of ties stretched much further and in all sorts of directions we're still discovering. To see them you don't have to look any further than Ugarit. The idea of East and West as separate and distinct places is a recent concept. It was convenient to the Europeans who invented it. In fact, trade and human contacts made a seamless, single entity of the globe a very long time ago. A World-Wide-Web has been with us for ages.'

Charlotte became even more animated when I told her about Samir and my scuttling out of Latakia.

'To hell with Samir! He's probably gone home now anyway,' she said. 'It doesn't matter if he hasn't. You must go back there. Latakia is a nice place, friendly, and quite unlike other Syrian cities. But it's Ugarit that you simply have to visit.'

'Why?' I said. I had a recurrent day-dream of being condemned by a people's revolutionary court to a life sentence of adult education with Samir.

'Well, two things, basically,' said Charlotte. 'First there's Ugarit's age. It was trading across the Mediterranean about 4,000 years ago. That's a couple of thousand years before Alexandria even came into being. It provided timber to the Egyptian Pharaohs. It had links with Cyprus and Mesopotamia. It exported bronzework to the Minoans of Crete. It was the first city on the Mediterranean to trade internationally.'

Charlotte turned back to her baklava.

'And second?' I asked. I needed all the reasons I could find to venture back down to the coast.

'Second is the small matter of Ugarit coming up with the world's earliest alphabet. Up until then the only two known systems of written communication used pictograms. But Egyptian hieroglyphics and Mesopotamian cuneiform were terribly awkward – literally hundreds of symbols were used to represent a complete range of words. The Ugarites reduced their own language to just thirty symbols. The communications revolution began there – it was the very beginning of easily stored and retrieved information. The city recorded everything from balance-of-trade accounts to its religious philosophy. The Ugaritic alphabet was likely taken over and adapted by the Greeks, making it the forerunner of modern European alphabets.'

'And the place itself?'

Charlotte only shrugged her shoulders. 'In some ways there isn't much to see at all. The site is quite degraded and there's not much more than foundations left. It's overgrown and poorly looked after. Oh yes, and one more thing. The sea has receded – Ugarit's a good way inland now. But go. You'll understand when you get there.'

It hardly sounded like a world-beating seaport. But I looked at Charlotte. If this woman could negotiate her way around the Middle East knowing only how to say 'quarter kilo' then I could face up to my own challenges. I decided I would be on the first morning bus to Latakia.

Charlotte was right. Latakia was quite unlike other Syrian towns. The port-city was a buzzy, busy place, and right away I got the feeling it was more outward-looking than the inland cities. Latakia was not just a centre of the Alawite faith, an offshoot of Shi'a Islam to which the Assad family belonged; between the two World Wars it had been a French colonial port and was still home to a large Christian population. As if starved of outside contact, Latakians literally stopped foreigners on the street to talk to them. After a day in the place I began to breathe a little more easily. Of Samir there was no sign.

I took a room at the Hotel al-Atlal, down by the harbour. It was run by an elderly Christian Arab with thick glasses and caved-in cheeks. He spoke slowly but precisely, and seemed to have taken a lesson in condensation from Ugarit's alphabet makers – he had almost as few words in English as he had teeth, but with them seemed capable of saying anything he liked.

There was one thing, though, he couldn't explain to my satisfaction. Where, I wanted to know, was the sea? From the hotel door the street ran two short blocks to a high wall and stopped. Above it I could see the tops of dockside cranes and the superstructures of cargo ships. The wall ran hundreds of yards in either direction. From nowhere in the city centre could you get the slightest glimpse of the water. It seemed a deliberate provocation – the construction of Syria's largest container terminal smack in the middle of an urban seafront. The city was cut off from the very element that had given it purpose since Roman times.

But seaports are open places by their very nature, and for all its invisibility the Mediterranean continued to work its cosmopolitan spell on Latakia. If the idea was to bar Syria's maritime gateway from importing new or different ideas it didn't appear to have had much effect. Latakia was liberal and tolerant in its habits. I saw few headscarves in the city. There were broad European-style boulevards, Christian churches and a Greek Patriarchate, tree-shaded avenues with outdoor café terraces, busy streets lined with bars and restaurants.

It was at night that Latakia really came to life. Was there any other provincial city in the Arab Middle East where women were quite as liberated? I doubted it. In the 'American Quarter', an up-market entertainment area close to the hotel, the sidewalks were thick with young Arab women in jeans; in skirts and boots; even in short blouses that occasionally but perhaps not inadvertently exposed a bit of belly-button. Does that fail to sound terribly daring? In Aleppo there were whole streets of dim, rundown nightclubs, little more than sleazy fronts for brothels. Now that's un-daring. What was impressive about the American Quarter in Latakia was its innocuous, international youth-culture style, its complete vapidity. In the Syria of the Assads exposed belly-buttons, MTV and teenagers crowding together for beer and pizza took a certain leap of imagination.

It was about eleven o'clock on a balmy spring evening when I walked out of the Stop 5, having had my own beer and pizza. Seeing happy couples holding hands made me feel a little forlorn, so I hiked off to the city Post Office to phone home. The building was long closed, but there were small-time scalpers by the outdoor telephone booths there who for a price would sell you a phone card.

Buying the card was easy, but the machine was unfamiliar and I couldn't make the connection. I tried three or four times, and then a hand reached over my shoulder and replaced the receiver. It wasn't what I had feared, the nightmare reappearance of Samir. The man behind me was stocky, grizzled, in his mid-fifties, and he was able to offer me help in the language of my choice – he spoke fluent English, French, German and Greek.

Home seemed far away that evening, and after I finished my call I had no objection to a bit of company. My new acquaintance, too, seemed happy to talk, so we strolled together through near-deserted streets. He was from Latakia, but had only recently retired as a captain in the Syrian merchant marine. He was blunt, his language was salty, but there was something appealing in his direct, no-nonsense manner. He had seen most of the world, and with a little prompting on my part could string together anecdotes about any port between Hamburg and Darwin.

But as we walked towards the city's old Roman gateway I began to get a little concerned. The Captain kept returning to the subject of his own home-port, Latakia. And what he had to say about it was not the kind of thing anyone said publicly in Syria. It started out discreetly, but each observation only seemed to make the man more agitated and outspoken. It crossed my mind that he might be testing my own desire to bad-mouth the regime, but I said nothing to encourage him. In the end there was such bitterness in his voice that I didn't believe he was anything other than an ordinary man who needed to let off steam.

As the city's stone Roman gateway loomed in the dark the Captain was complaining about the kind of shipping permitted to put in at Latakia. 'There are no regular freighters in the port,' he said. 'There are no passenger ferries in the port. It's all bastard containers. They want to keep the bastard port closed and under control. They want to keep us closed and under control, too. All we can do is pick our noses and act like monkeys and cheer the President.'

This was pretty strong stuff, but the invective against the state, the Ba'ath party and the Assads only got stronger. By the time we'd passed the New Mosque it had become more personal too. 'Do you know why I hate my fucking country?' he asked. 'Because they put me into the army for six years. A complete waste – six years! And now they have just put my son in the same damned army. I warned him to get out, but now it's too late. Do you think our wonderful army is any good no matter how many people they force into it? It's shit! Shit! Three weeks, I tell you! If we had to fight a day longer than three weeks the entire bastard army would collapse! I guarantee it!'

This kind of rant was all right out in dark and empty streets, but as we approached the centre again there were more open shops and more people. The Captain was so upset by this point he didn't seem to care if anyone was around or not. We came to the Saahat al-Sheikh Daher, a principle city square overseen by a large statue of Hafez al-Assad standing on a high plinth. The Captain, ignoring late-night shoppers inspecting tomatoes and flipping through pirate CDs on sidewalk stands, pointed an accusing finger.

'Look at the old dinosaur,' he raged, his voice far too loud. 'Look up at Jesus Christ and pray. Bastard! Bastard! Baaastaaard ...!'

I was thoroughly frightened by now, and even the Captain seemed sobered by his last tirade. But some of the poison was out of his system, and he seemed calmer as we walked back towards the American Quarter.

'You understand, things are changing here fast,' he said in a quieter voice. 'People used to know nothing but what they were told. That's coming to an end. Now we have satellite TV. We have Internet and e-mail and international telephone lines. People know what's going on. People know that the government speaks through this' – he pointed at his mouth – 'the way it speaks through this' – he pointed to his rear end. 'It cannot go on forever. I am sorry if I have disturbed you.'

We said goodnight and the Captain turned and walked away. The Stop 5 was close by, and still open. I needed a beer and a good dose of youth-culture vapidity. I'd had enough for one night.

Charlotte had been right about Latakia and she was right about Ugarit, too. It failed to overwhelm. When I arrived there the next afternoon there were no great ruins I could compare it to. It was not like the jungle pyramids of the Maya, the rock-carved tombs of Petra, or the ornate temple complexes of Ankor Wat. The old royal gateway into Ugarit looked like the outlet of a large city storm drain.

The whole place, in fact, reminded me of a vast, abandoned water-treatment plant. For the ancient Ugarites water was a vital element in all-important funerary rites, so the notion was not all that far-fetched – the place was a slough of wells, cisterns, stone-cut troughs, ditches, channels and subterranean conduits. Ugarit's engineers must have known a thing or two about hydrology, for the city, or what was left of it, sat on a little tableland elevated well above the surrounding country. Spread out below were the signs and sounds of more recent civilisation: neatly kept orange groves and vegetable plots, stands of dark cypress trees, white-washed, cube-like villages from which rose Arab music and the crowing of cocks. But Ugarit itself was anything but neatly kept. Its water works and foundations, its scattered stone blocks and the rubble of its once-great buildings were mostly hidden. They lay in a carpet of spring growth – spindly weeds, rich green grass and clusters of tiny wildflowers that waved in the breeze blowing off the sea. Ugarit was a place of serene and peaceful abandonment.

Apart from a gate-keeper who sold me a ticket there was no one about. I walked through the courtyards, halls and storerooms of the site's best preserved remains, its eighty-room royal palace. I strolled the ill-defined streets of its aristocratic quarter – like decayed teeth, its walls and houses had long ago crumbled to worn stumps. I jumped ditches, descended stairs into dank underground tombs and peered into dark cisterns. Behind the house of Rap'anu, where the first Ugaritic-inscribed tablets were discovered, I met a crippled hunter. Dressed in jeans and a ragged military tunic, he stood perched on crutches over a burrow-hole with a shotgun held awkwardly in his arms. Ugarit was the best place around for rabbits, he told me.

Finally, after a couple of hours of wandering over vast acres of ruins I came to rest at Ugarit's highest point, the city's sacred acropolis. In the temple of Baal I found a low wall with a view, and sat down on it. Late afternoon sun was streaming almost horizontally into the dead city. It lit up rough swathes of green grass, caught the tiny filaments on weed-stems and turned them incandescent, illuminated miniature clouds of gnats hovering low over fresh pats of cow dung.

More than 3,000 years ago ships bringing cargoes from across the sea used to drop anchor just below Ugarit's royal gate. Now I could see the seashore glinting through a distant curtain of cypress trees – it looked to be a fifteen-minute walk away. After a while I heard mooing and saw a cow passing through the ruins of the temple. It was being driven home by a man and his two small children, and when they came abreast of me they stopped. Ugarit was even better for cattle than for rabbits – the man, who introduced himself as Ahmad, said he grazed his milk cow here every day.

Ahmad wore a sky-blue New York Rangers jacket, but he'd never been further than Latakia. Of course he knew all about this place and what it used to be, he told me. This was where civilisation began. 'Every man has two homes:' he said in a soft voice, '... where he lives now, and his first home, Syria.'

I wasn't sure, in terms of strict anthropological descent, that he was entirely right, but I did understand what he meant. And as if perhaps I hadn't, Ahmad went on to tell me that the whole planet's population was related. We all had common origins. 'That is why I am learning English,' he said. 'It is the language of world communication. With it I can share with everyone else. It is the best thing today.'

I couldn't help thinking of another, less globally-minded Syrian I had met who was also learning English. This was an astounding assertion coming from a poor cowherd wandering around a forgotten port stranded high and dry a mile from the sea. Ahmad, despite present circumstances – his cow, these ruins, his morally bankrupt leaders and wayward nation – had kept faith with the ethos of an old city. I was glad we'd bumped into each other. When Charlotte Holloway told me I would understand why Ugarit was important I hadn't been convinced. Finally I was. Even here, even now, old cosmopolitan ways had left their mark.

I watched Ahmad as he headed off to his village. Was he right? Would he ever belong to a larger world? Behind him the setting sun was reflected in the Mediterranean like a broad, bright roadway. The sea wasn't likely to return to Ugarit in the near future. But perhaps one day soon, not far down the coast, it might make a reappearance in Latakia.

Seventeen

On the bus from Antakya to Adana cups of complimentary tea and coffee were handed out. The attendant who served them, a man in a spotless white shirt and black tie, behaved like a doctor about to conduct an intimate medical examination. Before making the rounds with his tray he carefully rolled up his sleeves, pulled on a pair of disposable gloves, and proceeded to handle plastic stir-sticks as if they were the latest in sterilised biopsy swabs.

I'm not saying this little demonstration was a sign of any great hygienic merit. When we stopped in Iskenderun to pick up more passengers the same man stood on the steps of the bus, studiously worked up a gob of phlegm and hawked it out onto the street. Above all, the gloves were a symbol of intent. For anyone who'd just crossed the Syrian border this felt like a get-ahead kind of place. Turkey had things on its mind and modernity, theoretically of the germ-free kind, was obviously one of them.

Coming over the high coastal pass separating the two countries the first Turk I'd seen was a peasant woman in baggy flowered pants hoeing a field. The next was a man in a flat cap and ancient suit, riding a donkey through a fruit-orchard carpeted in white spring blossoms. You couldn't help thinking in brochure-speak. It was quaint and it was colourful. It was timeless and unspoiled. And it all disappeared as soon as we got to the plain below. From Antakya onwards there wasn't much room for quaintness – it only got in the way of a busy, headlong rush of energy of a kind I hadn't felt in months.

Where exactly that rush was leading I couldn't say. Nor, I am pretty certain, could the other passengers sipping from their styrofoam cups. But it felt familiar. As the bus trundled along there was one franchise, one dealership, one assembly plant after another. There were Mitsubishi billboards, neon-lit Goodyear signs, yellow Opel banners flapping overhead in car-filled lots. Not only were they written in a non-Arabic script that I could read; I could understand them as well. They were telling me I had left a land arrested by sclerotic dictatorship and was back in the rough-and-tumble of a modern consumer society. Antioch, Tarsus, Seleucia ... long ago the towns along these shores had been the stamping grounds of New Testament evangelists caught in a fever of religious conversion. The Turkish Mediterranean coast should have felt ancient, exotic and biblical. But it didn't. After Syria it felt close to home.

I wasn't really convinced that I had driven into a horn-of-plenty – there were too many conflicting images lying just behind the billboards of moustachioed Turks driving new cars. On the far side of the Taurus Mountains, the steep range running behind the coast, I knew village Anatolia resembled Afghanistan more than it did any place in the West. Turkey was an old, poor place catapulting itself into the future. At one bus station I watched a whiskery country Turk in a ragged woollen hat abruptly hunker down on the platform, his knees to his chest, his posterior poised a couple of inches above the ground. He looked like he was preparing to answer a call of nature. Instead he settled down to take an incoming call on his cellphone.

But as we travelled along there could be no doubting one source of a vigour that was contagious even through bus windows. Along with rough-and-tumble capitalism came free-wheeling politics. I had stumbled into the middle of a Turkish election campaign.

The city streets we drove through were a sea of banners hanging from buildings, lampposts and overpasses. There were plenty of star-and-crescent Turkish flags. But most carried the symbols of the country's political parties: the light-bulb of the AKP; the radiating arrows of the CHP; the dove of the DSP; the horse of the DYP. I counted more than a dozen different party flags. Outside campaign headquarters on the main road in each town there were milling crowds and impassioned speeches over fuzzy megaphones. In suburban streets young men waving flags roared through traffic on motor-scooters. Even out in the countryside party militants were doing their best to rally the farming faithful – in the middle of nowhere we came across a campaign-parade of muddy-wheeled tractors stretching down the road and decorated with ribbons in party colours.

'Look, a rally for the Justice and Development Party,' the man in the seat next to me said as, pulling into the coastal city of Adana, we saw a crowd of long-coated, headscarved supporters gathering beneath a road-side marquee. 'The day after tomorrow there is a big election.' We rolled past the cheering throng, faces flushed and pink in their dark scarves, waiting to hear their candidate speak. 'Turkish women take their politics seriously.'

To me it was all fresh air – I had never seen such a strong contrast in neighbouring countries. All Turkey, left and right, Islamic and secular, was in a fever. And these were only municipal elections, a battle for control of towns and cities across the country. Before the bus arrived I made a change of plan.

I'd been intending to travel west along the Turkish Mediterranean, following the coast to the Aegean port-city of Izmir. But the sight of the great landmass of Asia Minor rising behind the shoreline made me restless. How far into the hills did the sea's sway extend, I wondered – did 'Mediterraneanness' spread right across Anatolia? Were inland Turks very different from coastal Turks? Now this election campaign decided it. I would watch the last day of campaigning in the Turkish capital and be in Izmir the following day for the vote. As we rolled into Adana I consulted my guidebook. It looked possible. I would head inland by road to Ankara. And then, with a little luck and a free berth, the Blue Train – one of the country's top expresses – would whisk me overnight to Izmir. At the terminal I stepped off one bus and straight onto another.

It was easy, for in Turkey all roads lead to Ankara. Once, when all roads led instead to the Sublime Porte, seat of imperial rule in Istanbul, Ankara was a remote town lost on the high, arid steppes of Anatolia – then it was called Angora, and known only for a local species of fine-haired goat. Today it is the beating heart of the country, the seat of republican power, and the hub from which a strong guiding authority radiates out to direct the lives of seventy million Turks.

All roads may lead to Ankara, but Ankara buses don't. They stop a little short, and deposit passengers in a brand new bus terminal that sits miles from anywhere. It was so modern and vast it looked more like a major air terminal. It had an air terminal's milling confusion, too, and could have done with a little strong guiding authority itself. I couldn't get anyone to direct me at all, and it was well after midnight before I hunted down transport into town.

It doesn't really matter, though, what time you arrive in the city. Ankara announces itself as a place of serious intent at any hour. Even in the dark it *felt* like a capital city. It had weight and dignity. It had gravitas. It had more broad marble steps leading up to more monolithic institutions than I'd seen since I'd toured Washington D.C.

The shuttle bus cruised stately six-lane boulevards, stopping here and there to drop off passengers. One great bureaucratic complex after another drifted past in the night. Ministries, state buildings, administrative head-quarters – all had grand facades, high, ceremonial doorways and, at one o'clock in the morning, anyway, a forbidding look. Official Ankara is built to make you feel small, and it does.

By the time the bus reached unofficial Ankara, the older, less opulent part of the city centre known as Ulus, I was the only passenger left. By now I had learned that travelling with an eleven-year-old guidebook to Turkey was not a wise idea – the country was changing too fast. But nothing had led me to expect the seedy doss-house the Lâle Palas turned out to be.

'The Lâle is a bit of old Ankara,' my dog-eared volume warmly enthused, 'with its marble and brass trim, faded grace and quiet welcome.' Since then the Lâle had acquired a dodgy nightclub with a couple of nasty-looking bouncers standing out front. When I found my way round to reception the welcome was all too quiet – it took me ten minutes to ferret out the night clerk, fast asleep in a room down the hall. Of marble and brass trim there wasn't a glimmer, but maybe that was because the whole place lay in the kind of eternal twilight that only 25-watt light bulbs can produce. All in all I could have done with a bit less of old Ankara, but it was too late and I was too tired to start looking elsewhere.

The first room the clerk showed me sat directly above the nightclub. The floor trembled and panes of glass in the windows vibrated. It was too loud to talk. I pointed upwards, and we tromped up four floors to the other side of the building.

The second room seemed all right. It was tiny. It held just four items – a bed, a bedside table, a cold-water sink and a telephone so ancient it appeared to be made of bakelite. More old Ankara. I dumped my bag, reducing the available floor space by half, and said good night to the clerk. It was only when I closed the door that I realised there was a fifth element, pernicious, invisible and inescapable, occupying the room – the smell of old cigarette smoke.

Turks, of course, are heroic smokers – if you can't get used to it you might as well leave the country. Had I complained the night clerk would only have looked at me mystified. But I'd never experienced stale tobacco like this before. The stinking pillow and blankets were the least of it. Uncounted generations of Turks had exhaled so much smoke into the room that it had become an integral part of its construction – it had condensed into a patina on the ceiling, been absorbed into the walls and impregnated the floor. In three minutes my own skin seemed to be exuding the same residue. Sleeping in the Lâle Palas was like sleeping in an ashtray.

I opened the window wide but it didn't change much. It only let in the blare of the constant radio traffic from the all-night taxi stand below. Nor was I any happier when I got into bed. The bottom of the sheet ended halfway down my calf and the springs were so badly bowed my bottom was a foot lower than my head and feet. I spent a restless few hours tossing and turning, and checked out early reeking like a Balkan Sobranie.

A hard, cutting wind was blowing up Atatürk Bulvari, the capital's main boulevard, and looked like it had been doing so for some time – the electoral banners and flags stretching across the street had been whipped to tatters. The morning was dark and overcast. Down on the Mediterranean the coast was green, the spring season full-blown. But here, almost 3,000 feet up on the Anatolian plateau, the city was still in the dead grip of winter. The trees on the sidewalks remained leafless and in the parks the grass was the colour of dishwater.

The few people out in the street at this early hour looked wan and washed-out too. Their coats were buttoned high and their faces were pinched as they leaned grimly into the sharp wind. There didn't seem to be anything Mediterranean about them. When Mediterraneans cross the street against traffic lights they dodge cars with careless insouciance. Here citizens didn't even try crossing the street against the lights. In fact I'd never come across a place that militated quite as actively against citizen-insouciance as Ankara.

When the traffic lights were red there was a visual display that gave pedestrians a second-by-second countdown of the waiting time remaining. When the lights turned green they showed a little electronically-animated figure ambling along; as pedestrian crossing time began to run out there was a sudden loud beeping and the little figure on the display broke into the energetic gate of a race walker.

'Marvellous', one might say, impressed with Turkish ingenuity and concern for traffic safety. But there is nothing like such devices for ratcheting up the general urban anxiety level in a place. Personally I'd rather see a few accidents. It might have been my own less-than-charmed mood after a night in the Lâle Palas, but I doubted it. Ankara that morning was a bleak city. The carefree *joie-de-vivre* of the Mediterranean does not penetrate to the heart of Anatolia.

Cold and shivering, I was one of the first visitors to Anit Kabir that day. The most austere and formal monument in a city of monuments, it sits on a low hill overlooking the city some way from the centre. But it was going to take more than a long trudge into a bone-cutting wind to stop me visiting the mausoleum of the greatest of all Turkish patriots. For here lay the man who had initiated the country's passion for secular republican democracy – Atatürk, father of the Turks.

The moment you set foot in the park that surrounds Anit Kabir you realise are on hallowed ground. Turks on the whole are an easy-going people, but one thing they will not tolerate: they might criticise his ideology or the acts committed in his name, but no one shows disrespect to Atatürk himself.

It was little wonder, then, that visitors accepted the admonishments of guards standing on the stone-flagged esplanade leading to the mausoleum. Asking Turks to put out cigarettes anywhere else is like asking them to amputate a limb. But here they meekly obeyed. Then they passed into a vast colonnaded courtyard overseen by an honour guard frozen to attention. Dominating everything was a national flag of a size you only usually see flying over US shopping malls.

Inside high bronze doors the atmosphere was more reverential still. There were glossy marble floors, more guards and the kind of brass ropestands and red velvet cords you get at the Cannes Film Festival. Visitors circulated clockwise, speaking in stagy whispers employed only for dramatic occasions. Atatürk's cenotaph, too, was exaggerated. His remains were actually buried in a smaller crypt below, but the focus of attention was a sarcophagus-like mass of carved and polished red marble. Twenty feet long, five feet wide and six feet high, it was built, like everything else to do with the man, on a larger-than-life scale.

The mausoleum left me cold; it was too grandiose and monumental to be appealing. Far more attractive, in a vast underground complex beneath the courtyard, was a stupendous museum collection of Atatürkana. Not only was there ample explanation of the historical context in which Mustafa Kemal, Ottoman general turned revolutionary nationalist, oversaw the birth of the nation. Here in room after room devoted to the man who incarnated the republic were ordinary possessions transformed into national icons. One of each was not enough. I counted a dozen walking sticks, five riding crops, half a dozen pocket-watches, nineteen cigarette cases, eleven cigarette holders, seven wallets, five notebooks, six pens, eight straight razors and Atatürk's personal rowing machine. That's not forgetting, of course, an extensive collection of fashionable Western formal wear – Atatürk was a snappy dresser – and the great man's dog, Foks, stuffed and mounted. I left feeling I knew as much about the father of the Turks' taste in smoking accessories and canine companions as I needed to.

No one down in the streets of Ankara, though, could doubt the seriousness of the man's legacy. In other Muslim countries to the north, south and east, other reformers had also single-handedly bent their nations to their will. But none of the Nassers, the Assads, the Saddams, Sauds or Pahlavis had given their people the kind of material and social progress, the democratic traditions that Atatürk had. And eighty years later that legacy was still being tested every day.

When I emerged from Anit Kabir early that afternoon there was just as much snow on the hills surrounding Ankara as there had been that morning. But downtown the political atmosphere had heated up. The streets were now thick with people and competition for public attention was fierce. There were long parades, speeches on city squares, campaign buses broadcasting party messages through giant roof-mounted speakers. Pamphlet-distributors were collaring voters on every street-corner. In one park, where a small anarchist party was holding a rally, there were more policemen in riot gear than there were participants. I wandered around for a long time, drinking it all in. Election day in the West was never like this.

At Kisilay, in the heart of Ankara, a young woman waylaid me on the sidewalk. Zahira was dressed in jeans and wore her hair in a ponytail down her back. She was studying political science and could have come from any university in any country in Europe. I wasn't Turkish and couldn't vote, I told her. It didn't matter, she said. She was happy to talk politics with anyone.

Zahira was campaigning for a small left-of-centre party. But she wasn't hopeful that socialism would sweep the polls in Ankara. The capital, she said, was a conservative place.

'I don't mean religiously conservative,' she added. 'Look around. You won't see many Islamic headscarves here – you'll only find them in the poor parts of town. But this is the heart of Turkey, the centre of power and politics and government. It's not like Istanbul or Izmir. It's far from foreign influences. It has no past but its republican nationalist past. Ankara doesn't look outward for new ideas – it looks to itself.'

As we were talking a car shot by, its horn blaring. A fist emerged from the passenger window and made a sign – to me the extended forefinger and pinky looked like the sign of the *cocu*, a gesture made all over southern Europe in ridicule of the cuckold. But here it meant something else.

'They don't like us,' said Zahira, frowning as she looked at the car disappearing down the street. 'They are supporters of the Nationalist Movement Party. They are on the extreme right and they make a lot of trouble.'

'And what's this?' I said, wiggling my two fingers.

'Don't do that!' Zahira said sharply, shaking her head. 'It's very bad. Those are the ears of the wolf. In Turkish mythology the lone wolf is a very old and powerful symbol. He is a mystical creature who led the Turkish people over the steppe to their ancestral home. The extreme right thinks that Turks are better and smarter than anyone else. These people are not intelligent. They hate Kurds. They hate Europe. They believe in a pure Turkish race.'

It was not extremism, in fact, but a broad-based movement that was Zahira's real worry. AK, the Justice and Development Party, had moved away from its radical Islamist origins – it was now seen as a moderate political force with religious tendencies. If AK militants frowned on liquor and encouraged prayer that was all right. More important, the party delivered – it was serious about paved roads, running water, well-lit streets and affordable transport. No one could object to efficient garbage collection, Zahira admitted, and AK's pragmatism had swept it to national power in the last general elections. The left would just have to learn to be better garbage collectors themselves.

Socialists, Communists, Nationalists, Islamists, Liberal Democrats ... in all there were fifty-five parties contesting the elections and every one of them was out on the streets. It was a battle getting through dense crowds and back to the hotel to pick up my bag, then carry it, still reeking of smoke, to the Ankara railway station. I found the last carriage of Train 314, the express 18:10 Blue Train to Izmir, just four minutes before departure, and collapsed gratefully inside.

Eighteen

Aboard the Blue Train, I had a two-berth compartment to myself and it was spotless. A uniformed steward knocked on the door and showed me how to fold the unneeded upper berth away. He also showed me a sink with hot and cold water, mirror and towel; a luggage rack; hooks to hang clothing on; a miniature fridge containing fruit juice and chocolate bars; a vent-control for fresh air; reading-light switches; a call-button for any hour of the day or night. Two carriages down, the steward told me, was the dining car – grilled lamb chops were being served even as we spoke. And if this sounds like a too-careful enumeration of what are really quite basic traveller's amenities, then all I can say is you've never stayed at the Lâle Palas Hotel.

I might as well have been floating on a cloud, and turned in early after dinner. All night long the Blue Train rattled and rolled, sometimes rushing, sometimes crawling cautiously ahead, sometimes lying-up silently as a goods train flew by in the opposite direction. I slept as one always sleeps on trains, intermittently. But I was happy anyway. I was closing in on Istanbul. Like a rail-carriage sliding in and out of sidings I slipped from one dream to another. I dreamed of Chechen generals in Sergeant Pepper uniforms, of scowling Samir in his sinister black security get-up, of Mustafa Kemal dancing like Fred Astaire in white tie and tails. And when I came to in the morning and raised the compartment's curtain I knew I was down off the Anatolian plateau.

The first thing I saw from the window was a yellow house in a field with two palm trees in front of it. The sun was shining and the leaves were back on the trees. It was warm outside. The Blue Train was too modern to have pull-down windows, but I would have opened them if I could, just for the smell of the air. Half an hour later, with the blue Aegean a ten-minute walk to the west, we were pulling into Izmir's Basmane Station.

I was tired of cheesy hotels and for once decided Mediterranean authenticity might be just as easily attained with a slightly higher level of comfort. Around the corner from the station I walked into the Hotel Baylan, a clean, pleasant place used by visiting businessmen. Dressed in suit, tie and crisp white shirt, Mr Ikbal Çelik, its cheerful general manager, offered me a glass of tea.

'Of course we have a room for you today,' he said. 'We even have a special reduction for you today. Because no one is working and no one is travelling. No one is doing anything but voting. The whole city is closed down.' Mr Çelik had a vigorous manner. 'You cannot buy a drink until eight o'clock this evening when polling stations close. You cannot carry a gun today, even if you have a licence for it. All you can do is vote.'

'Who is going to win?' I asked.

The manager needed no time to consider the question. 'In my heart I am Left.' He said it so proudly you could hear the capital L. 'But today the country is Right. AK will win.'

Like Zahira in faraway Ankara, Mr Çelik had to admit that AK, the party of moderate Islam, had brought efficient administration to Turkey. Nor were they any longer an extremist party; they were cooperating with the military, with business, with pro-Western parliamentarians, with the Kemalists. They were as interested in joining Europe as anyone else.

'The Kemalists?' I said.

'Yes. I am a Kemalist.' Mr Çelik sat up a little straighter, a little more officially in his chair. 'I vote for the CHP, the Republican People's Party, founded by Mustafa Kemal, Atatürk himself. It is secular and democratic and outward-looking ... like Atatürk himself,' he added.

'Will the AK win in Izmir as it's supposed to in Ankara?'

'That, most definitely not!' Mr Çelik said with alacrity. His mouth widened with a broad smile. 'Izmir is a progressive town. Ankara is a city of big politicians and big business. Izmir is a working-man's city, a place of industry and trade. We are too busy working here to spend time praying. We load and unload and assemble. We are a port – we do business with the whole world.'

Mr Çelik, with no clients to look after today, was enjoying himself. He took a sip of tea.

'We are international in mentality. When I was a child there was just one international trade fair in all Turkey. It was here, in Izmir. It was the time of the Cold War, but that didn't matter – the United States, the Soviet Union and every other country had trade stands and exhibitions. It was wonderful. I saw a model of the Apollo rocket. Very big. I even leaned over a railing and touched an American spacesuit, a real one. Do you think boys in Ankara could do that? Never!' said Mr Çelik. His eyes were bright with the memory.

'Now there are trade fairs everywhere,' he conceded. 'But Izmir is also the south-east headquarters for NATO. Behind the Hilton Hotel, by the NATO commissary, there are shoeshine boys who speak the best English in the city. And trade is getting busier all the time. Our port isn't big enough anymore. Izmir doesn't look in, Izmir looks out.'

Izmir, seen through Mr Çelik's eyes, seemed to be following a general pattern in this part of the world – cosmopolitanism was a coastal affair. I went for a walk. I didn't need a drink and I didn't need a gun, but I could see that Mr Çelik was right – the city was shut down. It was so quiet that when I passed by the Hilton Hotel there wasn't a shoeshine boy in sight. But what surprised me even more was that for a Mediterranean town Izmir looked practically new. Just down the coast lay the ruins of Ephesus, one of the largest and best-preserved cities of the classical age. But here there was little that looked even a century old. Most of the city was made of concrete, and not very pretty. Why, I asked Mr Çelik when I returned to the Hotel Baylan and found him still sitting idly behind his reception desk drinking tea. Mr Çelik was not only an enthusiastic tea drinker and Kemalist and toucher of space suits, he was proud of his city's past as well. He ordered an extra glass for me and settled in to explain.

In 1920, he said, Turkey had collapsed and the Ottoman Empire was in ruins. With the end of the war the victorious Allied powers had agreed not just on the dismemberment of the empire that had allied itself with the Germans, they had planned a carve-up of Turkey itself. By treaty accord Thrace in western Turkey was to go to the Greeks. Italy was to inherit a large part of the Mediterranean shore. Britain and France, already granted control of Iraq and Syria, were awarded much of the southeast, minus a portion slated for a future Armenian state. The Russians were to be given a chunk of territory in the northeast. The Dardanelles and the Sea of Marmara were to be jointly administered by the Allies. Turkey was to be left a land-locked rump-state on the arid central steppes. The arrangement was regarded as nothing less than historic desserts, the fate awaiting a major European adversary for centuries.

One country had not even waited for the Treaty of Sèvres to be drawn up, said Mr Çelik. Was the hotel manager an amateur thespian as well? His face grew suddenly clouded, his gestures oversized and dramatic. Already the year before Greece had embarked, with Allied blessings, on a military invasion of Turkey. The project was an old one – the Greeks had nurtured the *Megali Idea*, the Great Idea, ever since independence from the Ottomans in the 1830s. But their profound resentment went back a good deal further than that – what the Greeks wanted was in essence a refounding of ancient Greek Byzantium and its empire in Asia Minor.

They began, logically, said Mr Çelik, with Symrna, the ancient port-city that under the Turkish republic was to become Izmir. Whether Homer was a resident of Symrna, as tradition has it, remained unproven. Mr Çelik certainly believed he was. What was sure was that as long ago as the Homeric age Symrna was one of the most prosperous Greek colonies along the coast of Asia Minor. Later, as part of the Byzantine empire, it was one of the greatest of Mediterranean ports.

Symrna had retained its Western character even under the Turks. Less than a century after the Ottomans stormed Constantinople in 1453

Süleyman the Magnificent – a powerful but enlightened ruler, opined Mr Çelik – granted François I of France Turkey's first commercial treaty. It gave foreign merchants the right to live and trade in Ottoman territory, and before long Smyrna was the most Western and cosmopolitan city in the Ottoman Empire. Home to tens of thousands of foreign sailors, merchants and diplomats, the city claimed more Jewish and Christian residents than it did Muslims. A dozen nationalities shared in its sophisticated society and the Greeks, of course themselves Mediterranean traders *par excellence*, were pre-eminent among them.

But in 1919 the Greeks were looking to claim more than Smyrna alone. With the Ottomans' Grand Armies destroyed and their imperial administration in tatters at the end of the World War, the Turks could offer little resistance. 'The Greeks' big idea grew bigger every day,' said Mr Çelik, tension building in his voice. Soon they had taken the inland city of Bursa, and by September 1921 they were fighting on the outskirts of Ankara, the town declared Turkey's provisional capital by its desperate nationalist defenders.

Not only had Greece, a former Ottoman vassal, taken Smyrna; now it had marched deep into the Anatolian heartland as well. The shock of near-annihilation served to revive a demoralised Turkish people. 'It was then that Mustafa Kemal became a great national leader,' enthused Mr Çelik, who in telling his story seemed to undergo revival himself – his face was bright and lively. Under the general's direction the Turks reorganised and retaliated. In bitter fighting the Greeks were halted, held, then driven back. Their retreat became a rout. A year later, with Turkish troops in hot pursuit, decimated Greek forces were escaping from Symrna harbour by any vessel they found afloat. In the process the ancient city was destroyed, burned almost entirely to the ground. But the day that Mustafa Kemal – by now Atatürk – entered Izmir was the day he declared victory in the Turkish War of Independence. Soon after he declared the foundation of the new republic, too, and the Allies, bowing before a *fait accompli*, acquiesced to a re-negotiation of Turkey's treaties.

And so Izmir, Mr Çelik beamed, became a symbol of nationalist triumph born out of disaster. It showed that, given the right leadership and the kind of patriotism it inspired, a nearly decimated Turkey could become a potent force. What Mr Çelik didn't say, proud Izmiri that he was, was that under nationalism's thrall even an old and cosmopolitan coastal city could be shown up by a raw, brash new rival far out on the plains of central Anatolia.

But Mediterranean cities, like the phoenix of classical myth, have a way of rising from their own ashes. Izmir might no longer be a great mix of races. As I discovered the next morning, though, it has become its busy, cosmopolitan self again.

I stopped off at the reception desk on the way out. Mr Çelik was no longer there. His place had been taken by a clerk who stood poring over a newspaper. An enormous, bald man who would have had trouble with an 18-inch collar, he looked like a Turkish tag-team wrestler. But like his boss Mr Çelik he was an old-style republican, a dyed-in-the-wool Kemalist. He was both happy and sad. He turned the main page of the paper around on the counter to show me coloured maps and figures. AK Islamists had swept the country, winning more popular votes than the next three parties combined. They had taken Ankara and Istanbul with over half the ballot each. They had won three-quarters of the principle mayoral races. There was just one anomaly. The main opposition party, the Kemalist CHP, had easily won in Izmir. In fact all the eight cities won by the Kemalists were port-cities on the Aegean Sea.

'Why?' I asked.

The clerk spoke no English but understood the question. In answer he merely raised a large, horizontal palm high in the air, as if measuring the distance from the ground. '*Kultur Ege*,' he said, indicating the considerable height with his eyes. I spoke no Turkish, but understood the answer. 'We in the Aegean,' he was saying, 'are more sophisticated than the others – that's all there is to it.' The Turkish coast was a last hold-out of cosmopolitanism.

Leaving Mr Çelik's assistant glued to his newspaper, I walked through a busy bazaar area and emerged onto the waterfront at Konak Meydan,

Government Square. Like Alexandria, Izmir sooner rather than later pulls its visitors down to the sea, and it, too, has its Corniche. It is called the Kordon, after another French word, and much of the city's lively outdoor life is concentrated there.

The Konak Meydan was as modern and unexceptional as any other part of the city. But the sea beside it was anything but unexceptional. At the far end of the square began a great, deep bay, with the heavily built-up hills of the city running steeply down to the water on all sides. Out there on a sparkling roadstead freighters rode at anchor, tugboats nosed about arriving ships and hooting ferries plied their way through traffic to the far side of the bay. I had no need to cross over to the suburb of Karşiyaka, but then I saw the *Kapitan Mustapha Güler*, a ninety-foot, double-decker ferry gleaming white in the sun and about to leave. I couldn't resist it. Running to the terminal to buy a token, I made it through the turnstiles and hopped aboard just as the ferry was pulling away.

The breeze out on the water was glorious, not sharp like the winds off the steppe but fresh and inviting, full of hints of distant places. From out here I could see not just the path to the open sea but the inner harbour at the end of the bay. It was a mass of wharves and cranes, tall gantries for hoisting containers, silos for grain and cement, dry docks for big-ship repair. The other passengers had seen it all before. Having made the commute a thousand times they read their papers or drowsed in the sun. But as the *Mustapha Güler* cautiously tacked its way across a busy flow of traffic I watched ships.

There was the *Apache* out of Valetta, escorted on its slow way out to sea by a patient tug. There, too, heading the other way, was the *Georgos I* from Latakia. We dodged ahead of the *Rafik*, a rusty little coastal steamer flying an Egyptian flag, and wisely awaited the passage of the *Salerno Express*, a giant container-carrier flying the Maltese cross from her stern. There were other ships too far away for their names to be read, but as I stood by the rail peering out I noticed I was not the only passenger taking an interest. Sitting on the bench behind me was a small boy gazing out over the water and asking his father questions. There was a look on his face I had seen before. It showed the same curiosity, the same sense of intrigue with the unknown and faraway that I had seen in Ikbal Çelik's face when he described a now long-gone trade fair. The *Salerno Express* was hardly as impressive as an Apollo rocket. But of such contacts and curiosity are Mediterranean seaports made.

Twenty-four hours later, 150 miles to the north, I was looking at another sea and another port. The train trip from Izmir to the ferry-port of Bandirma on the Sea of Marmara had taken all day. I felt grimy and worn out. I was tired of trains, of buses, of hotels good and bad, of vast, unknown cities arrived at in the middle of the night. I'd been three weeks on the road, and was looking forward to settling down and not having to move at all. Istanbul lay just over the inland waters of the Sea of Marmara. Aboard a high-speed ferry, the *Turgut Ozal*, the crossing would take less than two hours.

I was looking forward to coming to a halt for another reason, too – I was growing lonely. Solitary travel is a process both sociable and isolating. Not far from the harbour-side café I was sitting in I could see a phone-box, and decided to phone Jany at home.

I had kept in touch with her from Egypt, Jordan, Syria and Turkey, and I thought I knew pretty well what was going on. But with Jany you never knew exactly what was next. Like the sea coast I was following she was Mediterranean, and just as unpredictable. She was lively, mercurial, emotional, demonstrative and voluble. Voluble, especially, on the telephone, and now what she had to tell me ran us through three phone cards.

The long and the short of it was that Easter was coming up and with it a break for Jany from teaching. When I had set out for Alexandria after the New Year I'd had no idea where I would be for Easter. Now that I'd finished my swing through the Middle East, she suggested, she could join me for three weeks. Wonderful, I said, Istanbul was still coolish, but free of the tourist crowds that would descend like Crusader armies later in the season.

'Istanbul wasn't exactly what I had in mind,' she told me from distant Aix-en-Provence, her voice loud and clear. Her voice was always loud and clear when she'd decided on a plan.

'I'd love to see Venice in the spring,' she said. 'We could meet there and then you could carry on eastward to Istanbul when I go back to teaching. You wouldn't miss an inch of the coast – you'd just be doing part of it the other way round.'

Most of my life had been the other way round since I'd met Jany, so I didn't see why it should be any different now. We talked a good deal more. But in the end I agreed, as Jany knew I would from the beginning, that I would fly out of Istanbul.

I boarded the *Turgut Ozal* in two minds. On one hand Istanbul, my goal for so long, was being snatched away. On the other I was feeling worn out and tired – the idea of a posh, pampered existence in one of Europe's most elegant cities rather appealed.

As we roared off across the water the sun sank, night fell, and the sea and sky outside the windows turned inky black. I was left with nothing to look at but ferry staff dishing out dinner in a brightly lit cafeteria. They wore little white sailors' uniforms with blue-trimmed caps and seahorses embroidered on their shirtfronts. They distributed clingfilm-wrapped sandwiches with efficiency, with panache and style even. But this was hardly the romantic sailing into Istanbul that I had imagined.

Nor was the landing itself. Instead of sailing up the Bosphorus and in under the harbour-lights of the Golden Horn, we berthed in a modern new ferry terminal miles to the west on the Marmara coast. The only lights I was going to see that evening were the runway lights of Atatürk International Airport. But it didn't matter. Venice, if half of what they said was true, was a city of some romance itself.

Nineteen

We hopped a train from Mestre, and rode a clattering metal causeway out into the Venetian lagoon. Two miles off the Italian mainland, Jany and I emerged from the doors of the Stazione Ferroviaria Santa
Lucia, a railway station among other railway stations. And from the top
of its broad steps Venice, a city among other cities, was suddenly like
nowhere in the world.

It was moving. Of course all cities move – constant, restless motion is
their nature. But Venice was moving *up and down*. It bobbed. Even at this
early hour the Grand Canal was heaving with traffic. Wherever we looked
objects were rising and falling on the agitated liquid surface that bore
them. Other travellers, like we train-passengers about to become boat-
passengers, were pouring past us and down to the quay beside the water.
But as generations of newcomers have done before, we stood wordless at
the top of the steps, agog at life.

Commuter-crammed *vaporetti*, the city-buses of Venice, cut heavy,
undulating swathes as they churned their way from one canal-side stop
to the next. Show-off *motoscafi*, the immaculate launches that make up
the city's snooty taxi fleet, cleaved faster, lighter trails over the water as
they scooted wealthy patrons to suites at the Cipriani or the Danieli. A
blue, square-ended garbage scow, its hydraulic claw poised above a heaped
cargo of plastic bags, floundered slowly by. Improbably, it, too, managed
to look like a superior kind of vessel.

There was every kind of craft dipping and dancing out there. There were vegetable barges bearing crates of bright tomatoes and shiny purple aubergines to market; post office boats carrying letters and parcels; raked-back, slate-grey pursuit vessels belonging to the *guardia di finanza*. There were the flame-red fireboats of the *vigile del fuoco*; vintner's boats laden with crated bottles and plastic-covered demijohns of wine; laundry-boats picking up dirty sheets from one hotel after another.

Coming and going amidst these specialised craft was the *topo*, the hard-used, all-purpose delivery vessel of Venice. I looked at the merchandise floating by on the battered decks of these Venetian work-horses – there were boxes of feather-light *biscotti*, half-ton office photocopy machines and just about every kind of cargo in between. And all of it was in motion, rocking up and down as boats criss-crossed paths out on the canal. Even unpropelled, inanimate objects like the floating *vaporetto* dock in front of us were semi-mobile – chained to the quay and staked between heavy wooden pilings, it couldn't help but jump and slew about as the wakes of passing craft fanned out to slap at the canal's banks.

I was mesmerised. The only other canals I knew were the three inter-secting canals of Little Venice in London. Now I could see just how little they were. The Grand Canal alone was two miles long. Radiating out from it, capillaries in a giant circulation system feeding fresh tide-water into the city, were 176 other canals. Narrower but only slightly less grand, they made up a maze whose total length exceeded twenty-eight miles. There were no proper streets in Venice, but more than 3,000 twisting alleys and bridged passages wending their way beside and over the water. There were no cars, no wheeled vehicles apart from delivery trolleys, prams and shopping carts. On the other hand, Venice could claim some of the most splendid palazzi in the world. And just as attractive, as far as I was con-cerned, was its collection of boats – the city harboured an armada of the most exotic and unlikely watercraft in the world. Venice was a boatman's paradise.

Jany was as enchanted as I. But other, more practical matters now lay before us. Somewhere in Venice, down one of those canals, our own small, homey version of a palazzo lay waiting. Jany dragged me back into the station to a bank of public telephones, and for the next few minutes she was busy talking.

A brief word, for a moment, about my wife's communications skills. Talk, for Jany, wasn't really a social skill at all – it was as necessary to life as breathing. If you stopped her conversing for very long you stopped her altogether. Nor was communication merely a vocal art; it was a visual activity as well. It involved her whole body, especially face and hands. I could follow Jany at fifty yards through a crowded street simply by watching for her hands. They were like restless birds attached to the end of her arms. In the event of a power black-out and complete darkness I wasn't sure Jany was capable of spoken exchange at all.

To a circumspect Anglo like me, such verbal conviviality was foreign – it was as good a symbol of Jany's thoroughly Mediterranean character as any. That she had become a language teacher was no accident – it gave her talents for communication the fullest scope possible. Her gift for sociability was operative in all places and at any time. On the bus, at the bank, in a supermarket check-out – in two seconds she'd fall into conversation with strangers, and strangers would soon become friends.

Planning for Venice had been no exception. Spending weeks in a hotel there, I knew, was going to be near-unaffordable. Like its garbage scows, even modest hotels in Venice affect superior airs – they are happy to command some of the most inflated rates in Europe. I'd raked the Internet and there appeared to be no other option.

Then Jany put more human skills to work. She taught Spanish at a *collège* in Aix-en-Provence, and had a network of teachers, teachers' friends and friends of teachers' friends that stretched from the Pyrenees to Andalusia. But she could just as easily follow other lines of communication extending in the opposite direction.

At a school in Marseilles Jany knew a teacher of Italian, who'd introduced her to an artist living in Montepulciano, who'd put her on to a Sicilian couple who'd moved to Venice and were on friendly terms with ... I won't bother continuing, but on it went, one link leading to another in a coil that wound its way up and down Italy, crossed the lagoon at the head of the Adriatic, and ended up in a small apartment by a minor canal on the eastern edge of the Venetian district of Cannaregio. Pinella, the apartment's owner, was visiting her mother in Ravenna for a few weeks. In the meantime it was ours. All we had to do was get in touch with Pinella's ex-husband, Caesar, an abstract painter and creator of fragile objects pressed from hand-made paper.

Such was the convoluted trail by which one telephone call and twenty minutes later we found ourselves standing on the *vaporetto*-landing at Ca' d'Oro, on the great S-bend of the Grand Canal in the heart of the city, eyes peeled for a man we'd never met before. Caesar, when he arrived, appeared every bit a bohemian artist of Venice, his fingers long and delicate, his goatee greying, his waistcoat vented and cut from elegant silk. So we weren't surprised, either, on being led through a labyrinth of narrow alleys, to find an apartment that looked every bit a bohemian apartment of Venice.

It was old, and reached by a worn flight of stone steps from a dim ground-floor hallway. Half a dozen umbrellas stood in a stand inside the door to the street. The hallway walls, in the baroque style called *scagliola*, were painted to imitate marble. Inside the apartment the ceiling was high and painted in geometrical patterns of sienna and dull mauve, old yellow and pale rose – colours so faded and obscured by time they now threatened to disappear altogether. In other rooms twisted wooden beams, dark with age, straggled across the ceiling. The floors, too, were ancient, a pressed assemblage of the tiny coloured pebbles, polished to a dull sheen, known as *terraza alla Veneziana*.

But it was the marriage of the traditional to the minimal that I enjoyed. The kitchen was all sleek design elements of burnished steel and the tropical hardwood floor in the bathroom reflected a rich halogen glow. The paintings on the wall were modern, and Caesar's own.

'Spaghetti,' said Jany after he'd closed the front door quietly behind him, leaving us alone in proprietal splendour. She was looking at a painting of long, wavy parallel strands scraped down to white canvas through dark paint.

'The Grand Canal and its lesser confluents,' she added, switching her gaze to another tableau of the same type, a single, broad wavy strand surrounded by a confusing trail of narrower ones. She may have been right, but I wouldn't have counted on it – she tended more towards the figurative than the abstract.

We didn't know where to look first.

We opened shutters in the rear bedrooms and gazed down onto a green garden, and in it a terracotta-tiled house whose walls radiated a patina of lush red. There was a tall magnolia tree on the lawn, a glistening bay laurel, stone benches, a trellised vine and singing birds. Best of all, when the windows swung open an odour of raisins and spices, cinnamon and warm pastry wafted into the rooms. Someone nearby was baking.

We unpacked – in my case, a bag you could take in the cabin of an aeroplane; in Jany's, a suitcase not much smaller than a steamer-trunk.

'Couldn't you have brought a little less?' I asked as I dragged it down the hall and into the bedroom. In a city without wheeled transport such luggage is inadvisable. But Jany seemed to have made her travel arrangements according to some bizarre law of inverse proportion.

'Well, I could have brought less if I'd had more time to pack,' she said as if it were the most obvious thing in the world. 'It's not what you take; it's what you have to decide what not to take that makes it difficult. I didn't have time.'

I said nothing more. For I had been around Jany long enough to know that there were differences between us, most of them having to do with two ways of looking at the world – one Anglo, the other Mediterranean – that were not worth debating. It was better to simply accept and adapt. Jany's peasant-farmer ancestors had accumulated and hung on to tiny plots of earth through the centuries – not a square inch was ever willingly given up. Did her Mediterranean world-view extend to the aggregation of baggage as well? I wasn't sure. All I knew was that often enough it took something less crucial than a Samsonite suitcase to provoke a clash of civilisations. So I kept my peace.

We put our things away. There were women's dresses hanging in an armoire, folded shirts in the drawers. Jany sniffed at soaps and toiletries in the bathroom. I inspected small bits of clay statuary and art books stacked on living room shelves. We poked at pots and pans in the kitchen. There were olives and apples, pecorino cheese and jars of jam in the refrigerator. On the counter beside it was a half-finished bottle of Valpolicella. We felt a little odd, as if we had unaccountably stepped into someone else's life. But already we also felt a little Venetian, and when we had unpacked I went out to shop. It was almost like coming home.

Twenty

Just down the way lay a supermarket, a small place provisioned, like all shops in Venice, by boats from the nearby canal. It was mid-morning now, and the stone-flagged passages of the quarter were crowded with shoppers. Without cars or other transport, Venetians cannot carry too much at one time, so shopping is an almost daily expedition conducted at the helm of little two-wheeled carriers. Even then they take up too much space in narrow aisles so they're left outside – there were a dozen of them standing by the supermarket entrance when I arrived. I found a space and parked my own carrier, a nifty little number patterned in red plaid I'd found behind the apartment door. It was as close as I ever got to a traffic jam in Venice.

Jars of antipasto, mushroom-stuffed ravioli, mozzarella and tomatoes for a salad – I stocked up on whatever lunch-things took my eye. But what interested me as much as the items on the shelves were the customers perusing them. This was not Harry's Bar, the Venice Biennale or a private beach at the Lido, so I wasn't expecting svelte and slinky starlets. But neither was I expecting the quiet diffidence and decorum of these buttoned-up matrons.

You couldn't call Cannaregio's middle-class housewives dowdy. They were well dressed, in a formal, conservative sort of way. Nor were they haughty or standoffish. Here everyone knew everyone else and, when two friends met, long and detailed were their consultative deliberations over the ripeness of the asparagus or the thickness of the Parma ham sliced by the aproned girls behind the meat counter.

But Italy is Italy, and one grows used to its effusiveness, its loud voices and warm, uncalculating spontaneity. That kind of thing was absent here. This wasn't Naples or Rome. Neither was it one of the cooler and more self-possessed north Italian cities – Turin, say. There seemed to be something else, a distance tinged with some unobtrusive element I couldn't identify that morning. It wasn't something that announced itself with a flourish. But the longer one stays in Venice the more one senses in Venetians a habit of reserve and quiet dignity. It is a quality that seems to have its source in the past.

It is not a character that has anything to do with the city's flamboyant commercial marketing of its history – its carnival or a thousand smaller fêtes and celebrations. You wouldn't find it in a day or two of tramping through noisy museums and across crowd-swept squares. It is something foreigners sense most easily in the atmosphere enveloping the physical city itself, as if it were an element discharged from old brick and undisturbed stone. They are not wrong – such emanations tend to concentrate in obscure places, in still back alleys and along minor canals after dark. But the mood is everywhere, and it was here, too, in the women in the aisles of an ordinary shop on a busy Thursday morning. And it made Venetians seem unlike other Italians.

Was it just a lagoon that separated Venice from the mainland? Or was there a wider distance which made for this quiet sense of a different and largely unconnected past? For a thousand years the Venetian Republic had gazed not to the nearest shore, but eastward, over the lagoon and across the sea. Long ago Venice was the focal point of the Mediterranean, the meeting place of Occident and Orient, an exotic maritime bazaar that became the wealthiest market of commercial exchange in the world. Venetians don't trumpet their past as they once did – their glory is, after all, now well behind them and their foreign ambitions have long fallen away. Today they are simply Italians – and bourgeois, provincial Italians at that. Yet that extravagant Eastern history is always there, no further away than the nearest palace or the faint trace of nostalgia in a Venetian face.

What also remains is a demure regard for the manners of another age.

The only uncalculated spontaneity I saw that morning was when a carefully made-up shopper, a woman of a certain age, emerged from the supermarket doors with her arms loaded with shopping bags.

'*Ecco la Mamma!*' she trilled effusively to a little white dog tied to a rail beside her carrier. The dog, in return, jumped and wagged its tail, pleased as punch. '*Cara mia! Ecco la Mamma!*' the woman sang again, and if she'd had a tail and no one was watching she might have wagged it, too.

I trundled my own shopping bags back to the apartment, we had lunch, and afterwards Jany stretched out for a siesta. I took myself off outdoors in search a quiet bench in the sun. Less than a hundred yards and just a canal-bridge away from our door lay a large, light-flooded *campo*, one of the squares providing open space in an otherwise cramped and densely-packed city. The Campo dei Gesuiti was silent and deserted when I arrived – in the early afternoon it was inhabited only by a tinkling fountain, by cooing pigeons and sparrows that flitted between trees. Occasionally I had to move benches as the sun slid westward from its zenith, pushing shadows from surrounding buildings across the *campo*'s bright flagstones. But it wasn't enough to disturb my contemplation of what had overnight become our neighbourhood church, the baroque Chiesa dei Gesuiti.

Its façade was vast, an ornate confection of white columns and heavy pediments. Vying for space, an entire community of stone-carved angels, saints and bearded patriarchs cluttered the front of the building. Some were housed in deep, arched niches. Others gave cause for alarm – less cautious, they stood poised on high parapets or teetered precariously from the edge of steep eaves. Of course they ran no risk – from the very top of the church roof, assuring the safety of her heavenly entourage, reigned the Virgin Mary herself.

It was an extraordinary exterior, but nothing compared to the stone-worked wonders that awaited inside. The church's makers seemed to have had a greater love of cloth than stone – they'd contrived to make every surface in the church appear to have been sewn from the softest and most pliant of fabrics. Fat silk pillows, curtains of rippling brocade, an altar covered in bunched swags of damask – all were carved from hard, cold marble. Even the walls themselves appeared to be surfaced in upholstered flock wallpaper. It all made the painting on the first altar to the left, nothing less than an oil by Titian, look meagre and insignificant.

But there was something even more extraordinary about the Gesuiti. Anywhere else such a church would be mobbed, the centrepiece of endless gawking and celebration. But in Venice it was simply a church among a hundred others. For the moment, at least, there were no vast crowds. There were no crowds at all.

The quarter around the Gesuiti slowly came to life after the siesta, and when it did its parishioners hardly seemed to hold the church in special regard. It was mere background to the stuff of daily life. Young mothers in jeans arrived with small children and plonked them down to play on the steps of the church. Dog-walkers stopped to let their dogs lift their legs on its more convenient corners. A pair of girls wobbled around outside it on roller skates. A raucous gang of small boys began slamming a football into its front wall.

'*Goal! Goal!*' they shouted.

'*Va fanculo,*' the goal-keeper, unperturbed and equitable in manner, replied to them all. No one, mothers, babies, dog-walkers, roller-skaters or football-players, gave the Gesuiti a second glance. It was wonderful, this unselfconscious, cheek-by-jowl co-existence of High Baroque and Low Campo. It was all the more wonderful that, apart from me, there wasn't another tourist in sight.

Eventually Jany sauntered by and together we wandered on past the Gesuiti to the Fondamenta Nuove. Behind a broad quay land came to a sudden end and the lagoon spread out before us. There were half a dozen *vaporetto* stops along the waterfront. Boats were making off across the water, following staked channel-markers through the lagoon's sand-banks and mud-flats. The islands of San Michele and Murano lay close at hand. Others, further out, sprawled low and indistinct on a flat, hazy horizon.

We carried on past the *vaporetto* halts. There were small restaurants on the quay, where at sunny outdoor tables diners lingered over the detritus of lunch – sauce-stained plates, empty wine bottles and tiny, drained cups of espresso. There were ice cream shops splashing the afternoon with a gaudy touch, a dozen different flavours of *gelati* lined up side by side. Just as colourful was an antique shop dedicated solely to squids – glass squids, brass squids, nimble squids in yellowed lithographs, agile, oil-painted squids in carved and gilded frames. Jany wanted to go inside, but out on the lagoon I was following a different kind of marine traffic.

There were ambulance boats coming our way. They came from various directions every few minutes, some following the shoreline from different parts of the city, others arriving from islands across the lagoon. Like land-bound ambulances they carried red crosses on their sides and blue lights on their roofs. One, an emergency case accompanied by a police boat escort, arrived at high speed in a wash of waves, its lights flashing and siren blaring. The craft were all converging on the same spot, a dock a couple of a hundred yards ahead of us.

'*Ospedale Civile*', it was sign-posted, and from freshly arrived boats uniformed nurses and medics were jumping ashore to wheel their patients directly into a quayside hospital complex. I had never seen waterborne health care before. I dragged Jany inside.

The Venice hospital's lagoon-lapped entrance led to even more surprises. The place was vast and ancient, and barely resembled a hospital at all. How could it? It was 600 years old and had seen its beginnings as the Scuola Grande di San Marco, one of the professional associations through which pious Venetians displayed their wealth and benevolence. It had everything a modern hospital could wish for – emergency wards, outpatient clinics, operating theatres, busy staff striding along with stethoscopes around their necks. They all just happened to be housed in the dim, quasi-monastic surroundings of late-medieval Venice.

We wandered about gloomy stone cloisters. We walked down superbly dismal, high-ceilinged hallways. In semi-gloom we passed blue-gowned patients pushing I.V. drip-stands on squeaky wheels. We stumbled across magnificent chapels. We gazed up at ornate ceilings, at religious statuary and age-darkened oil paintings of Christ crucified. I didn't think I'd like to be a patient here. As hospitals go there were too many reminders of the Great

Beyond. You got the feeling that in its Christian devotion the place would be more than happy to pack you off into the afterlife at a moment's notice.

But, still, it was pleasing for the same reason that the Gesuiti was pleasing. This was no ordinary institution, yet patients, doctors and visitors all went about their business in an everyday way. Here the sacred blurred into the profane without anyone noticing. The *Ospedale Civile* was humdrum and heavenly at the same time.

It took us twenty minutes to work our way forward to an antique, pillar-lined reception hall. By now we were used to anachronism. It wouldn't have surprised us to stumble out into a street filled with noxious miasmas, masked plague-doctors and tumbrels stuffed with cadavers. But even then I wouldn't have minded. I was beginning to enjoy myself.

Not even confusion on the way back upset my mood. It is one thing to wander out into the streets of Venice, and quite another to get home again – in the narrow alleys on the far side of the hospital doors we began going around in circles. We squinted at the map. We pored over the guidebook. We took conflicting advice from passers-by. I gave up on conventional navigation and tried Far North survival techniques – I gauged compass direction by the sun, took bearings from prevailing winds. Nothing worked. No visitor, as far as I can make out, has ever explored the streets of Venice without becoming utterly lost.

We wandered for more than an hour, never far from home but never quite there. Finally I realised that maps were useless, grid references a waste of time. In your own neighbourhood you use neighbourhood ways. At the end of a side street I spied a spiffy little shopping carrier pulled by a Venetian matron of a certain age. I had never seen her before but I had little doubt about which supermarket she was headed for.

'*Ecco la mamma! Avanti!*' I said in my best Italian. We followed her, sticking close behind. It took just two right turns, a canal bridge, and a left turn before we were able to drop our pursuit and unlock our front door. It was quite unaccountable: Venice was extraordinary and dramatic, but at the same time ordinary and domestic. Venetian tourism, I decided, was my kind of tourism.

Twenty-One

After our first outing we barely strayed from our own little corner of Cannaregio. If we ventured further it was not towards Saint Mark's Basilica or any other sublime, mobbed monument, but along quiet backwaters and alleys. For the truth was that we had a fairly good idea of the tourist mayhem that lay out there – we just weren't ready to face it.

We wandered minor lanes aimlessly. I began to appreciate small Venetian things – the delicate arch of a bridge reflected in a still canal, the water-eaten stone and crumbling red brick of a once-gorgeous palace, the sudden bright flare of window-boxed geraniums perched high over a dim passageway. The more slowly we went and the less distance we covered, the more of itself Venice revealed.

Jany became even more local than I did. As sociable as ever, she refused to let a small thing like the Italian language hold her back. She used a composite of her own invention, a sort of Esperanto construed on the spot and stitched together from bits of other Latin languages. The astonishing thing was that, helped along by gestures of hands and expressions of face, it actually worked. She used it to chat to Roberto Puppo, the baker from whose next-door *pasticceria* those wonderful drifting odours rose each morning. She used it to gossip to her new friend Monica, a woman so tiny she stood on a raised wooden platform behind the counter of her corner shop. And she used it as she nudged me through the door of every establishment in the neighbourhood.

Together we examined rods and reels laid out on varnished racks in an old-fashioned fishing-tackle shop. In an even more out-dated millinery she guided me through the arcane mysteries of women's foundation garments, hooked, elasticised, flesh-coloured objects so complex in make-up their purpose was unimaginable. In a hotel-trade supplier's we examined chefs' toques, maids' starched caps and yellow-and-black-striped butlers' waistcoats. It wasn't that Jany was actually interested in buying any of these things. She liked them because she liked the people selling them – they were part of the quarter and its solidly-knit neighbourhood life. The shops were old. They were unfashionable. They had personality. And in a fashionable and impersonal place like Venice, a tourist town with an incoming and outgoing population that renewed itself as frequently as the tide, they were a rarity. They were a vaccination against the trials to come.

We couldn't hole up in Cannaregio forever, and a couple of days after our arrival those trials duly arrived, as we knew they must, when we marched in hazy spring sunshine to the *vaporetto* stop by the Rialto Bridge. We might just as easily have gone into the heart of the city on foot. But arriving by water, I enthused to Jany, added a certain Venetian pomp and dignity.

Once the Rialto had been a banking district funding trade between Venice and the East – if you wanted to invest a fortune, exchange currencies, charter a ship, sell a cargo or mount an expedition to the Levant, this was the place to come. But things had changed. We had to fight our way past the tourist-jammed souvenir stalls that now sat at the foot of the humpbacked marble bridge. Where Venetians had once financed an empire they now traded tat.

Mouths agape, we threaded our way through the crowds past Rialto snow-globes and revolting Murano blown glass that looked like glazed vomit. There were pizza plates, Piazza plates, canal calendars and yachtsmen's caps with 'Venezia' scrolled in gold across the brim. And there were gondolas of all sorts – plastic gondolas, key-chain gondolas, blinking plug-in bedside gondolas, battery-operated gondolas that played popular Italian music selections. There were gondolas in bottles, bottles in gondolas, bottles shaped like gondolas.

They were among the more tasteful items. By the time we got to the Italian silk ties printed with anatomically detailed images of female genitalia Jany was snuffling derisively about Venetian pomp and dignity. The greatest days of Venetian commercial glory, I had to admit, seemed to have come and gone. But I wasn't worried. Just a short boat-ride away lay Saint Mark's Basilica and the Ducal Palace. Hadn't Ruskin himself called the palace 'the central building of the world'? If Venice was making money flogging pornographic neckties to all the peoples of the earth it also did a profitable line in art and high culture.

Fifteen minutes later we jumped off a *vaporetto* onto the most frantic stretch of waterfront in all Venice. In front of us lay Saint Mark's Basin, that broad expanse of water which funnels traffic into the mouth of the Grand Canal. But it was not nearly as busy as the Riva degli Schiavoni, the quay that lines it. Joining the crowd on the Riva was like falling into a fast-flowing current. One moment Jany and I were standing on its edge, marvelling at the force of its surge; the next we were swept helplessly along on a human tide. There was no end to the restless, roiling mix of races and languages and nationalities. Away it tumbled in a fluid, continuous spate, the upheld flags and umbrellas of tour-group leaders showing the speed of the crowd's advance.

It was no good trying to make for calm backwaters. Once we got snagged at the end of a stand selling carnival masks and bell-tinkling court jester's hats. Once we swirled about in an eddy of hotel guests struggling to the front door of the Danieli. Once we were caught in a log-jam of photographers snapping pictures of the Bridge of Sighs. It was only a couple of hundred yards further on that the torrent slowed and finally came to a halt in the great arcaded space of the Piazza San Marco. Like victims of shipwreck washed ashore, we were at last deposited in front of the Ducal Palace in the heart of Venice.

I had no complaints about a Japanese tour-group, the large party that preceded us up the Scala d'Oro and on through the Palace – they were as inconspicuous and self-effacing as any couple of hundred people can be. But I can still hear their buzz of excitement, see the massed video cameras swing back and forth in unison as a Japanese guide's commentary unreeled at high speed. In the world of art and culture the Palazzo Ducale has become a supreme example of European architectural refinement. In my own memory, though, its great halls will remain forever more a venue for the holding of large oriental sporting events.

Around we went. The palace was huge, the pace relentless. Not speaking Japanese, the details of the building's transition from Gothic to Renaissance remained a mystery to me. But I think it would be fair to say that both periods relied heavily on lavish displays of gilt. There were huge swatches of it everywhere. Burnished and gleaming, it encrusted walls, dripped from cornices, and ran in crested waves across ceilings. Much of it surrounded even huger swatches of oil painting.

Still feeling fresh and curious, we walked around the Sala dello Scudo, the Shield Room, a hall in which the Doges received foreign visitors they wished to impress. In other rooms we had seen works by Venetians whose names are known by millions – Tintoretto, Tiepolo, Veronese. In the Shield Room I looked at works by artists I'd never heard of before. I'm not sure that Ramusio, Gastaldi or Zorzi were household names for other people, either.

Why, then, had their artistry so impressed the Doge's foreign visitors? It hadn't – it was the theme they'd depicted. Spread across the Sala della Scudo's high walls were painted maps, representations of the Venetian Republic's once vast and scattered maritime trading empire.

I looked up at oil-painted charts of the Dalmatian littoral, of Cyprus, Crete, the Peloponnese, the scattered islands off Asia Minor, the wide coast sweeping around the eastern end of the Mediterranean. Everywhere there – by negotiation, by purchase, by stealth and sometimes by outright aggression – Venice had acquired the imperial possessions she used to promote trade with the East.

I strained to read the script on the maps. Zara, Zakinthos, Monemvasia, Negroponte, the Morea ... they were hardly place-names that reverberate in the annals of global trade today. But even at the height of her power most of Venice's territories were small and isolated coastal sites – islands, seaside cities, ports, sometimes nothing more than fortresses on rocky and defended headlands. Yet with them Venice established an imperial network, multiple strings of possessions rarely more than a day's sailing apart, joining the head of the Adriatic to the great trading terminals of the Levant.

For 500 years they had made her the richest and most powerful maritime nation in the eastern Mediterranean. It was the empire shown on these walls that was the source of the city's great wealth, that spawned her power, prestige and displays of opulence. It was the empire's trading prosperity that had allowed painters like Tintoretto and Veronese to exist in the first place. If Venice had produced the most sophisticated art of its age, it was sophisticated trade that had produced Venice.

Jany had moved on down vast, wide hallways. Alone, I continued gazing up at far-flung islands and thinking of how they had become Venetian. This was one of those moments, inevitable in a place where you could hardly sidestep the Mediterranean's rich and complex past, where I was going to have to confront a large chunk of history head-on. It was daunting – the island in the lagoon might have been called *la Serenissima*, the Most Serene Republic, but her centuries were long and crowded and anything but serene.

Venice, I knew, had never been interested in acquiring the territorial holdings of a true overseas empire. While she had possessions on the Italian mainland, her ventures there had more often than not got her into big trouble with powerful neighbours. Her good luck lay precisely in *not* being on the mainland. The lagoon gave her protection, and in her isolation placed her strategically between West and East. Her opportunity came in linking the two – she made it her business to connect the wealth of Europe with the valuable and hard-to-obtain resources of Asia. And so her aims were not ownership of land on either continent, but control of the sea that lay between them.

One result of this was that Venice had little use for the kind of moral rationale required by other huge empires. Unlike Alexander the Great before her, she felt no need to impose political unity on the world by force of arms. Unlike the British after her, she claimed no improving mission, no need to export a superior way of life to lesser peoples. Unlike the Spanish in the New World, she was inspired by no zeal, driven by no religious ideal to convert the heathen – Venice, in fact, was often cursed by other Christian powers for her willingness to do business with Muslims even in times of holy war. In Venice, profit drove all before it.

But every nation, even those unashamedly bent on commercial gain, needs ideological unity, some sort of cohesive, underlying spirit that justifies and propels its venture forward. Where, I had to ask, was Venice's? Then I walked a few short feet into the next room of the Ducal Palace. Here was my answer. The Sala Grimani was a lair containing half a dozen winged, stone-carved lions.

They served merely as reminders, for lions, of course, are everywhere in Venice. One sentence alone – a rather long one at that – ensures that readers of Jan Morris's superb study *Venice* are given ample feeling for the leonine presence in the city: 'The city crawls with lions, winged lions and ordinary lions, great lions and petty lions, lions on doorways, lions supporting windows, lions on corbels, self-satisfied lions in gardens, lions rampant, lions soporific, amiable lions, ferocious lions, rickety lions, vivacious lions, dead lions, rotting lions, lions on chimneys, on flowerpots, on garden gates, on crests, on medallions, lurking among foliage, blatant on pillars, lions on flags, lions on tombs, lions in pictures, lions at the feet of statues, lions realistic, lions symbolic, lions heraldic, lions archaic, mutilated lions, chimerical lions, semi-lions, super-lions, lions with elongated tails, feathered lions, lions with jewelled eyes, marble lions, porphyry lions, and one real lion, drawn from the life, as the artist proudly says, by the indefatigable Longhi, and hung among the rest of his genre pictures in the Querini-Stampalia gallery.'

That, surely, is a sufficiency of lions; I won't bother readers with the slightest account of the six specimens I bumped into the Doge's Palace. But Morris's description only further begged the question, and I lingered on in front of them. Venice was lion-obsessed. What was this heraldic icon so deeply buried in the city's psyche? Obviously it could be nothing less than essential to Venice's existence, a symbol of the energy that drove her.

Of all Venice's lions its most famous is the three-ton bronze beast who lives atop a granite pillar on the waterside Molo just outside the Doge's Palace. Probably the most didactic lion as well, its placing in this prominent public place reminded Venetians of their city's origins.

For the winged lion is, of course, the apostolic symbol of Saint Mark. And even if the saint's association with Venice is largely based on myth, it was as necessary to the greatness of this port-city as Alexander's legend was to Alexandria. Only with Saint Mark's posthumous elevation to the post of supreme patron of the Republic did the city itself climb to its dizziest heights.

Early Venice, by contrast, couldn't have started from a lower point. When the western half of the Roman Empire collapsed in the barbarian invasions of the 5th century Venice did not collapse with it – barely exposed mud-banks have nowhere to go but up. Of no interest at all until then, the uninhabited islands of the lagoon became a refuge, a haven for mainlanders escaping waves of attacks by murderous barbarians. Safely isolated, Venice gradually grew into permanent island-communities built on wooden piles driven into the muck. And with them also grew the self-reliance of a people with no other resource to exploit than the liquid expanse that surrounded them. From the start Venetians were as happy afloat as ashore, as amphibious in their lagoon as swamp frogs in a pond.

If the first Venetians made a living trading across the lagoon, they had to search further for their religious needs. And there was only one direction to look in – eastwards. With the West overrun and Rome in pagan hands the capital of Christianity was transferred to the eastern half of the empire. It was from Constantinople, the new Roman capital established in AD 324 in the old Greek city of Byzantium, that the power of the church radiated. Patriarchs and governors dispatched from Constantinople dispensed not just holy communion in Venice, but political instruction, too. Byzantine by administration, Venice became partly Eastern, also, in her taste and outlook, her love of refinement and sensual display. It was one reason why Venice was so at ease in her later trade in the East – she felt pretty well at home there already.

Venice may have begun as an oriental city, but as she grew so did the contest with authority in faraway Constantinople. Venetians, always independent spirits, elected their first Doge in the early 700s. It was a move towards self-rule which under 117 successive Doges was to develop into a kind of government found nowhere else. And it was rule with staying power – more than a thousand years were to pass before the *Serenissima*'s republican independence was finally extinguished by Napoleon.

I watched a teenage brother and sister slouch into the Sala Grimani behind their parents. They were bored stupid, and suddenly, in front of the lions, they declared they'd had enough. In this day and age, of course, bucking parental authority is expected – despite protests they simply told their father they wanted money for pizza. He gave it to them and they stomped off.

For young dependencies in the medieval age telling parent-states to go and get lost wasn't quite as simple. A century after Venice's first elections, a line of Popes was re-ensconced in Rome and dual Christian empires, Eastern and Western, had agreed to separate spheres of influence. The city on the water, squeezed between the two, wanted neither of them. Determined on a separate existence, she looked about for some way of signalling her intentions.

What Venice needed was a symbol, a talisman whose divine power would protect her identity and autonomy. In fact she already had a patron, the saint who today still bravely shares the top of a second granite pillar on the Molo with a crocodile. But Theodore was ignored – he was a symbol of Byzantine origin. Had that other evangelical power, Saint Peter, been available, he might have been enlisted instead. But he was already employed by the Holy See in Rome. With both protectors in the service of other states, the Venetians, never ones to let religious principle stand in the way of practical need, came up with their own source of domestic help. They engaged Saint Mark, concocting for him a CV that was doubtful from the very beginning.

Mark, so the Venetian creation-myth goes, set off one day for Rome from Aquileia, a city lying on the Adriatic to the east of Venice. Why he would choose to navigate the dangerous and deserted channels of the lagoon is not explained, but during the crossing a great storm arose and Mark's boat, propelled by a divine wind, was pushed onto a mudbank. An angel sent from God then appeared before the saint and intoned, '*Pax tibi, Marce, Evangelista Meus. Hic requiscet corpus tuum*' – 'Peace be unto you, Mark, my evangelist. In this place your body shall rest'. What the angel went on to say, the legend insists, was that Christians would one day settle the swamps and build a magnificent city as a repository of Mark's body.

Such a prophecy, put about many centuries after Mark's supposed marooning, was all very well and good. But a body was needed – this was still an age in which the physical remains of early Church leaders bestowed a potent aura upon any city that possessed them. And so a body was found. In 828 two Venetian merchants removed the remains of Mark from his tomb in Alexandria, the city where he'd been bishop for the last forty years of his life. His shroud, so the accounts go, was cut open and the body of another saint, which by good fortune happened to be lying nearby, was stuffed into its place. The deception failed – so aromatically scented with heavenly purity was the odour exuding from Mark's 800-year-old corpse that the theft was noticed and the alarm immediately raised. When the Venetians hauled the body aboard their ship only the ruse of hiding it in a consignment of pork saved it from discovery by suspicious Muslim harbour officials.

So did Venice, celebrity body snatcher, come into possession of a relic that gave it a spiritual mystique just slightly less prestigious than Rome's. (Only in 1968, in a commemoration nineteen centuries after Mark's martyrdom, did the Catholic Church consent to return the relic – and then merely a portion of it – to Alexandria.) Once she had the saint, Venice set about building her distinctive character around him. A gorgeous reliquary was built to house Mark's remains – it would later become Venice's great Basilica. '*Pax tibi, Marce, Evangelista Meus*', the words that appeared on the book held in the paw of Venetian lions, became a slogan of Venetian identity. For centuries Saint Mark's banner sailed ahead of Venetian fleets of massed war galleys. It flew before Venetian armies who trumpeted '*Viva San Marco!*' as they stormed into battle. From Spalato to Famagusta and throughout the Venetian domains the saint's standard fluttered over ports and palaces, churches, fortresses and governor's residences.

Not even a great fire that destroyed the early basilica and obliterated Mark's remains in the 11th century could hold the city's patron back. Mark's body had not been consumed in the flames, it turned out. It had simply been misplaced. For in the middle of a commemoration service held by the Doge after the basilica's rebuilding a miracle took place. There was a cracking sound from a church column, a sudden fissuring of stone, and lo! Saint Mark's hand abruptly emerged into the daylight, to be duly followed by his entire and wondrously-preserved body. It was hardly a surprise – with a sponsor of this resilience at the helm, Venice could only move from strength to glorious strength. Saint Mark, a direct witness of the word of God and incombustible to boot, could guarantee nothing less.

Suddenly Jany was pulling at my shirtsleeve. She barely glanced at the weathered, stone-cut lions I was still standing by.

'Are you asleep? she said. 'You haven't moved an inch in the last ten minutes. I've been through outer waiting rooms and inner waiting rooms, the Sala del Collegio, the chamber of the Senate and the Scala dei Censori. And there's still a lot more. Aren't you coming? It's exhausting.'

So off we moved, this time on the heels of a frantically noisy Italian tour group. Our ears ringing, our eyes slowly glazing over, we trudged through one thronged and gilded room after another. The larger the hall, the more spectacular the paintings became. By the time we got to the Sala del Maggior Consiglio – a meeting-room so massive it could accommodate the 2,500 members of Venice's Great Council – we had ceased to take in anything at all. The further we went the less we cared. We were tired, thirsty, overheated and becoming claustrophobic. The last bits of the palace went by in a forgettable blur, and finally we were out on the Piazza San Marco again.

I stood on the edge of the jammed square, thinking not just of the acres of gilded halls that lay behind us, but of the myth that went with them. Is there any point in trying to separate the historical from the fictional in a city built on the legend of a Christian saint? It would be like trying to demystify Che Guevara or the cowboys of the American West – historical reality, in the end, is driven by such fictions. What is certain is that in Saint Mark Venice found a figure around which a new kind of pride could coalesce – nationalism.

It was a more focused kind of pride than that which had caused the two ice cream-licking backpackers in front of me to sew Canadian flags on their rucksacks. Of all the Italian city-states, Venice was the only one to escape centuries of feudal autocracy.

Over time she moved from a rough kind of egalitarian democracy to an unyielding patrician rule that muzzled popular expression. But throughout, the city remained a mercantile city. In other societies across Europe the development of a commercial class was held back by its conflict with an aristocracy. In Venice a commercial class *was* the aristocracy, and its values pervaded the whole society.

The religious fervour that surrounded Saint Mark transformed itself into tremendous civic self-esteem and an identification with the Republic and its institutions. Allegiance that elsewhere might have gone to the nobility or the church was in Venice attached directly to the state. 'They want to appear as Christian before the world,' Pope Pius II complained from Rome, 'but in reality they never think of God and, but for the state, which they regard as a deity, they hold nothing sacred.'

Unity, in its turn, led to single-minded energy in Venice's pursuit of profit. If the *Serenissima*'s overseas adventures were primarily undertaken for the benefit of her wealthy merchant-princes, they were also seen to contribute to the greater glory of the city and all its inhabitants. And in art, in architecture and music, in the prestige and prosperity of the population as a whole, they did. Venice became the envy of the world. It was this fierce proto-nationalism, combined with unrivalled ability in all matters commercial and seafaring, which kept Venice far ahead of her competitors – for a time, at any rate.

A good deal of that commercial skill had remained – square yard for square yard, I was willing to bet there were more tourists packed onto this piazza paying higher prices for ice cream than anywhere else on the continent.

But success has its price – nowhere else on the continent is mass tourism so at odds with its surroundings. Behind the Canadian backpackers an overweight child fed pigeons while his overweight father took photos. Sandals removed for a picnic, toes pale in the grime that rimmed them, a woman sat on the Piazza steps beside us spreading cream cheese on crackers. Around us milled tour parties, families and school-groups from every part of the planet – hip-hop boys in baggy clothes and baseball caps; punks with barbed-wire tattoos around their biceps and beer cans in their hands; parties of silver-haired, name-tagged retirees; files of small children winding their way across the Piazza. Off in the distance tourist queues snaked away from the doors of the Basilica and Campanile only to disappear around far corners.

Closer by, a band in dinner jackets was stationed outside the Caffè Quadri and racing through a frenzied medley of Eastern European gypsy music – the end of each refrain concluded with the violinists, madly sawing away, flinging up their bows and shouting 'Hey!' Jany wandered over to the Caffè Florian to see if it looked any more restful, but wandered back to report it was crowded with tourists taking photos of other tourists drinking €14.00 aperitifs.

We were all the same. We had come to be amazed and entertained by Venice. In her Mediterranean conviviality Jany was as sociable as anyone on the entire square. But this kind of sociability was beyond her.

'Did you know,' I observed, 'that your compatriot Napoleon called the Piazza the finest drawing room of Europe?'

'Yes, I did,' Jany replied. 'But I doubt he ever imagined the whole continent trying to barge its way in at the same time. Let's go home. This is awful.'

I had to agree. Just at the moment our own little drawing room looked even finer. So dragging sore feet, we headed for home and a bath. We'd had enough art and culture for one day.

Twenty-Two

Why does tourism make us all so stupid? It was something I had to ask myself as, day in and day out for the next week, we were swept with countless thousands around the marbled magnificence of Venice.

Dutifully, we ascended the three floors of the sprawling Correr Museum, there inspecting Venetian coin collections, ducal regalia, hideous ceramics and Carpaccio's arresting 'Young man in a Red Hat'. We marched solemnly through the church of Santi Giovanni e Paolo, gawking at the family tombs of the Mocenigo Doges, the foot of Saint Catherine of Siena, and an urn containing the flayed skin of Marcantonio Bragadin, the Venetian commander peeled alive by his captor Lala Mustafa Pasha at the Turkish siege of Famagusta in 1571. Battling through crowds, we discovered furniture suites of green and gold lacquer in the Ca' Rezzonico, canal views by Canaletto, and a beast by Longhi – not a lion drawn, as the artist proudly says, from the life, but his equally animated 'Rhinoceros'. Few creations of any kind escaped our attentions.

And yet the more I saw the more I wondered about the impetus that drove us relentlessly around Venice like voracious army ants.

When we leave our homes for holidays in places like Venice we set out as functioning human beings. We're more or less in control of our lives. We have jobs that demand capable performance, relationships that need subtle handling, household tasks that require regular attention. We manage in a complex world. If we are not able to fix a car ourselves we know where there's a Midas Muffler that can.

Then we arrive at our destination and suddenly there is barely an area in which we have any competence left at all. We don't know the difference between a Tintoretto and a Veronese. We stumble through restaurant menus even when they're in four languages, one of them our own. We can't get around the corner, much less from the Palazzo Gritti to the Galleria Franchetti, without getting hopelessly lost. We might as well be mentally impaired three-year-olds.

In the normal course of travel these things aren't a problem – they are what make travel interesting and worthwhile in the first place. You learn that you prefer Bellini to either Tintoretto or Veronese, you discover that *figadini* delights your tastebuds and *fegato* doesn't. Eventually you even find your way from the palace to the gallery. You make the world a bigger place. But as time went by I began to wonder if the world was really becoming bigger at all – more often it seemed the same confusing place with just a lot more people in it. Venetian tourism was starting to bother me in a serious way.

Was I becoming a travel snob? Or were these vast tour parties, herded by their group leaders through one gallery and palace after another, really as sheep-like as they looked? In the circumstances it was difficult to be anything else. It was the scale of the operations that made it all so doubtful. Venice, a vast concentration of art, was also a vast exploitation of art.

'It's like the Vegas Venice, only much, much better,' a woman marvelled to us one day as, standing in a *vaporetto*, we steamed past Gothic arches and flamboyant tracery on the Grand Canal. Who cares what Venice really is, or was? Today's kind of tourism doesn't offer a lot of scope to find out. It is a hungry maw down which ordinarily competent people disappear to be transformed into dim-witted gawkers. The really odd thing is that they welcome such transformation and go to it willingly.

For me it all came to a head on the afternoon we finally decided to visit the Basilica. Day after day we had been putting it off because the lines stretching away beneath its domes and golden kiosks had been so long. It was the one place that not only I, but everyone else in Venice, especially wanted to see.

And with reason. Inside and out, it is the most extraordinary sight in the city. No one could take it for a simple church. It is too gaudy, too wild and extravagant to be a place of worship. The poet Petrarch thought it the most beautiful thing on earth. Mark Twain enjoyed it for its 'entrancing, tranquilizing, soul-satisfying ugliness'. Ruskin thought it 'a treasure-heap ... a confusion of delight'. Herman Melville saw it as charmingly impermanent, as if 'the Grand Turk had pitched his pavilion here for a summer day'. Not even Twain, though, a man who devoted an entire book to the still new and baffling spectacle of tourism, had any idea how big the monster he was describing would eventually become.

And it remains more baffling than ever. Why would people wait an hour, even two hours or more, I wondered, only to rush through the Basilica in less than ten minutes?

For here was the building, a sort of sacred trophy-house, that lodged the city's soul. Much of its treasure was plunder, pure and simple. No matter – such booty honoured God, Venice and the ideal of material gain equally, and for centuries a dazzling exhibition had encouraged congregations to ever greater efforts. Here were worked porphyry blocks filched from Acre; sculpted columns stolen in Syria; the stone-carved Tetrarchs taken from Roman Alexandria; the Horses of San Marco, looted from Constantinople. And that was just on the outside of the building. Inside, pickings from the same Byzantine adventure were everywhere. Nor did the Venetians feel any need to dissemble their ill-gotten wealth as art. The vast majority of gold and silver objects ransacked from Constantinople lay in the Treasury, a glittering horde of reliquaries, chalices, incense burners, icons and candelabra. Having heard of these things, I was anxious to see them all.

But I didn't. The visit didn't go well from the beginning. We queued for forty minutes. I was told I would not be allowed inside with the shoulder bag I was carrying. I returned breathless from the apartment to find Jany already gone in. I waited another hour to get to the front of the queue again. Out of nowhere a brazen German stepped into the line in front of me. I objected. He said my objections were useless. I said if he went ahead of me he would be breaking the rules of acceptable conduct. He said if I went ahead of him he would be breaking my face. So did matters proceed until I finally entered the Basilica.

Inside the doors stood movable metal railings, the kind used at terrorist bomb scenes, Jamaican carnivals, British cup-final victory parades and other lunatic gatherings. Here parallel lines of railing formed a corridor, about six feet wide, running up one side of the church and down the other. It was jammed with bodies and we shuffled along, looking left and right as we proceeded.

I suppose there were arterial corridors leading off to the Treasury and up to the Horses on the roof. I didn't see them. I was so dismayed by the whole pack'em-in-'n-move'em-along atmosphere that I didn't see much of anything at all. Even the Basilica's floor-mosaics, a display of colours and patterns almost as astonishing as the wall mosaics too distant to see properly, were invisible beneath our feet – they were covered by a protective layer, a sort of springy grey Astroturf. Moving at the same speed as everyone else, I was through the church and out into bright daylight once more almost before I knew it.

Venice's thousand years had passed before my eyes in just over nine minutes. I couldn't be bothered to queue up to repeat the process, and never saw the wonders of the Basilica again. The place left me speechless.

Twenty-Three

Mid-morning had passed and still we lay in bed, listening to the upstairs neighbour's piano and wondering how to spend the day. We were burned out, wholly fed up with churches and museums. Then, stepping out to buy *pan di Domenica*, the special bread Puppo's Pasticceria sold only on Sundays, Jany had an idea. For the residents of Cannaregio Sunday seemed to be made for excursions and family visits – dapperly dressed and fresh from Mass, customers emerged from Puppo's with bunches of spring flowers in one hand and boxed cakes tied with ribbons in the other.

Why didn't we make an outing of it too, Jany suggested, and get away from Venice altogether? Not far away lay the islands of the lagoon. The idea of not seeing another alabaster-cheeked cherub or Madonna and Child for an entire day cheered us tremendously.

Down on the Fondamenta Nuove the sun was shining in a limpid sky. Waiting on the quay with other island excursionists, we gazed out across the lagoon. For all its brightness the Venetian day was restrained – soft and pearly-hued and a little blurred.

The atmosphere played games with distance and perspective. The horizon seemed to sit too high and it was difficult to say how far across the water church or campanile lay. I reminded myself, as I often had to, that this was still part of the Mediterranean. Not far away from our own home the Marseilles sun, like the working-class city it rose upon, was plain and unambiguous. There the light was strong, contours were clear and objects simply defined. And so it was elsewhere in this sea. But nothing is quite as simple in Venice. It has no hesitation in informing you, through a thousand variations of light and colour, that it is a more subtle place. It stands apart from its sister cities and, despite common origins, denies kinship with any of them.

Soon our *vaporetto* slid into the landing. Passengers piled on and piled off, and with a sudden thrust of propellers and a back-surge of water we were away. It seemed as easy as boarding a city bus, but just how the passenger ferries coped was a mystery to me. I watched our skipper throw his engine into reverse and nonchalantly flip the spokes of his wheel to turn his boat's stern, allowing an incoming *vaporetto* all of six inches' clearance. Could anything but maritime genes a hundred generations old allow such calculation?

Jany and I passed on through the main cabin of the *vaporetto*, a place of crowded wooden benches and loud chatter. Through glass doors we spotted two unoccupied seats on the boat's tiny, open rear deck. There was a sharp, fresh tang in the air that never seemed to reach the confines of narrow Venetian streets. Gulls hovered so close we could see their greedy eyes casting about for passengers to toss them food. As the vaporetto rounded San Michele we sat filling our lungs and looking behind to the broad, milky-green arc of our wake. It didn't matter that we were sailing on a shallow lagoon and surrounded by hidden mudbanks. We had escaped – after the closeness of Venice we felt we'd cast off on a wide and liberating sea.

Murano was far too busy to disembark. So were Torcello and Burano. But at Mazzorbo nobody got off, so we did. The little island was quiet and peaceful. On a day of Sunday visits, the busiest people about were the living paying their respects to the dead in the island's green and leafy cemetery.

We walked beside the sun-flooded lagoon and I felt more relaxed than I had in weeks. Water has that effect. So, too, does lunch eaten outdoors in spring sunshine. When we came to the little waterside Trattoria della Madalena and saw tables overlooking a quiet channel we sat down without even consulting each other. I had the sole. Jany had the *frutta di mare mista*. She looked happier than Tintoretto's 'Virgin Ascending to Heaven'. It wasn't just the food. It was the sweetness of the day and the softness of the lagoon air that made for our humour. That, and perhaps the steadily descending bottle of wine.

By the time we were finished the world had become the mellow kind of place where all things are reconciled. We sat basking in the sun watching boats come up the channel. A few were tour vessels – packed, double-decked craft with loudspeakers mounted in the bow. More were local, families in small day-cruisers or young men impressing girls in speedboats. But the happiest-looking Venetians to go by were three crewmen on a *topo*, one of those tireless delivery boats found in every canal in the city.

Taking the day off, they lay splayed on the foredeck, their torsos bare, their tanned faces giving way to dead white in a sudden V at their necks. They may have been the hardest-working people in the city, but at the moment they had about them the satisfied appearance of men who owned all they surveyed.

I couldn't help thinking that once, long ago, it had been more than just appearance. But history's wheels had turned and Venice's maritime prerogative was lost. There wasn't much left but floating delivery jobs. It seemed a tiny inheritance from an extraordinary past. Did nothing else remain?

In one sense it did. Venice had in fact lost none of the business flair that had generated such prosperity for so long. The city had adapted to circumstances. Having created history through its wealth, it had turned around and learned to create wealth through its history. Instead of going out to the world for money, it was clever enough to persuade the world to bring it to Venice. And no matter how quickly the city slimmed down the fattest wallets, it did so with manners and style. The tourists, despite great crowds of other tourists, kept on coming.

But it seemed to me that there was something deeper that Venice had lost for good – its cosmopolitan character.

It didn't matter how worldly the guests at the Gritti Palace were. It didn't matter which languages were spoken on the Piazza or how many races and nationalities blended on the Riva degli Schiavoni. Real cosmopolitanism comes from exchange based on mutual interest. Mass tourism might have its own exchanges, its payments for services rendered, but the relationship is one-sided and temporary. Today tourists arrive at destinations all over the world, pay for what they want – sunshine or sex or art – and then leave. Of genuine shared benefits in the largest industry on the globe there are few.

Sitting on the edge of Mazzorbo and watching those *topo* men pass by, it came to me I wanted another kind of Venice. And I knew, too, that I was looking straight at it – a more watery Venice. Painting and architecture might be the elegant froth that floated on the city's surface, but beneath it lay the lagoon and the sea, long the basis of Venetian existence. I'd had enough tourism for a while.

I spent the rest of the day quietly plotting a mutiny, and the next morning, bright and early, presented myself at the Palazzo Loredan, Venice's town hall.

Escorted upstairs, I was shown into the office of Caterina Faloma. It was a small, busy place, full of stacks of paper and people shouting 'Pronto!' into telephones. Signorina Faloma, blonde and energetic, had plenty on her hands. But when I explained what I was interested in, she showed all the vigour and organisational talent the Venetians are renowned for.

'The sea?' she mused. 'You want to know how Venetians live with the sea? Yes, it is a big question. How could we not live with the sea? You must give me a minute.'

It hardly took longer than that. Soon she was on the telephone, and before lunchtime had presented me with names, dates and telephone numbers – a whole sheaf of suggestions.

'First, you must see the Arsenale, this very afternoon. It was the world's first shipyard, the place where they built Venetian galleys. I have spoken to Comandante Calzavara – he is arranging it. And you should visit the Archivio di Stato. It is wonderful, an old monastery full of monks' cells – it holds every Venetian document ever written about land or sea. The

Dotoressa Alessandra Schiavon is the archival director, and she will help you.

'Do you like sailing? There is a yacht, a famous racing boat called the *Moro de Venezia*: next weekend it will escort a regatta through the lagoon. You will meet Corrado Scrascia, a Venetian sailor. And rowing, you like rowing? A few days later there is a race for *caorlinas*, the market boats that used to deliver vegetables to Venice. They are very heavy, and need seven rowers. You can follow the race with Umberto Sichiro – nobody knows more about rowing. You are interested in gondolas, too? There is only one man to see – Gianfranco Vianello. He is a champion rower, and one of the best gondola-builders in Venice.'

I was thrilled – here was a watery Venice I had only glimpsed from a distance. I could hardly ask for more. But then I did. And before she sat down to her antipasti Caterina Faloma put a call through to yet another Venetian waterman, Renato Barich, of Barich Trasporti. I was enlisted, if only temporarily, as a canal delivery man. *Topo* toil wasn't easy, I was warned – the work was hard and the hours long. But walking back to my own lunch I felt happy. I might have been a *sandolo*, the lightest and most dapper of Venetian craft, floating exuberantly on a rising lagoon tide.

Twenty-Four

Overheard in the Museo Storico Navale, the historical naval museum that sits outside the walls of the Venice Arsenal: English father to teenage son – Here's an old British Army joke. How many gears does an Italian tank have?

Son – I don't know. One?

Father – No, four. One forward and three in reverse. Ha, ha!

It wasn't the world's funniest joke, but if it had to be told I could see why it was being told here. Venice's vast naval museum was partly devoted to recent history, including the last World Wars – the rooms I was strolling through held underwater mines, models of camouflage-grey destroyers and the bells of famous ships. But there were also a number of Italian 'secret weapons' of 1940s vintage. In technological terms they might have appeared devilishly cunning at the time, but they didn't look that way now. They looked like the kind of fiendish device that Q might have designed for James Bond if Q had just had a lobotomy.

The apparatus that father and son were standing in front of was a tiny metal vessel with a powerful motor, an open cockpit and just one seat. Labelled 'Explosive Speedboat' in English and Italian, such craft, the accompanying notice explained, had been employed in the Second World War in action at Suda Bay. It carried a powerful charge designed to detonate on contact with a target, and its use was simple: 'at about 200 metres the pilot blocked the rudder and jettisoned using the floating seat-back.' A floating seat-back! Those Italian naval engineers had certainly thought of everything. Still, I had my doubts. Why was the explosive speedboat used on only one occasion?

There was more zany-scientist stuff. There was a 'Waterproof Container for Carrying Assault Craft' – a sort of outsize cigar tube holding a cylindrical attack-boat designed to be 'attached to a submarine deck and used in a concealed approach to the entrance of enemy bases'. Was the assault craft waterproof, too, and launched from a submerged submarine? How were the expelled attackers – wet or dry – to get back into their submarine? It wasn't explained. But clearly the Italians had been conducting daring and innovative underwater experiments. There was also a mannequin dressed in an Italian frogman's prototype wetsuit. He had his oxygen tanks on his chest and wore aqua-dynamic rubber shoes so tapered and foppishly pointy that a 14th-century courtier would have loved them. It all seemed a little medieval.

But then I walked a little further and suddenly Venice's naval museum *was* medieval. And the older it got the more impressive it became. How can you not be impressed by a 400-year-old tiller more than nine feet long and adorned with a dragon's head? A tiller, what's more, that belonged to an oar-driven war-galley, a ship whose design was already old when it was adopted by the Greeks and Romans? So confident were the Venetians in the efficiency of their formidable galleys that they used them well into the 17th century. Looking at that tiller, a small remnant of what was in effect the Venetian marine version of a tank, I could practically guarantee it – no opponent seeing one of Venice's earlier triremes bearing down on him, its three tiers of flashing oars powered by 250 men, would have found time for making jokes. Venetian galleys didn't go in reverse and their top gear – ramming speed – wasn't funny at all.

And so I continued walking on around the museum, cutting my time as fine as I dared – I didn't want to miss my meeting with Comandante Calzavara and his assistant, Patrizia Rigo, at the gates of the Arsenale. But who could resist the carved wooden stern-ornament from Admiral Morosini's 17th- century flagship, a top-knotted Turk bound in chains?

Or a 300-year-old glass ship's lantern, surmounted by a fretted-metal lion of Saint Mark, the size of a Volkswagen van?

There were models of galleons and galliots, fustas and frigates, barques, brigantinos, and a dozen other kinds of Venetian craft. And they, too, surprised me – most of them were propelled by oars. The Venetians, having started life in a shallow, difficult-to-navigate lagoon, were always more comfortable with manpower than sails – they still prefer to row today. What astonished me were the distances they rowed back then.

From the beginning Venetians had rowed their warships. But from the 1300s they began to row their cargo-ships, too. It didn't sound like a brilliant move – it sounded like a step backwards. But it came down to a question of speed. With the growth of their markets in the East, with the rise of competitors like Genoa in the West, with the dangers of piracy along the way, the Venetians had to be fast. And, quite simply, given the technology of the day, they could row faster than they could sail. Perhaps they also had more incentive than most galley-rowers – the men weren't slaves, but free and well paid. Nor were they ever more than a day's row from rest in a Venetian port. When the winds were right they even got a little help by hoisting sails. Nonetheless, just imagining it gave me lumbar spasms. Men who could row from Venice all the way up to the Black Sea, load freight and then row back again were not men to be ignored.

Nor was their successor, Comandante Calzavara. What very nearly made me late for my rendezvous was a detailed scale model of a boat that had never been rowed very far at all. The state ship, the *Bucintoro*, rarely made it past the mouth of the lagoon. And maybe that was a good thing – it was built more for ceremony than seaworthiness. Not even Cleopatra's royal Nile barge had been quite as extravagant.

I gazed on. The *Bucintoro* had been 140 feet long and powered below decks by 168 men, four to an oar. Above decks the Doge, pre-eminent among Venetians at sea as on land, had presided from his high throne at the head of a spacious salon. State dignitaries sat in attendance below him. No matter how grandiose their behaviour, how rich their robes, not even they could add a great deal more to the lavishness of the display.

Festooned with heavy gilt, ivory, satins, embroidered damasks and other precious materials, the *Bucintoro* was a voluptuous symbol honouring the *Serenissima*'s eternal ties to the sea. From the winged lion on her bowsprit to the proliferation of carved sphinxes, mermaids, dragons and sea monsters disporting themselves across her hull, she was a declaration of the glory of maritime Venice.

Ten minutes later I was at the gates of the Arsenale, a decorative entrance set in two miles of high and forbidding walls. The gates continued to hint at maritime fantasy – carved, trident-wielding sea gods still guarded the way in. But on the other side of the wall all self-indulgence stopped. The Arsenale remains an active naval base and out of bounds to civilians – once through a check-point I was surrounded by the kind of spit, polish and purposeful bustling only the military can affect.

Impeccably turned out in a tailored uniform, the Comandante had a round face, a clipped moustache and the jovial disposition of the PR man. He was going to have to disappear, he apologised – he was working on the last-minute details of an Arsenale yacht show. But Signora Rigo, he said, clapping his Number Two on the shoulder, was a very able seaman. She would show me around.

Signora Rigo didn't look like a seaman. She looked like a socialite at a cocktail party. She was dressed in a tight skirt, had dark, bouffante hair piled onto her head, and wore shiny patent-leather shoes with high, spindly heels. As soon as we stepped onto the soft earth of the Arsenale lawns I knew they were going to be trouble. But the Comandante was partly right – Signora Rigo was supremely able, at least when it came to the Arsenale's past. Immediately she was off and running, bombarding me with a rapid fire of names, dates, figures and the forgotten achievements of long-gone naval architects.

We walked away from modern buildings, past Second World War bunkers and bomb shelters, into the middle of installations centuries old. Close to the edges of stone-lined boat basins were ancient dry docks and covered boathouses. There were mills and rope-factories, warehouses and wood kilns. The further we wandered the more dilapidated grew the buildings and the longer the grass surrounding them. Signora Rigo's ankles were growing wobblier; she was stumbling about like a fresh rating on a rough sea. At the same time she was lobbing statistics – galley tonnage, sail square-metreage, cannon weights, oar lengths, mast heights, per-unit requirements in wood, tar, canvas, manila, flax-fibre, iron and copper.

It was too much to take in. Gazing around a hundred silent, disaffected acres, I tried instead to imagine the site at its most productive. More than five centuries before Britain's own revolution ever got off the ground, the Venice Arsenale was turning out ships in literally industrial quantities.

Venice, the urban historian Lewis Mumford claimed, was the first place in the world to have consciously planned for industrial production. With the development of its arsenal in the 12th century it had become 'a new type of city, based on the differentiation and zoning of urban functions'. Its name was old, a corruption of '*dar al-sin'a*', the house of industry, and like many things Venetian it had been borrowed from the Arabs of the eastern Mediterranean. But the Arsenale's techniques were new. They resembled those of the modern factory complex.

On two occasions the poet Dante came to Venice and was toured through the Arsenale's noise and smoke and seeming confusion. He was so struck by it that he used images like the caulker's vats of boiling pitch for his elaboration of hell in *The Inferno*. But the production-line process was anything but confused and its unrelenting pace brought results. By the beginning of the 1400s the Arsenale was the base for 300 commercial shipping companies operating some 3,000 trading vessels. At the height of Venice's 16th century wars with the Turks it employed 16,000 workers, almost all of them specialists, turning out fully-equipped warships at the phenomenal rate of one a day.

The rare foreigners who visited the Arsenale – its secrets were closely kept – were astounded by the assembly-line methods evolved there. One of them recorded the process by which ships were towed past a series of canal-side loading bays. From them, each ship was successively provisioned with food, drink, ammunition, sails, rope and other equipment;

in the time it took a ship to reach open water it was fully equipped for a long sea voyage. If the Grand Canal was admired around the world for its leisurely elegance, the Arsenale was a byword for the organisation and industriousness that had brought Venice its dominance of the sea.

I looked around at buildings in an advanced state of decay, mortar slowly crumbling and doors hanging from hinges. What goes up must come down – even empires. Only one solid building by the water, its façade stone-carved, its triumphal doorway high and arched, recalled grander days.

'The *Bucintoro* boathouse,' said Patricia Rigo, wiping mud from her now not-so-shiny shoes. 'But it's empty – there's nothing inside. The last *Bucintoro* was stripped of its wealth by Napoleon. It finished its days as a prison-hulk, and was finally burned.' Understandably the Signora, like most Venetians, had little love for the man who'd once famously declared his role as 'an Attila to the state of Venice'. 'Napoleon didn't treat what was left of the Venetian naval fleet much better,' Signora Rigo added. 'It was confiscated and put under French command. The French tried to invade Ireland with it. When that didn't work Napoleon sent it after the British in the Mediterranean. But he wasn't very careful with it – along with the French fleet it was sunk by Nelson at the battle of Aboukir.'

We ambled along, Signora Rigo continuing to rake me with statistics. But I was no longer listening. For a fleet that had once dictated terms across the Mediterranean its final sinking in the hands of a disdainful conqueror seemed ignoble. Perhaps such an end was inevitable in the city-state's ever-accelerating competition with bigger nations. It was easy enough to look back in hindsight – almost from the start one could see in Venice's rarely satisfied ambition her eventual dissolution. With a little imagination I could even picture the Arsenale shipyards as they long ago set about preparing the Venetian triumph that in the end was to lead to the city's profound decline.

It started in the spring of 1201 with the arrival in Venice of a small party of Frankish knights. They had an urgent request. Anxious to recapture Jerusalem, wrested from them by the Turks a decade before, the chivalry of Western Europe was in the midst of mounting yet one more Christian Crusade.

The fourth in an attempt to rid the Levant of Muslim supremacy, it wasn't a struggle for which Venice itself had ever shown much taste. Venetians were above all traders, and it was peace, not war, that was good for business. In dispute Venice preferred the subtle arts of diplomacy and negotiation, and if she fought it was usually in defence of trade, not God. On the whole buying and selling in the East meant friendly relations with local partners – as business plans go, firing boulders at Muslims with siege catapults made little sense.

But on this Fourth Crusade the nobles of Europe were not asking the Venetians to take up arms. The Franks had a logistical problem – the transport of a vast crusading army across the Mediterranean to the Levant. And Venice was the only power with the maritime resources to do it.

Sea transport for 4,500 knights and their horses, 9,000 squires, 20,000 foot-soldiers, food and supplies for nine months ... it was a massive undertaking for a small city. Its completion would require the full-time labours of 30,000 *Arsenalotti* and sailors, fully half the Republic's adult population. Yet the Venetians, under their wily Doge, Enrico Dandolo, soon enough agreed to the proposition.

Dandolo's role in the events that followed has been debated ever since. But most concur that the venerable leader was attracted by more than the exorbitant sum he demanded – 85,000 marks, twice the annual income of the French and English thrones combined. There was also the Crusaders' promise, in return for the provision of fifty Venetian galleys, of half the territories they might conquer. And if Dandolo was blind and approaching his ninetieth year, none doubt his ambition and inner vision. Some scholars believe that even from this early point he had already set his sights on the greatest prize of all – Constantinople.

Relations with the Christian empire of the East may have soured over Venetian success in Levantine markets, but to the Doge's contemporaries the idea of taking Constantinople by force was, of course, preposterous – Crusades were work done in the name of God.

Venice rolled up its collective sleeves and the Arsenal laboured as it had never done before. And in a frantic year and a half the job was done. In the autumn of 1202 the Fourth Crusade assembled in Saint Mark's Basin. There were so many ships, nearly 500 of them, that the fleet stretched all the way across the lagoon to the Lido. It included an escort of fifty war galleys, 240 troop-ships, seventy supply ships and 120 cavalry carriers, the last equipped with flat keels and ramped hull doors for amphibious equestrian landings. For its era not even the transport of men and materiel to today's Gulf and Iraq Wars could compare to it. 'Never did finer fleet sail from any port,' wrote the proud knight Geoffrey de Villehardouin. 'Our armament could undertake the conquest of the world!'

But the fleet was in deep trouble even before it weighed anchor. For there were in fact several cities in the world which were now candidates for conquest by the Fourth Crusade. Behind the scenes there had been duplicity and double-dealing from the beginning.

The Frankish soldiers in the holds of the troop-ships had always believed they were to head directly to Jerusalem. It wasn't the case – the Crusade's leaders had judged Egypt to be the weakest point in the Arab's Middle-Eastern defences. But they had withheld revealing their intended destination in the justifiable fear that the rank-and-file would refuse any less prestigious target than the Holy City itself. As for the Venetians, they had probably never planned to land an attacking force in Egypt at all – they had recently concluded a highly lucrative trade agreement with the ruler of Egypt, and almost certainly informed him of the Crusaders' plans.

Dandolo, who despite his age and blindness sailed in splendour from the lagoon on a Venetian flagship, had drawn up for himself a wholly different itinerary. When news had leaked out before departure that the Holy Land was not the intended landfall, the disillusion was huge – fully two thirds of the fleet's compliment failed to show up in Venice. It was a mortal blow, for it meant that the self-financing Crusaders could not pay the Venetians the huge sum they'd been promised. But a deal was a deal in Venetian eyes, and the Doge now saw that he could work Crusader insolvency to his own advantage. Not far down the coast the Dalmatian city of Zara, until recently a Venetian possession, had fallen into Hungarian hands. The Doge now proposed that if *en route* the Crusaders would help him reclaim it, payment could be deferred and the Crusade proceed.

The Franks were aghast. Zara was a Christian city, and under the protection of the Pope. But Dandolo had the upper hand and, short of annulling the entire venture, there was little choice. Arriving at Zara, Franks and Venetians stormed the walls, took the city, and promptly began fighting over the spoils. Just as promptly, the Pope excommunicated the lot of them. Venice had consolidated her power in the Adriatic, but the action hardly spoke well for what was supposed to be a band of brothers, true believers embarking against a common infidel enemy.

The horizon ahead only grew darker when, just prior to sailing on from Zara, the fleet was joined by a hopeful young man, one Alexius Angelus. The son of Isaac Angelus, the former Byzantine Emperor who'd been deposed by his brother, Alexius had also cut a deal with the Doge. If the fleet escorted him to Constantinople and there assisted him to his rightful place on the throne of Byzantium, he'd agreed to show the greatest gratitude – he would pay the Crusaders 200,000 marks, supply them with 10,000 soldiers, and guarantee to protect Frankish possessions in the Holy Land. And finally, he promised, he would return the Byzantine Empire to the authority of the Catholic Church.

This was the clincher. To mend the Great Schism, the theological rift that for 150 years had irreconcilably divided Rome and Constantinople, would be an undreamed-of achievement. For apostate Crusaders who looked on the invasion of yet another Christian city with dismay, it was a moral green light. Alexius' money could pay off the Doge and finance the bankrupt force's invasion of Egypt. But the return of Constantinople to the Papal fold would buy the eternal blessings of the Pope himself.

There were other Crusaders, though, who didn't see the opportunities offered in Constantinople in quite such a Christian way. To most soldiers in the ragtag armies that marched across the medieval world the storming of cities meant one thing only. Muslim or Christian, they held out the prospect of loot. And it was not long after the fleet rowed up the

Bosphorus, dropping anchor off the walls of the Byzantine capital in June 1203, that they forced open the most splendid treasure-chest of them all.

Constantinople, Greek-speaking, Christian Orthodox and 1,800 years old, was at the time the capital of the most sophisticated civilisation on earth. Its urbane citizens had long regarded their Catholic co-religionists as primitive bumpkins. The Crusaders in turn regarded the Byzantines, long used to the luxurious ways of the East, as effete. But however sissyish they may have been, their city, many times the size of any Western capital, made Venice's magnificence pale by comparison. To the Franks gazing up at Constantinople from the decks of their ships for the first time this was the stuff of legend – a repository of classical Greek and Roman tradition, a city that had preserved Christianity amidst barbarian onslaught, and a place overflowing with unimaginable wealth.

At its heart stood the Basilica of Hagia Sophia – Holy Wisdom – a miracle of engineering far grander than any European cathedral. Yet it was just one church in a capital where there were more than a hundred others dedicated to the Virgin alone. Constantinople was a metropolis of stone-carved palaces, a city of bazaars without end. And everywhere there were statues, monuments and columns, holy relics and priceless works of art from across the ancient world.

There were wood-carvings from Troy, marbles from the Acropolis, bronzes from the foundation of Rome, copper-sheathed pillars erected by Constantine himself. There were, of course, the famous four horses of the Hippodrome, cast in an alloy whose composition had been forgotten altogether. Nor was Constantinople simply a gallery of pagan art. The legendary Crown of Thorns; the spear that pierced Christ's side; the Virgin Mary's Robe; the finger of the doubting Saint Thomas; not one, but two heads of John the Baptist – these and countless other relics were collected in the treasure house at the centre of the world.

And in that catastrophic visitation from the West it was all destroyed, a great civilisation either smashed to pieces or dispersed to the far corners of Europe. Headed by blind Dandolo himself, sword in hand, a Venetian assault led to a breaching of the sea-walls beside the Golden Horn.

Constantinople was taken in a day, Isaac was hauled up from the dungeon in which he'd languished, and his son Alexius was installed beside him on the Byzantine throne. Where now, demanded the conquerors, was the promised cash?

Heavy taxes were imposed. The silver lamps of Hagia Sophia were melted down for coin. Resentment and hatred grew by the day. Payments slowed down and finally stopped. The Franks threatened retribution. The Constantinopolitans tried to set the Venetian fleet aflame. A Byzantine nobleman, determined to have done with foreigners, deposed father and son, both of whom were shortly after murdered. With the death of Alexius went the last chance of any kind of negotiated payment. The Franks decided to pay themselves.

Rape, pillage, murder and destruction – few sacks in history have measured up to the sack of Constantinople. For three days sword-wielding Crusaders, half-crazed with blood and lust and drink, rampaged about the city in a riot of wanton destruction. Whole quarters blazed. Palaces were smashed, churches stripped, libraries burned, mosaics ripped down, bronzes wrenched from their plinths. In Hagia Sophia, the holy of holies, a drunken prostitute was installed on the Patriarch's throne, where she screamed blasphemies, and 'sang bawdy songs, and danced immodestly in the holy place'. It was little wonder that the Byzantines saw the Crusaders as heralds of the Antichrist.

As the Franks were destroying what they couldn't carry off wholesale, the Venetians were far more selective in their choices – they moved calmly about the city crating up its greatest treasures. But the most valuable possession that Venice carried home from the sack of Constantinople was not gold or silver – it was dominance of the entire eastern Mediterranean.

Dandolo was perfectly happy to allow a Flemish nobleman to assume the throne in Constantinople – he knew that feudalisation and inevitable squabbling would only keep his rivals, and the Byzantine Empire itself, weak and divided. But what he did secure with great satisfaction was the foundation for the Venetian empire of the future. Assuming the poetically sonorous and topographically-correct title of 'Lord of a Quarter and Half a Quarter of the Roman Empire', Dandolo accepted the Venetian portion of the carve-up of Byzantium – Crete, the western coasts of Thrace and the Greek mainland, the Ionian islands and the Peloponnese. His agreed-upon three-eighths of the spoils were carefully chosen – it was these lands that now gave Venice an uninterrupted chain of ports from the Venetian lagoon to the Black Sea. Before Venice had been a trading city. Now it was a trading empire.

So in the end it was not German, French or Flemish knights who were the real beneficiaries in Constantinople. It was the power that had engineered, or at the very least facilitated, its downfall – Venice itself.

Within a few decades the empire and its capital were retaken by the Byzantines. But Venice hung on to the commercial colonies she had won, used them as a base to acquire others, and for 250 years made huge profits from them. By the end of that time Venetians had become the greatest shipbuilders, sailors and traders in the world, and their city the most beautiful in Europe.

Many European historians now say that an earlier invasion by Turks or Mongols would have been preferable to Constantinople's Christian sacking – the damage to Western heritage would have been less. They go further still, maintaining that the destruction did more than simply annihilate a great civilisation. For while the Byzantine Empire of the Greeks was to linger on, it never recovered. A strong Byzantium might have provided protection on Europe's southeastern flank, but a weakened Byzantium was no match for Turkish armies. In 1453 the city was once again invaded, this time to become Istanbul, capital of the Ottomans. The greed that brought about the destruction of eastern Christendom by western Christendom was to result in the Ottoman domination of much of Eastern Europe for five centuries. And Venice, inevitably in the front line through much of the conflict, was to suffer greatly for Doge Dandolo's overarching ambition.

Empires come and go, and so do conducted tours. As I'd been reflecting Signora Rigo had been directing me towards the grand gate of the Arsenale. The spate of facts and figures had nearly dried up. But oddly enough, as we reached harder ground and my guide ceased wobbling uncertainly on her heels she seemed to lose the firm confidence she had so far displayed.

Around the gate were ranged four stone-carved lions, so famous in Venice, affirmed the Signora, that erudite scholars had written entire volumes about their history and provenance. One had probably been removed from the Lion Terrace at Delos to commemorate the short-lived Venetian recapture of Corfu from the Turks in 1716. Two others had been taken from Piraeus to mark the temporary reconquest of the Peloponnese by Francesco Morosini in 1687.

But the origins of the fourth lion, my guide had to admit as we shook hands goodbye, left her stumped.

It was an odd-looking creature. Was it Greek? Syrian? Roman? Did it celebrate a victory in Venice's centuries of straggling rear-guard actions against the Turks? Signora Rigo shrugged her shoulders. 'I just don't know,' she said. 'To tell you the truth, I believe the specialists got it wrong. To me it doesn't look like a lion at all. I think it's a dog.'

Such are the occasional uncertainties one comes across in the recounting of the Venetian past, I thought as I walked home. But of the folly of the sack of Constantinople there could be little doubt at all.

Twenty-Five

There was an early-morning fog lying over Venice when I made my way to the church of the Friari a day or two later. In the muffled and empty medieval streets I must have circled around it two or three times, quite lost, before it loomed out of the mist before me like a brick cliffside.

It wasn't the grand Gothic entrance that I made for, but a smaller doorway on the far side of the church. When the Franciscans were in their Venetian heyday there could have been no shortage of monks to serve the Friari. Nor did they have to walk far to get there. Fifteen hundred of them were housed in the vast adjoining monastery I was now entering.

I hoped for their sake that all those bodies had generated a little warmth. Outside a humid chill in the air went right to the bones. Inside it seemed even colder. No wonder the monks had spent summer and winter in the same thick woollen robes. Seven hundred years later the building was still damp and unheated, and I wondered how the staff of the Venetian State Archives coped.

I wasn't expecting to be met by a robed and cowled abbot, but I imagined that the archival director of such a place would be something like that – no one, I was sure, could spend a more than a month or two in these gloomy corridors without becoming distinctly monkish. So when I was collected at the reception desk by the Dottoressa Alessandra Schiavon, twenty-four years in the business and still as bright and lively as the young women in Tintoretto's 'Mercury and the Three Graces', I was taken aback.

The Dottoressa was a step or two ahead of the monks. Not only did she wear a warm woollen skirt, she fought the cold radiating up from the flag-stoned paving with thick stockings and high leather boots as well. But monkish she was not. Her fingers flashed with jewellery and gold rings, her face was surrounded by a nimbus of curly dark hair, and her smile was warm and animated. It didn't seem to matter where I went – the women of Venice were vivacious and formidable. No one, surely, could deal with the cold, dead hand of history more effectively. Alessandra Schiavon loved what she did – for her the Venetian past had never stopped living at all.

The archivist led me through an arched and columned reading room, once the monastery refectory. A few scholars were already installed there, heads lowered over tomes and documents. Every day hundreds of tourists passed through the Friari next door, but here a serene calm reigned. Did non-academics ever arrive, I whispered, to disturb the peace?

'Sometimes,' the Dottoressa said as I followed her towards the heart of the monastery. 'Journalists and photographers like the Archives, although they're more interested in the setting than the documents. Occasionally we get filmmakers, too, although that doesn't always work out. The last bunch, a German documentary crew, thought things needed livening up. They tried to bring a Venetian lion onto the set – a real one.'

Passing through the monastery cloister we paused at a tall Franciscan monument, all marble saints and winged angels, that rose over the monks' well.

'Nobody in Venice much likes Napoleon, but we should be thankful he knew an opportunity when he saw it,' Signora Schiavon said as she admired the well. 'He was a record keeper himself. When he closed down the city's powerful religious orders and threw out their clerics he saw he suddenly had a space large enough to house all the republic's documents. And it had to be large. In the 8th century a Venetian widow gave thirty-five baskets of olives to a monastery in Friuli. The donation was recorded, and not much has happened since that wasn't. Deeds, wills, property pur-chases, marriages, inheritances, bills of sale ... barely a scrap of parchment or piece of paper has been thrown away. It all ended up here.'

It sounded dreary enough to send even a conveyancer into a state of rigid catalepsy. But it wasn't really. The Venetians were thorough, systematic and secretive rulers, and public consultation was not the order of the day. The Great Council, the Senate, the Collegio, the Signoria, the Council of Ten ... the higher one climbed through the levels of power the less one knew of their deliberations. Yet like most such tightly-run organisations, the Venetian Republic had an obsessive mania for taking down and preserving its minutae. What lay inside these walls went some way beyond olive transactions – it was the most detailed record of early modern state rule in the world.

On the far side of the cloister we plunged into a confusing, multi-floored maze where windows were few and far between. In all directions lay long corridors, high-ceilinged chambers and tiny monks' cells. All were stuffed from top to bottom with paper – faded paper and folded paper; paper in boxes old and new; paper rolled into scrolls and tied with coloured ribbons; paper worm-eaten and mildewed and reeking with age. It seemed unlikely that one small city could have produced quite so many written words.

In a moment I was lost. The halls went on forever, running off into the distance like an exercise in Renaissance artistic perspective. In an earlier age so little was known about this hidden world that rumours of the Archives were rife. They were wild estimates about how many hundred rooms it contained, how many million volumes. Jan Morris tells the story of the number-addled geographer Andrea Balbi, who calculated there were 693,176,720 pages of paper in the Archive which, if laid out one after the other, would create a trail 1,444,800,000 feet long and go eleven times around the globe.

It was all exaggeration, the Dottoressa assured me. In total there were seventy-eight kilometres of shelves in 300 rooms. Inspired by the brain-fevered Balbi, I made a quick calculation. That was a mere 255,840 linear feet of documents – hardly anything at all, really. Still, said the archivist, she could probably find something here that would interest me.

And she did. Signora Schiavon assured me no one could know the entire Archive. But as we walked through corridor after corridor she had no difficulty picking out items relating to the great *Stato del Mar*, the sea-state that was Venice.

'Water, water ... let me see,' she murmured, running her eyes over ancient document boxes. 'Yes, here we are. These are the proceedings from meetings of the *Savii ed Esecatori alle Aquae* – the Wise Men and Executors in the Ministry of Water. They were responsible for advising on water in all its states – river, lagoon or open sea. We have 1,200 boxes of theirs in this room. This one contains ... ah ... a map and directives on water control in the Venetian mainland city of Vicenza.' Suddenly I was looking at a detailed, coloured map of canals and irrigated rice-fields that the great hydraulic engineer, Leonardo da Vinci himself, might have admired.

From there we moved outward into deeper and faster-flowing waters. In scarred leather volumes we looked at a neat hand, 500 years old, that had recorded debates and disputes over navigation on the Brenta River. Miles of shelves away we pored over the inner workings of the Mercanzia, the body that regulated the finances of mercantile transport. We strolled on to look at packets of trade correspondence, listings of maritime cargoes, catalogues of anchorage fees, sailors' employment registers, customs records, edicts on the provision of shipyard timber from Dalmatian forests, insurance claims for shipwrecks, retirement regulations for master mariners, cannon production in the Arsenale. There was the daily log of the ship *Sacra Famillia* sailing to Constantinople; of the *Nova Caesarea* setting out for Alexandria; of the *Calima* beating eastward against a stiff scirocco on her way to Salonica.

After a while I began to feel quite as worn out as any struggling crew member on the *Calima*. The State Archives were exhaustive and exhausting. The Dottoressa was indefatigable, but my feet were beginning to complain. And still we hadn't covered the tiniest fraction of Mediterranean material.

What, I asked my guide, hoping the question might delay a proposed hike over to Maritime Diplomacy on the far side of the monastery, was her own favourite topic in the Archive?

She didn't hesitate for a moment. 'Veronica Franco,' she said. 'Do you know of her?'

I shook my head.

'She was a celebrated 16th-century courtesan, a beautiful woman of strong character, famous for her affairs with Venice's greatest painters and writers. Living with poets, she became a poetess herself. She wrote excellent sonnets and verse epistles. She was an early feminist – she refused to conform to the ideal of the silent and obedient Renaissance woman. When I began reading Veronica Franco I felt an extraordinary complicity with her – it was research into her letters that got me interested in Venetian history in the first place.'

Being a woman in the Venice of the 1500s, said Signora Schiavon, especially a woman who had to live by her charms, was far from easy.

'But she was fiery and gave in to no one,' she enthused. 'Once she was insulted by Maffio Venier, a poet from a powerful and aristocratic Venetian family. She dared to stand up to him. In fact she challenged him to a three-part duel – first in bed, second in poetry and last in arms.'

Lara Croft, I thought, curl up and die.

But Veronica Franco's most celebrated bedfellow, I learned, was not a poet, although she later wrote two sonnets for him. In 1574 Henry III of France, twenty-three years old and recently proclaimed king, arrived on a visit to Venice. It was from the first moment an extraordinary occasion. Escorted into the lagoon by fourteen galleys, he rode on a Venetian ship rowed by four hundred Slavs, sailing past triumphal arches built by Palladio and decorated by Tintoretto and Veronese. Around him was a fantasy armada – boats got up as dolphins and Neptunes and a raft upon which skilled artisans blew glass objects in a flame-breathing, dragon-shaped furnace.

Things only got more fevered from there. Henry was installed at the Ca' Foscari on the Grand Canal, sleeping in bedsheets of crimson silk and surrounded by the finest furnishings and works of art the Venetians could lay their hands on. Dinner for 3,000 guests at the Doge's palace was a sumptuous offering: 1,200 dishes on silver plate and delicate white damask serviettes that on handling turned out to be fashioned of spun sugar. After the banquet the King went to the opera, only to emerge to a naval miracle. Before dining he had been shown all the elements of a war galley laid out before him in pieces – now the galley was fully assembled and riding the water by the quayside, its deck embellished with a 16,000-pound cannon, still hot, cast during dinner.

How could such delicious evenings not end in the company of Veronica Franco, selected by the French King himself from an album of painted miniatures thoughtfully provided by the city fathers and featuring the most acclaimed prostitutes of Venice? It is said that after his visit Henry returned home in a somewhat fuddled state of mind; despite all the luxuries and romances the French court offered he spent the rest of his life quite overwhelmed by Venice.

Henry's visit left almost as indelible a mark on Venice itself. For the occasion was an exception, a moment's happy and carefree celebration in an age in which dire writing had been on the wall for some time. By the 1400s Venice had reached her apogee. She was to live on for another three centuries – in fact as her power and influence dwindled in the world she maintained a pretence at home with ever more splendid balls, masques and decadent revels. But her long decline was there for everyone to see. Usually it was characterised by a steady nibbling away by the Turks at her Mediterranean possessions. But occasionally it was marked by sudden revelations of catastrophe. One such disclosure lay in the shelves of diplomatic correspondence on the far side of the monastery.

We got there some time around midday after an arduous slog. I trailed down one corridor after another behind the energetic Dotoressa, wishing there was a faster, more convenient route. By this point I would have said yes to an electric wheelchair, a Smart Car or any other modern vehicle that could have negotiated these halls. But my guide would not have approved. As she was about to show me, innovations in transport can sometimes have disastrous aftermaths.

In 1499, seventy-five years before Veronica Franco was to fête Henry III, appalling news arrived in diplomatic letters from King Manuel's court in Lisbon. A Portuguese sea captain, Vasco da Gama, had travelled to India and back via the southern tip of Africa.

It took some years for the full weight of the disaster to penetrate Venetian minds. After all, another Portuguese, Bartholemew Diaz, had already rounded the Cape of Good Hope. But more farsighted men at the Rialto could see that a successful sea trip to India and back spelt ruin. It meant nothing less than the end of Venetian global trading supremacy.

For no longer would Oriental silks and spices have to be carried thousands of miles on horse- or camel-back across the trading routes of Central Asia. Nor would water-born cargoes from the East have to be trans-shipped – unloaded in Suez or the Persian Gulf, carried overland and then reloaded in Levantine ports. Goods could now travel in a single vessel, bypassing the Venetian-controlled eastern Mediterranean altogether. If they were headed towards the rich markets of northern Europe – Holland, England or the Hanseatic ports – they didn't have to enter the Mediterranean at all. Lisbon, not Venice, would now become Europe's entrepôt for eastern goods. The Middle Sea was no longer vital to European commerce. In one stroke da Gama had transformed the Mediterranean into a backwater.

Foreign technology was partly to blame for Venice's suddenly diminished prospects. Challenged by a vast, unknown ocean, the nations of Atlantic Europe had developed better ships, more advanced navigation techniques, more highly skilled sailors. Venice, born to the sea, had finally been outperformed in her own liquid element.

But in the larger view her out-classing was part of a more important global shift. It was an historic change that moved the entire centre of the world's human gravity north-westwards. The Mediterranean, so long the principal stage of European civilisation, was no longer to be the focus of the Western world. There were new economic forces at work, new political ideologies forming, new social classes emerging. And they took shape on the shores of that other, larger body of water, the Atlantic.

In a short time the silver pouring eastwards from the recently discovered Americas would make Venice's wealth look paltry. It would turn

Spain into the superpower of the West, and make her the main rival to that superpower of the East, the Ottoman Empire. Out-performed by both, Venice was destined to become an irrelevance, a charming but powerless anachronism: she would end up one of the first tourist curiosities in the world, a place where pleasure came ahead of any other business.

It was my own pleasure, after the morning's exertions, to sit and chat for a few minutes. Before she left me Alessandra Schiavon took me up to a small office under the monastery roofs and sat me before a diminutive woman in her eighties. Grey-haired, dressed in warm, tweedy clothes, Maria Francesca Tiepolo had passed the morning hours working on the Latin text that lay on her desk.

The elderly Signora had, in fact, spent an entire lifetime unravelling the secrets of Venice – an employee of the State Archives for three decades, she had for her last thirteen years been its Director. And now in her retirement she continued research on her favourite subjects. I asked about her name. It was one of the most famous in Venetian history, belonging to a family that produced admirals, governors, aristocratic conspirators, dukes of Crete and two celebrated 13th-century doges.

The Signora modestly admitted that she counted Doge Lorenzo Tiepolo among her direct forbears. History lives on everywhere in Venice, she said. It is in its old papers, in its monuments and palaces and paintings, and in its people, too. Time, she said, is a continuous flow connecting everything. And as I watched her talk, her eyes bright, her smile warm and strong, I had the curious feeling that I might have been watching the Dottoressa forty years on in the future. Or looking at Veronica Franco 400 years ago.

It was an eerie sensation, and it pursued me back down the long monastery corridors and across the silent refectory. Then I was through the tall doors of the Archives and away from the damp world of paper secrets. And suddenly it was hard to believe that time, for all its connective power, could even join the two halves of a day. For outside the thick fog of morning had vanished. It might never have existed at all, and the great brick façade of the Friari lay basking in a warm and dazzling afternoon sun.

Twenty-Six

Il Moro de Venezia II – the Moor of Venice – sat docked at a quayside directly in front of the *Bucintoro* boathouse. It was as if by simple proximity alone, by rubbing herself against stones where the older boat must have often tied up, she might appropriate to herself some of the same prestige and grandeur. I was no expert in multi-million dollar high-tech racing yachts, but as I sat there waiting she looked pretty grand anyway.

I had returned to the Arsenale to rendezvous with Maurizio Vecchiola, scion of the family who owned the *Moro*. The Vecchiolas were not just simple sailing folk – they also owned one of the largest industrial PVC manufacturing firms in the world. But the *Moro* was their pride and joy. The yacht was, by all accounts, a well-known international racer, although she wouldn't be racing today. Instead she would be overseeing a different kind of race, a regatta of traditional wooden sailing boats organised by the Venice yacht club, the Compagnia della Vela. The *Moro* would merely be lending a little mystique to the event.

Already on board were the *Moro*'s skipper and mate. When the yacht was in full racing fettle she required a crew of twenty-two energetic young men, experts who flew at stainless steel winch handles like furies and counted time lost in microseconds. But even out of season, laid up and inactive, the *Moro* had its skeleton crew – you don't leave a million-dollar baby without a nanny. We introduced ourselves and the pair got on with loading the largest canvas sacks I'd ever seen. The *Moro* carried enough sail to fit out a small armada.

A small knot of men came striding down the grassy path where Patrizia Rigo had wobbled a few days before. They were no more naval officers than she was. I doubted they were yacht club officials, either. Unshaven, wearing black clothes and dark sunglasses, they looked more like a Mafia hit-squad. They turned out instead to be Gucci men. The Vecchiola family sold PVC to Gucci for the making of Gucci shoe-soles. Men of lesser vision might entertain esteemed associates in corporate hospitality tents at public sporting events. Maurizio Vecchiola, for his part, had a floating hospitality tent that provided its own sport. Having sustained the indignity of an inspection of their own footwear by the *Moro*'s crew – no ordinary street-soles ever touched the boat's fabulous Kevlar-carbon composite deck – the Gucci shoe men sat around looking fashionably bored.

Another party approached, looking much more like sailors. It was Corrado Scrascia, the official from the Compania della Vela, and his little team of yacht-club officials, judges and time-keepers. Signor Scrascia was no Gucci man. No one bothered to glance at his shoes. From the white smile in his tanned face to the buttons on his multi-function chronometer he looked every bit a saltwater yachtsman.

The team with him also looked nautical. They had brought along orange marker buoys, aerosol-powered starting horns and a whole boxful of folded signal-flags you had to be a sailor to understand. They began preparing the *pilotina*, the little outboard motor-boat tied behind the *Moro*'s stern, that would accompany the race along its course.

Finally Maurizio Vecchiola turned up. He didn't look like a sailor at all. He looked like a kid out of a private prep school. But his responsibilities were large, he told me – his father had put him in charge of the company's North American operations, a large and expanding chunk of the business. Still, I found it a challenge to associate the young Vecchiola with either competitive yacht racing or cutthroat corporate business. He wore nerdy glasses, loafers with tassels and a bespoke button-down blue shirt whose tail hung out of the back of his trousers. In fact he did little sailing that day. His main function was to entertain.

The white wine secured, the cocktail sausages safely stowed away, we started the engines and cast off. The marine approaches to Venice are busy. Once outside the Arsenale basin we motored through the thick of weekend traffic, small craft going in all directions in an unrelenting flow. There were sleek speedboats with curvaceous young women perched on their bows like exotic car hood-ornaments; small sailing dinghies with parents and children plump in bright life-vests; wide, multi-decked car-carriers piggy-backing vehicles from the mainland to the roads of the Lido; sightseeing tour-boats of the Azienda del Consorzio Trasporti Veneziano, operators of the city's *vaporetto* services. But for sheer size the most impressive boats were the international ferries running the Adriatic routes southwards to Greece. Ten stories high, they reared sheer out of the water in front of us like giant icebergs. From the sundeck of the *Ikarus Palace*, escorted out of port by two black and white tugs and bound for Patras, tiny figures gazed down and waved. All of us, the Gucci men excepted, waved back.

'Welcome aboard,' said Maurizio Vecchiola as the *Moro* veered to port, entering a busy navigation channel leading towards the barrier island of the Lido. 'The first thing you should know is that the *Moro* is one of the most important boats in the world.'

'You must tell me why,' I said as he indicated a free place beside him in the cockpit. But I knew he was not going to need any encouragement.

The technical explanations that followed were complex, and I won't pretend I understood them. Suffice to say it was impressed upon me that the *Moro* was a member of that elite and blue-blooded caste of yachts, the Maxi-I.O.R. I had never heard of them. The International Offshore Rule that defined this class of boat in fact no longer pertained and Maxis were no longer being built. More confusing still, other changes of rule meant that the *Moro* was now considered a 'Mini-Maxi'. To me the boat was sounding more and more like some kind of revolutionary new sanitary pad. But no matter – at seventy-one feet long, she was among the fastest, costliest and, above all, largest racing yachts ever designed. It was craft like this that had brought international renown to such races as the Fastnet, the Sydney-to-Hobart and the America's Cup.

The *Moro* was now twenty-two years old, Vecchiola told me, and no longer the innovative racing craft she had once been. But that was not the point. The point was that she was a noble boat with noble owners who had made a place for her in yachting history. In fact the list of personalities associated with the *Moro* over the years seemed more important to Vecchiola than the yacht herself.

She'd been owned by the greatest captains of Italian industry. She was designed and built for Raul Gardini, agro-chemical industrialist, once owner of the second biggest corporation in Italy, and the yachtsman who'd put Italy on the international racing map. Later, among other illustrious owners, she'd also belonged to Carlo De Benedetti, then head of the Olivetti Corporation.

The names rang a bell. Hadn't Raul Gardini committed suicide in a notorious financial corruption case in the 1990s? If it came to that, hadn't Carlo De Benedetti also been brought low in a series of Italian kickback scandals? But there was no time for questions. Vecchiola Junior had moved on to Dennis Conner, the yachtsman who'd won the America's Cup back for America. He, too, had sailed the *Moro*. Why, even royalty, in the person of King Juan Carlos of Spain, had skippered this boat. And, in a way, the circle had now been completed – the Vecchiolas bought the raw materials for their PCV from the Porto Marghera chemical factory across the lagoon that had once been owned by Raul Gardini. It really was a return to the source, wasn't it?

I had to agree it was. What else could I say? By this point I was drinking the man's wine and nibbling his canapés. But Maurizio Vecchiola's bedazzlement by the great and the good of the yachting world was rather worrisome – nobody that young should be so impressed by status and money. What was really worrying me at this point, though, wasn't yachts at all, but wind. There wasn't a breath of it, either for the *Moro* or the little flotilla of aged craft we were now slowly approaching.

They were beautiful old boats, cutters for the most part, some of them built close to a century ago. Lovingly maintained, their long bowsprits and wooden hulls glowed beneath multiple layers of varnish. For the moment they looked rather sorry, their rust-coloured sails hanging limp as they waited in a small knot on the still, glassy water. Until a minute or two before we had been in the lagoon, motoring behind the protected lee of the Lido. But now we had cleared its north end through the Porto di Lido – the main passage to and from Venice – and sailed out into the open Adriatic. And still there was no wind.

Signor Scrascia called his men together at the stern of the *Moro*. They searched the heavens, gazed at the horizon, sniffed the air. After lengthy deliberation they issued their verdict: we would hang on. Given their reading of the skies, to say nothing of the weather forecast printed in the day's local paper, there was every chance that an afternoon wind would eventually pick up. We would just have to be patient.

And so we sat. Tillers hard over, the antique boats floated nearby, drifting slowly in desultory little circles. Bored by the seafaring life, the Gucci men banded together over a second bottle of wine and got down to Milanese fashion gossip. Corrado Scrascia strung a taut cord between two mast-stays and hung up a series of signal flags with clothes-pegs. It looked like an especially colourful laundry line, but apparently informed the world at large that the old-boats regatta was on hold. Signor Scrascia's men jumped into the *pilotina* to lay out buoys marking the regatta's course. Maurizio Vecchiola conferred with his father on his mobile telephone, then joined the men in black to regale them with stories of shoes and the sea. I sat down, my feet hanging over the bow, and gazed out over the water.

Not far away stretched the groomed beaches of the Lido, so close I could see long rows of bathing cabins and regularly laid out beach umbrellas. It was too early in the year for anyone to be using them. Behind loomed the bulky Palazzo del Cinema. It was there that every summer for seventy years the prestigious Venice Film Festival was celebrated. But in my mind's eye I was already picturing another annual event. It had been held for a good deal longer, was even more prestigious, and in its way was just as cinematic. It was here, on the very spot where we were floating, that for 800 years Venice had celebrated her Marriage to the Sea.

It had begun with nothing more than a naval campaign against piracy, a scourge that had troubled shipping in Mediterranean waters for centuries. On Ascension Day in the year 1000 Doge Pietro Orseolo II sailed out of the lagoon to rid the Adriatic of some particularly troublesome Croatians. His pacification programme went well – when he returned the sea was a Venetian sea, amenable to the establishment of commercial outposts, trade and profitable voyages. To commemorate the event a yearly Ascension Day celebration was organised. Led by the Doge in the bows of the *Bucintoro*, the churchmen and the people of Venice sailed out to the Porto di Lido in a great decorated fleet for a service of invocation.

At first things remained simple – a short prayer of thanks was followed by the singing of psalms. But the Venetians, ever in love with spectacle, were not ones to let such a dramatic opportunity pass them by. As time went on a simple act of propitiation – the Doge's casting of a gold ring into the sea – began to invest the ritual with overtones of matrimony. In a short while the service, a 'sign of our true and perpetual dominion' over the waves, became a full blown *Sposalazio del Mar*, a symbolic marriage of the city to the sea.

Only the Venetians could pull off such a spiritual union with the pomp, style and extravagance it merited. And only the Venetians, with their eye for material value, could encourage such a hasty recuperation of their marital investment. There was no hoard of 800 gold wedding rings lying on the shallow sea-bed beneath our keel. At the end of each ceremony, Venetian citizens were free to dive in and look for the ring. Not only was it 'finders keepers' – the successful diver was exempted from all taxes and state obligations for a year.

An hour passed, then another. I was enjoying the soft light, the low green islands off in the lagoon, the tall campaniles of Venice rising above the Lido. The Gucci men were less happy and rapidly growing mutinous. Corrado Scrascia could only smile politely at their impatience as we bobbed about directionless. Just as I was deciding it was all over I felt the faintest hint of cool air on my cheek. We all felt it. Even Maurizio Vecchiola, crestfallen at the prospect of a public-relations failure, perked up. Stronger by the minute, the wind was soon blowing steadily.

Signor Scrascia changed the colours on his signals line. The skipper and his mate hauled sails up onto the *Moro*'s deck. The old cutters, their own canvas now taut, positioned themselves as the aerosol horn sounded a series of race-start warnings. Then they were off.

They were only a tiny armada of fragile old leisure boats. But as they set a course south, small bow waves pushing up at their prows, I transformed them into another, more formidable flotilla of wood and canvas. Growing ever smaller in the distance, they became the Venetian warships that once sailed out past the Lido to rendezvous with other ships of a 'Holy League' that included Spain and the Papacy. Two hundred war galleys strong, this was the giant fleet that in 1571 took on an equally large Turkish armada in the Gulf of Patras off Greece. The battle of Lepanto was the largest naval action since Caesar Augustus had destroyed Anthony and Cleopatra's fleet at Actium 1,500 years earlier, and the last major engagement to be fought with oared galleys.

The writer Miguel de Cervantes, serving aboard a Spanish ship, was thoroughly impressed; not even three wounds and the loss of the use of his left hand – 'to the greater glory of the right', as he wrote – could dampen his enthusiasm. For him Lepanto was simply 'the greatest occasion that past or present ages have witnessed'. Certainly the figures were impressive: in sinkings and hand-to-hand fighting 30,000 Turks were killed, 8,000 were captured, 113 Turkish galleys were destroyed and 15,000 Christian galley slaves freed. But if the battle was counted as an unqualified triumph – the coalition itself lost a mere 15,000 men – the Holy League was really only tilting at windmills. More vigorous than ever, the Turkish navy immediately began building an even larger fleet. In the end Lepanto did little to halt Venice's long decline in the eastern Mediterranean.

Having taken time to raise its sails, the *Moro* was now gaining on the wooden boats and once again I could see them clearly. There was no sign of shot or shell in their hulls. They were no bodies floating in the water behind them. Nor did it really matter who won their competition – the wind itself was triumph enough. With the *pilotina* following closely in their wake, the *Moro* was now free to take on the wind herself. Ratchets purred, winch cogs turned on precision-fitted bearings, and a spinnaker rose high into the air. Looking up, I could see the vast face of a Venetian lion ballooning on the canvas spread above us.

The deck heeled over. Nine knots was no great speed for the Moor of Venice. I don't doubt that even a Turkish galley, given a little extra effort by a few hundred galley slaves, could have outpaced us. But soon we had left the little fleet far behind, and were rushing forward on our own. I was exhilarated. The Gucci men were exhilarated. Even Maurizo Vecchiola appeared to be enjoying not just the way the *Moro* made him look, but the way she looked herself. Proud Venetians, we might have been sailing to Byzantium.

Twenty-Seven

I t was a sunny Sunday afternoon and I hadn't been waiting more than two minutes on the Fondamenta Nuove before Umberto Sichiro hove into view, right on time.

He arrived in that most patrician of Venetian water craft, a *motoscafo*. Its superstructure gleamed white and the teakwood planking of its hull was buffed to a high sheen. Even the august figure standing in the motor launch's cabin, his shirt crisply laundered and suit freshly pressed, had a costly look about him. He wasn't Umberto Sichiro. He was the water-taxi's chauffeur, but if he hadn't been holding the pilot wheel in his hands I would have taken him for a visiting merchant banker. Given the hourly rates that Venetian launches charge he might as well have been. The lagoon's annual Mestre Regatta was a popular event, an affair of ordinary people celebrating simple working life. But that was no reason for its contingent of Venetian journalists to show up in a boat any less well turned out than they themselves.

There were four or five photographers and reporters from local papers ensconced in the launch's plush cabin. Lounging about in marine décor – upholstered white armchairs and settee, navy blue carpet, mahogany trim – they suggested a Venetian version of those bored and sophisticated Roman *ragazzi*, the press-pack in *La Dolce Vita*.

Being not just a senior journalist but a member of the regatta's organising committee, Umberto Sichiro stood slightly apart from his younger colleagues. He remained on the *motoscafo*'s rear deck, feet planted wide in the manner of an experienced sailor, chatting to a pretty female committee member. His sunglasses were expensive, his tan shoes highly polished. Only the tie beneath the dark blue windbreaker hinted at any nautical bent – in discreet miniature it featured the same marine signals that Corrado Scracia was fond of flying. But Umberto Sichiro obviously had more than nautical charm – he had the allure and seductive manner of a middle-aged man who still attracted women. Despite his years his hair was sleek and dark. His smile was self-confident, his moustache neatly trimmed, his gestures practised. Not many people can make smoking look attractive these days, but Umberto Sichiro could. An elegant Latin sophisticate, he had all the smoothness of Mastroianni himself.

The launch touched the quay just long enough for me to hop aboard, then headed down the channel past San Michele towards Murano. I preferred to stay outside on the deck, too, not just for a better view of the race we were going to follow, but to hear what my host had to say about it.

Halfway between the two islands a couple of hundred small outboard motorboats milled noisily about nine other boats that sat calmly, waiting, with no motors at all. They were powered instead by seven rowers apiece, three on each side and one astern. The boats they manned were *caorlina*s, lumbering, flat-bottomed vessels that used to bring fruit and vegetables from the farming islands of the lagoon to Venice. To innocents like me they were simply old work boats, an awkward means of heavy transport whose day had come and gone. But to experts like Umberto Sichiro such craft were objects of complex and unending appeal. For all his Venetian sophistication Signor Sichiro was passionate about Venetian rowing craft. He had studied them all his life, and in the end I wondered if in their nuanced subtlety they were not more delectable to him than Venetian women themselves. From the slim and delicate *pupparin* to the generous, wide-hipped *sampierotta*, there wasn't an oared craft in the entire lagoon the man did not venerate.

The press launch nosed its way through the buzzing, expectant crowd floating on the water to take up its official position beside the *caorlina*s.

My host cast a practised, calculating eye over the crews, and those who saw him waved and smiled. Everyone knew Umberto Sichiro.

'It's a good crowd today,' he said with satisfaction. 'These events attract all sorts of people. The contestants are mostly gondoliers and fisherman, so they draw other gondoliers and fishermen. Look at all the women and children, too – some of them are the rowers' friends and families. If the rowers have rowed before and performed well, they are neighbourhood heroes – the whole quarter turns out to see them.'

I looked at the rowers standing relaxed and happy in their boats. All wore striped jerseys, red waist sashes and white trousers rolled up to the knee. They also wore the racing colours of their boats, bright primal splashes that gave the gathering the festive look of a land-bound race-meet. But these racers didn't have the physiques of jockeys – under the finery they were large, weathered, brawny men who had spent most of their lives in outdoor work.

'They have to be strong,' Umberto said, as if reading my thoughts. 'Those boats are heavy. They curve up nicely at bow at stern, but they are eleven metres long and broad across the beam.'

He held up his hand and tested the air. From out of the south-east, where a mass of dark cloud troubled an otherwise clear sky, a strong breeze was blowing up the Adriatic. 'Today physical strength is going to be especially important. On other days technique might count for more. But that wind is blowing across the *caorlinas*' bows. The last rower, the steersman, is going to have to expend some of his energy keeping his boat on a straight course. It can make all the difference. It's the compensating strength of the forward rowers which will count most.'

The course ahead was cleared, a rope was stretched over the water to form a starting line, and for a moment everything – the crowd, their boats, the rowers themselves – was still. Then a horn sounded and the rowers heaved into action. Blue lights on police boats flashed, sirens on fire boats wailed, and the whole flotilla sprang to life, moving ahead with the *caorlinas* at a steady seven knots.

Seven knots might not sound like much of a speed, but anyone who has watched the exertion of *caorlina* rowers will tell you it is positively hair-raising. Mediterranean rowers, of course, are not like northern rowers. They do not sit with their backs to their destination and put their power into pulling on oars. It is a position they find illogical. They prefer to face forward, standing upright, and put their energy into pushing on oars instead. Their outside legs ahead, their whole weight pivoting on their front feet, the *caorlina* rowers came down on each forward push with a terrific surge of muscle power. It was a demanding, synchronised rhythm they would maintain unrelentingly for the next three and three-quarter miles.

For the moment there was no apparent difference in the relative strength of the rowers. Could he, I asked the expert, predict any winners? Did he have any favourites?

Umberto looked at the boats racing over the water, then without hesitation delivered his verdict.

'The blue team will win,' he said, as if there wasn't room for the shadow of a doubt. 'Orange will come in second, pink third and violet fourth.'

'Really?' I said, surprised at the assurance in his voice. 'You can be that certain?'

'Of course,' he replied, as if he were the coach and personal trainer of each rower present. 'It is only a question of scientific knowledge. I know the technique and strength of all of them.'

That didn't stop other spectators from worrying about who might win and lose. Everyone was shouting, but from a motorboat some way behind us came an incessant, bull-like roar. A middle-aged woman wearing an orange armband was shouting so hard and heaving about so uncontrollably she was being held back in the boat by two other women.

'That's Igor Vignotto's mother,' said Umberto. 'She tends to get emotionally over-excited. It is unnecessary. Igor's a good, steady rower, very scientific.'

Apart from the rowers there was other science here I didn't understand at all. Why the need, I asked Umberto, for that grotesquely twisted bit of wood, full of strange angles and concavities, when a simple single-position, English-style oarlock would do?

'Ah,' he replied. 'The *forcola*, a most interesting piece of equipment. An oarlock couldn't possibly do the same job. You cannot even begin to row properly unless you understand the principles of the *forcola*.'

He took out a piece of paper, and using the pitching top of the launch's cabin as a desk began drawing a series of diagrams. They were complex, schematic plans with arrows running in different directions and points labelled *'fuerza,' 'fulcro'* and *'resistenza'*. I think they were meant to show what happens when a given impetus, augmented and redirected through leverage on a fulcrum, encounters a natural field of resistance like water. But did that mean that by slotting the oar into a higher position on the *forcola* it gave the rower more manoeuvrability but less power? Or did it provide less manoeuvrability and greater power? I was confused. I have kept the diagrams, and from time to time even study them, but they haven't become any less puzzling.

I quickly gave up trying to understand things on paper, for out on the water things were taking shape. As predicted, Celeste, the blue team, had taken the lead and was looking strong. Rosa, the pink crew, was not far behind. To Signora Vignotto's partial satisfaction Igor was giving it everything he had – Arancio, the orange team, was running a close third. But the distances between boats were gradually widening – after fifteen minutes of vigorous rowing the lead boat was more than a hundred yards ahead of Rosso, the red team that lagged last.

By now we had left Murano far behind and were running parallel to the elevated railway track that crosses the lagoon. Straight ahead of us lay Mestre, the industrial town that sits on its shores. After weeks spent in the confines of the lagoon such things as smokestacks, motorways and concrete blocks of workers' flats looked oddly foreign. I had almost forgotten their existence. But there they all were, looming before us. In a little while I would have to face them straight on. For the moment I was perfectly happy to see them from a boat pitching and yawing in the confused wakes of a hundred other boats.

The flotilla wasn't more than a couple of minutes from the finish-line at the San Giuliano bridge when Signora Vignotta roared especially loudly.

213

The Oranges had called on their last reserves of strength and pulled up level with the Pinks for second place. Water streamed from oars, bodies rocked furiously, the crowds cheered their favourites hoarsely on. For a moment it seemed uncertain. Then, of course, Orange pulled slowly ahead. Umberto Sichiro smiled with pride, as if it were he himself who had won the race. Blue crossed the line first, followed by orange, pink and violet. His prediction was spot on.

'*Mamma Mia! Que spettacolo!*' the master of ceremonies kept repeating at the prize-giving on the quayside fifteen minutes later.

'*Mamma Mia! Mamma Mia!*' said my host, rolling his eyes as we stood watching winner after winner come forward to receive his award and be loudly cheered. 'Our announcer has had too much to drink again.'

Umberto was enjoying the sight of champion rowers being photographed with girlfriends, babies and proud mothers. He applauded judges long and loudly, praised organisers and time-keepers for their unstinting contributions. But towards the end it seemed to me he was becoming slightly impatient, anxious to wind up the official ceremonies. It was only half an hour afterwards, at tables set up in the garden outside the San Giuliano boating clubhouse, that I discovered the unofficial ceremonies the organisers had organised for themselves.

I had wandered off to look at the *caorlina*s and by the time I arrived a feast was in full swing. Up and down the tables there were tubs of small red fried fish, sardines grilled over charcoal, and *sarde in saor*, a Venetian specialty of sardines marinated in onions, wine, raisins and pine nuts. Everybody, even the most elegant of race-committee ladies, was enjoying slumming – jewellery and gold rings flashing, they ate fried fish with oily fingers, bit the heads off sardines with their teeth, and reached over their neighbour's plates for the wine.

This last item, especially, was popular. It was drunk from plastic glasses and disappeared down thirsty throats in surprising quantities. I had never seen Venetians, generally so reserved and well ordered, quite so unbuttoned. In no time they were laughing loudly, calling for more bottles and singing boat songs. They were executed in three-part harmony – this *was*

Venice, after all – but they were relaxed and joyous just the same. And in the middle of it all, suavely dominating the tables with charm and elegant discourse, was Umberto Sichiro.

The songs were about rowing and so, inevitably, was the conversation. There are 120 boat regattas in Venice each year, most of them celebrating rowing, so there was plenty to talk about. Racing techniques old and new; the exploits of former champions; the precise specifications of the two-man racing *gondolino* – all came under review. But simply talking boats was not enough. When someone from the local rowing club suggested we inspect a boat being built in the workshop next door, there was a general emptying of tables.

We crowded into a room that smelled of glue and fresh wood shavings, an odour to which we added our own winey exhalations. The boat we surrounded was far from finished and the structure of its hull, a complex series of delicate, arched ribs, still lay exposed. Tapering evenly away towards either extremity, they formed part of a perfect, diminishing geometry. The joins were flush, the angles precise, the wood sanded to a satin finish. This was both art and science, a work of love exactingly executed.

To me it was a beautiful thing. To everyone else, too. There were low whistles, murmurs of approval, expressions of admiration. And then there was a grunt, loud and monosyllabic and disdainful, that unmistakably signified the opposite.

It came from a shambling bear of a man in a sleeveless down jacket. I had seen him officiating at the start of the *caorlina* race, and wondered who he was then. He was squat and powerfully built. Grey hair straggled down a massive head into an unkempt beard. His hands were large and rough, his blunt fingers stained with varnish. He had a kind of raw, animal force you couldn't ignore. Without his saying a word, the room had fallen silent.

'That's Gianfranco Vianello,' Umberto whispered to me over his shoulder. 'He looks primitive, but he is intelligent. Watch.'

And so I watched. Gianfranco Vianello, son of a gondolier, master boatbuilder and legendary twelve times winner of the Regatta Storico, the greatest rowing race of all, was hard not to watch. The conversation that followed was too fast and excited for me to follow, but you didn't have to speak Italian to get the drift of things. Vianello clearly disapproved of the boat before him.

He glanced up and down its elegant lines. The construction was OK, he admitted. That wasn't the problem. The boat failed to respect the rules and style of Venetian *tradizione*.

Perhaps it didn't have to, some brave soul emboldened by wine ventured to remark; it was a handsome craft none the less, and superbly built. The effect on Vianello was remarkable. He flushed red, clenching his fists at his side. I thought he was going to hit someone. Instead he launched into a tirade, talking louder and faster by the second. Words like *'capriccioso,' 'fantasia,' 'innovazione'* came and went in a flash. It was like a dam bursting. In a minute he was joined by a conservative supporter or two. Then, able to address someone apart from the formidable Vianello, proponents of innovation weighed in. Soon everyone had jumped into the fray and the whole room was arguing furiously about change and tradition. *'Calmi! Calmi!'* shouted Umberto, doing his best to control tempers and keep things constructive. But not even he could get a word in.

I thought Vianello was drunk. Later, I visited his workshop on Giudecca, watched him building a gondola, and realised he'd been stone-cold sober. He hadn't been purposely provocative – he was always like that. He was a force of nature, and passionate about boats.

It was difficult to explain rowing to a non-rower, Vianello told me in Giudecca as he took a break from placing ribs in a new hull. It was very personal, something to do with harmony of movement. Perhaps boxers and dancers felt the same way. But for him it was enough that he was a Venetian, and attached to the old ways of doing things. If he had to build deeper gondola hulls to take today's increased motor turbulence into account, so be it. Otherwise why not stick to the way things should be? Vianello might not have looked like a philosopher, but he struck me as being a bit like Plato. Peacefully floating somewhere in his mind were the ideal forms of every worthwhile boat that had ever been designed, built or rowed. They were perfect, eternal, immutable and unchanging. And every last one of them, of course, was Venetian.

But if Gianfranco Vianello had been in total control on the evening of the *caorlina* race, the rest of us definitely hadn't. We had all overdone it with the Friuli white.

'Never mind,' Umberto said when the last boat song was sung, the last plastic glass emptied. 'It's not far home – just over the bridge. I've got a lift for us.'

Joining two other companions, we stumbled over to a parking lot and the smallest vehicle that has ever carried four inebriated, full-sized adults over the lagoon to Venice – a baby blue, 1960 Porsche sports car in mint condition.

'We'll never get in,' I protested as its owner opened miniature doors and Umberto proceeded to fold himself into a back seat two feet wide and a foot deep.

Umberto replied with a kind of enthusiastic gurgle. I think he was saying it was no problem at all, but the roof of the car was so low his chin was jammed into his collarbone. Eventually I, too, got myself bent into the back seat. The driver and his other passenger installed themselves, and off we roared.

Their cramped state did not stop the passengers of the baby-blue Porsche from picking up the debate where it had been left off before the Vianello incident. It had to do with alternate rowing stances, and which ones were most effective on heavier, slower lagoon boats. But the theme didn't discourage the driver from his keen Italian racing-style. Up on the causeway high above the water we were shooting in and out of lanes and passing everything in sight. I closed my eyes and wondered what would happen if we crashed through the barrier and headed to the bottom of the lagoon. Would take it us as long to get out of the Porsche as it had to get in?

Barely two miles separate Venice from the mainland, but it seemed a lot further to me. Umberto argued rowing all the way. When we parked and he'd finally managed to extricate himself from the back seat, he immediately took up a graceful stance and began demonstrating his alternate rowing stroke.

The other two gathered about, one criticising, one approving. Then they took up other stances to demonstrate their own preferred styles. All in all they looked pretty silly, without oars or any other props, rowing away up there on the fourth floor of the Tronchetto multi-storey car park.

I might have stayed on to debate pros and cons, too, but I had an early start the next morning. Besides, the weather had grown threatening. The wind that had been blowing up the Adriatic all afternoon had finally brought black clouds over Venice. They opened up as I scurried home, and by the time I was standing at our door in Cannaregio I was soaked.

I towelled off, refused the dinner that Jany had cooked, and was soon in bed. But I found it difficult to get to sleep that evening. I had eaten and drunk too much. Besides, I simply couldn't figure out how Umberto Sichiro had managed to predict the first four *caorlina*s over the line. It wasn't science at all. It was downright uncanny. In the end, I decided before I drifted off, you just had to be Venetian, an oarsman from the start.

Twenty-Eight

The Adriatic rain, once it started, didn't know how to stop. It fell heavily all night, and when I got up at 5.30 to go to work it was still coming down. The wind was strong and gusty. Hunched into the weather on the Strada Nuova in the grim half-light of dawn, the few early pedestrians already on their way to work were battling with umbrellas. Two minutes from the apartment my own umbrella promptly turned inside out. Having no other wet-weather gear, I returned home and asked Jany to help me out. Half an hour later I met my Barich Trasporti co-workers at Tronchetto wearing a green plastic garbage bag with holes cut out for my arms and head.

Tronchetto lies at the working end of Venice and is not terribly chic, so I didn't feel too embarrassed – it wasn't as if the men from Gucci were skulking about on the quays there at six o'clock on a wet Monday morning. But it was surprising how many other people were. Apart from harbouring the city's road, rail and ferry terminals, Tronchetto is the site where all mainland merchandise destined for the city is trans-shipped from trucks to delivery boats. The place was crawling.

Like a pontoon bridge leading nowhere, the Barich fleet, five boats painted in the company colours of red and black, were tied gunwale to gunwale not far past the Venice wholesale market. On either side on the busy quay other transport companies had their own *topos* similarly moored to allow everyone a place. Crews in bright waterproof jackets and pants swarmed across rain-soaked decks. Some were loading wine and beer. The men of Soligo Dairy Products were stowing crates of yoghurt in their refrigerated *topo*s. The employees of the Merlini frozen fish company were packing cod and calamari into their own cold-storage hulls. Bananas in soggy cardboard boxes, wooden flats of green peppers, trays of aubergines glistening with drops of rainwater, all were being passed from hand to hand and carefully stacked on boat decks.

There were other items that couldn't be loaded by hand at all. Weighty acetylene welding tanks had to be lowered into a *topo* with chains and winches. A wooden spool of heavy-duty electrical cable six feet high required the ministrations of a quay-side crane. Bulk-liquid transport presented a whole other set of problems: when a sewage carrier, having filled its hold at some Venetian hotel septic-tank passed by in all its stinking splendour, there were good-natured jeers and nose-holdings from the men on shore; they were answered by the rude gestures of their smelly but equally good-natured friends on board. If Venice sits sparkling and indolent upon the morning waters when the tourists wake up, it is only because someone has already done the dirty work, the hauling and heaving, the mucking out and resupplying, that keeps the city going.

Of all the *topo* outfits pressed for time, Barich was one of the most pressed. It didn't carry fish or wine or dirty laundry. It was a courier service, a sort of floating UPS guaranteeing the fastest waterborne delivery possible. Its employees, who regarded themselves as the upper class of delivery men, had to hustle hard for the privilege – each boat made up to 300 separate deliveries a day. In the lead-up to Christmas things were even busier.

As I shook hands with Rene Barich his crews weren't simply passing their documents and parcels from hand to hand – that wasn't fast enough. Standing in the back of a truck reversed onto the quay, the deliveries dispatcher was lobbing smaller packages through the air with all the verve of an American football quarterback firing off snap-passes. Each *topo* was assigned a different *sestiere*, or district, of Venice; shouting out the name of the *sestiere*, he would simultaneously send the object winging off through space to the boat concerned. The crewman standing on its slippery decks had to be fast to catch his package, stow it out of the rain, and be ready and waiting for the dispatcher's next projectile, possibly intended for him. In the mornings I spent at Tronchetto I saw a few spectacular saves, but never a single package dropped in the water or even fumbled.

Moustachioed, greying, Rene Barich was twenty-five years older than his athletic young employees. He ran the office ashore, and he worked hard – he showed up on the quayside early each morning like everyone else. He got along well with his crews because he was like them: he'd risen through the ranks and made good, but he was a local boy. There was no other way to do it.

'Rene Barich is pure Venetian,' Daniele said to me, as we pulled away in the *Alvise*, the 24-foot wooden *topo* I'd been assigned to. 'It doesn't matter how rich you are or where you came from, there are three professions in this city you can't buy your way into. If you want to be a gondolier, a water-taxi driver or a *topo* man you have to be Venetian, born and bred.'

I repeat this exchange as if Daniele had been talking to me in English as the two of us sat in armchairs calmly facing each other in a quiet room. In fact Daniele, ringed of ear and pierced of nose, larded his Italian with Venetian slang and banged it out at high speed. He shouted it to me, as he shouted bits and pieces of information to me all through the morning, through wind and driving rain over the hammering of a marine-diesel engine. Luckily, Daniele had a spare rain-jacket for me. It not only kept me dry but it allowed me to hear him – after a few minutes in the howling gale my heavy-duty garbage bag was reduced to ragged bits of flapping and fluttering plastic.

It didn't matter if I didn't understand everything Daniele said or not. From the moment we turned a watery corner into the Grand Canal there were other voices out there, too, and I heard them perfectly well – the storm beating at the water-stained palazzi that stretched away on either side of us, the hoarse greetings snatched by the wind from topo crews heading past us in the opposite direction, the angry hum of a million raindrops hitting the water all around us. Standing beside Daniele in the *Alvise*'s open stern-well, I didn't mind that my fingers were numb with cold or that icy water was trickling down my chest inside my shirt. All these sounds were telling me there was only one way to see Venice: from the rear of a *topo* heading down the Grand Canal in a rainstorm at 6.30 on a windy morning. There was nowhere else I wanted to be.

The euphoria wore off as the morning progressed, but still I preferred *topos* to tour-groups. I don't know how many items we delivered. I couldn't possibly remember the route we followed along dozens of canals. And I certainly couldn't recall the streets we followed deep into the heart of the *sestiere* of Dorsoduro. Every time we tied up we would remove the wooden planks covering the hold of the *Alvise*, pull a stainless steel wheeled dolly off the bow, and load it with dozens of packets and parcels. Then we would plunge off into what for me was unknown, unexplored Venice.

'*Attenzione*! *Attenzione*!' Daniele would cry as we made our way through narrow alleys, our passage complicated by the deadly umbrellas that congested them. There is no place like a crowded Venetian thoroughfare in a rainstorm for losing an eye. '*Avanti*! *Avanti*!' I would shout as I helped the dolly up and over the steps of a humpbacked bridge. But neither of these obstacles was as challenging as hunting down the houses to which our packages were destined.

For the Venetian house-numbering system is not like any other in the world. Instead of assigning each street with a new set of numbers, the Venetians count buildings consecutively through an entire *sestiere*. Thus in the *sestiere* of San Marco the Doge's Palace is No. 1 San Marco, while the last house numbers in the 5,000s. In between is an endless maze of crisscrossing alleys, passages, lanes and courtyards, at whose intersections the steadily increasing numbers can meander off in any direction. Daniele had been making courier deliveries for six years, and often he still found it baffling. And bafflement is bad when you're in a hurry – every minute lost is a minute to be made up by the end of the day.

By noon I'd walked miles, hopped ashore with the *Alvise*'s bow line a dozen times, and searched for countless house numbers. We had delivered textbooks to universities, dentures to dentists, legal briefs to law courts, tubes of blueprints to architectural firms. We'd been inside a noisy children's crèche, a steamy restaurant kitchen, a ceramic tile-furnisher's showroom, a dance studio, a carnival sequin supplier's, an ancient book-binding shop and a funeral home. We had penetrated draughty and half-ruined private palazzi, snug luxury hotels, a casino, an art auctioneer's and a prison. I saw more of Venetian life in one morning than I had seen in three weeks. No one gets around the city and its hidden places more handily than a *topo* driver.

Even Venetian delivery men eventually find time for lunch. In Arca, the little restaurant where the Barich crews met most days at a long table at the back of the room, pizza was taken as seriously as *topo* work. As they downed massive, molten pizzas laden with raw prosciutto they talked. What do Venetian *topo* workers talk about? Like workmen on breaks everywhere, about women. Like most Venetians, about the dismal per-formance of the city's football team, Venezia Calcio. And, perhaps unlike anyone else at all, about inboard-motor piston-ring specifications, marine crankshaft lubrication, and the idiocy of the water-cops who enforce Venetian canal speed limits. It's hard not to talk shop at lunch.

Afterwards I jumped ship and joined Paolo to make deliveries further across the lagoon. If Daniele was all talk of football and boat engines and his slinky girlfriend Chiara, Paolo was a little older and more contempla-tive. We braved heavy rain in the *sestiere* of Castello, bounced through rough chop on the way out to Murano, fought the wind on the way back around Venice to Giudecca. It was fraught and soggy, and only after we had dropped off a consignment on a Lido quay late that afternoon did things calm down. The wind died and the rain let up. Abruptly, as we were cruising past Saint Elena on the approaches to Saint Mark's Basin, a single bolt of sunshine shot down through the black clouds above to light upon the surface of the lagoon.

It was dramatic, a dark, stormy seascape pointed with gold and silver. Paolo was as tired and wet as I was but the sight entranced him. He slowed the engine just to watch it for a moment.

'Don't you ever get tired of Venice?' I asked in my broken Italian. 'To me it seems not real, an extraordinary place in a dream.'

His freckled face, framed in ruddy hair tied back in a rain-soaked bandana, broke into a smile. 'I see this every day,' he said. 'It is normal reality. And still I'm like you. I think it is an extraordinary place, like a dream.'

I told him about other Venices I had seen – Little Venice in London; Venice Beach in California; Amsterdam, Venice of the North. He accepted their attractions, acknowledged they might well have a history and life of their own. 'But none of them,' he said, 'none of them could have a life like Venice. There is nowhere else I could live.'

By now we were in the Basin, and from the mouth of the Grand Canal there emerged three gondolas, their gondoliers taking advantage of the first dry weather of the day to take a party of Japanese tourists over the water. In the lead gondola, facing backwards to a beaming audience, were an accordion player and a tenor singing 'O Solo Mio'. It made the music that issued from the battery-operated gondolas sold on the trinket stalls on the Rialto sound almost good.

Paolo screwed up his face and smiled again. 'You may not believe me, but nothing, nothing at all could make me want to live anywhere else.'

Twenty-Nine

The days slipped by, the rain continued to fall, and life on the *topos* came to seem like something I'd always been part of. It was one of the rainiest springs Venice could remember. Every day I was wet and cold and every evening I was overheated in the crowded, smoky *osterias* where we ate. After a while delivery by boat became too much of the same thing to be able to distinguish one day on the water from another. I did it instead by remembering meals and the places they were eaten – a terrific dish of squid in its own ink at the Vedova, an especially savoury sausage on polenta at the Bomba. Then, around mid-May came something more memorable still: *aqua alta* – high water.

Nothing special marked the beginning of the day. At Tronchetto Marcello had clowned around with a rendition of 'Singin' in the Rain', complete with twirlings of an umbrella and swinging around a lamppost. I liked working with Marcello not only because he spoke good English – it relieved me of using bad Italian and an Esperanto nowhere as good as Jany's – but also because he'd seen what life could be off the canals: he'd worked as an orderly in a psychiatric hospital and counselled in a clinic for teenage drug-addicts. Incurably cheerful, Marcello counted himself a lucky man.

He was also the hardest worker at Barich. He had a phenomenal memory, and was faster with difficult addresses than anyone else.

'I am the *putana* of the Barich employees,' he told me happily one morning when he was switched from working the Castello *sestiere* to

San Polo. 'Paolo, Daniele and the others only know one *sestiere* and are faithful to them – they don't go anywhere else. I know them all. So when someone goes sick I'm the one called to replace him. I am the *putana* who whores around all Venice.'

Marcello's memory for numbers was so developed that he knew most public places better by their postal addresses than their names. Walking together, I would sometimes test him.

'Dorsoduro 3757,' I would say.

'The Arca restaurant,' he would fire back without a second's hesitation.

'San Polo 3002?'

'The State Archives.'

'San Marco 1243?'

'The Luna Baglioni Hotel.'

But it wasn't numbers above doorways that Marcello was scanning as we tied up outside the Santa Lucia railway station on this mid-May morning. It was the water in the canal below us.

'What is it?' I asked, watching him minutely inspecting water swirling against the wall of the quay where we had docked.

'Nothing,' he said, still watching as the rain spat down on us. 'The tide seems to be running faster than usual, that's all.'

It wasn't five minutes later, as Marcello was asking a news-kiosk owner in the station for a signature of receipt, that a siren began a low, loud moaning. Like every one else Marcello stopped talking and listened in silence. Then he shook his head, looking troubled. 'It's a flood warning – the *aqua alta* siren. But there shouldn't be any high tides at this time of year. They come in winter.'

'Well, that's no problem for us,' I said cheerfully. 'We're in a boat. We float.'

Marcello looked at me for a long moment, the greenest deliveryman he'd ever worked with.

'We float too much,' he finally said. 'Just try running a *topo* under a canal bridge in *aqua alta*. You'll leave your head and the superstructure of your boat in the water behind you.'

Back on the Grand Canal we stopped in at the Municipio in the Palazzo Loredan. In the lobby on the ground floor there was a sophisticated piece of machinery that gave the current height of the water and a forecast of exactly how high above the average high-tide mark the *aqua alta* would rise. The bright red figure on the current-height display was increasing by the minute. Pushed to the end of the Adriatic by the strong sirocco that had been blowing for days, augmented by ceaseless rains, the waters of the noon high tide were forecast to rise to 115 centimetres above average. It would be enough to flood the lowest-lying parts of the city.

An hour later seawater was overflowing the tops of the canal-banks and spilling out into the city behind. With water climbing the streets we no longer stepped from our *topo* onto dry land, but into a cloudy green soup that rose to our knees. Marcello lent me an old spare pair of the hip-waders that all *topo* crews carry, but they didn't do much good – the rubber had perished and within minutes there were litres of water slopping around inside.

Metal walkways raised two feet off the ground were installed along major pedestrian routes in the city. Shopkeepers and ground-floor residents busied themselves in a flurry of last-minute barrage-building. They slid steel gates into rubber-rimmed flanges running around the lower edges of their door frames, screwed them tight, and gave the joins a quick brush of silicone stopper. Then they waited to see if their entrances would remain watertight.

We didn't help much. Stepping over dammed-up doorways, we sloshed in leaving dark, wet trails wherever we went – the water that had collected in my waders drained out onto every polished floor and carpet I walked on. It seeped onto the tiling in the law courts, dripped onto the meticulously waxed floor-surface of the ladies' lingerie department in the Coin department store, and dribbled into puddles in the geriatric ward in the ancient *Ospedale Civile*.

But nobody took much notice of the mess. They were far more interested in getting the latest news on the flood outside – soon they'd be on their way home to lunch.

'How's the water out there?' they would ask. 'Wet, very wet,' Marcello would reply, as if Venetian water was possessed of properties that more ordinary water was lacking.

The tide rose, hit the promised 115 centimetre mark, caused minor havoc among those Venetians and tourists unprepared for a late spring flood, and then subsided. That evening, sitting in the Portega over *baccalà mantecato* and white wine, we watched the entire bar came to a halt as once again the *aqua alta* siren began its low moan. This time the water would rise to 125 centimetres. When we ordered more wine and some little crabs cooked with lemon and parsley we were served, but also warned to get back to Cannaregio well before high tide at midnight.

But even at ten o'clock we failed to return dry footed. The Fondamenta Nuove was wholly impassable and the back streets further inland inundated, too. You can always tell locals from tourists in a flood. The Venetians, equipped with knee-high rubber boots when they go out, see *aqua alta* as an unfortunate inconvenience. The foreigners, especially those returning from winey restaurant dinners to their hotels, find it romantic, or hilarious, or both. As we made our way home we crossed paths with men grinning like small boys as they ploughed along through calf-high water, their trouser legs rolled up and shoes and socks held aloft. The women they were carrying on their backs found the whole thing even funnier.

Roberto Puppo didn't find it so amusing. He had to get up before dawn to begin baking but now, as dark water lapped ever higher about his doorsill, he was busy installing and waterproofing his doorway. Two or three doors down a neighbour's daughters had failed to arrive home before their apartment was sealed up. Now they came begging a ladder from Puppo's and, leaning it against an outside wall, climbed to a first-floor window and slithered in, head-first and giggling. From our own first-floor window an hour or two later I looked out to see the street completely flooded. Later, asleep, I had a dream that all I had to do to make a delivery anywhere in the city was lean over the side of the *Alvise* and slide my packet through a window. Jany said it was a dream with deep Freudian implications. I said it was just a *topo* crewman's fantasy – those delivery dollies are hard work.

The next morning there was yet a third *aqua alta* warning for the following high tide. I went down to Tronchetto as usual but asked for the day off. I had three good reasons. For the first time in a week it had stopped raining, and that alone was worth celebrating. Second, I wanted to see the Piazza under water. And third, Jany would soon be flying back to Aix-en-Provence and I setting off in the other direction for Istanbul. I wanted us to see the city together one last time.

We wandered down towards Saint Mark's, where the crowds were thicker than ever. Flooded streets had reduced access to the square to just two or three points, and everyone was jammed on to the raised metal walkways that bordered the Piazza. The square itself was an open lake, as calm and flat as a millpond, its surface reflecting the ragged grey sky and the arcades that surrounded it.

Nothing, though, was going to stop the main business at hand, the purveying of art and culture to the world at large. In front of the Basilica a walkway stretched out of sight around the corner, its human load slowly, patiently moving forward to Venice's very heart. Another walkway carried more visitors, anxious to see the flooded square from above, to the door of the Campanile. Where the two paths crossed there was, inevitably, a traffic jam. Policewomen in rubber boots and dark blue raincoats splashed up and down beside the walkways blowing whistles, gesturing furiously and, as I myself had grown fond of doing, shouting '*Avanti! Avanti!*'

Jany took my hand. 'It's romantic, isn't it?' she asked.

I was going to splutter something sharp and cynical. But I held off because this might be the last time we looked at Venice together, and such moments are supposed to be tender. So instead I simply looked down to the reflecting water in front of me and in it considered the extravagant pavilions of the Basilica, the gorgeous tracery on the Doge's Palace, the winged lion on his granite column in front of Saint Mark's Basin.

And slowly it dawned upon me that Jany was right. The city might no longer be a seat of power, a display of unimaginable wealth, or a jumping-off spot for the East. The great era of its truly cosmopolitan existence was long over, the age of its maritime dominance past. Not even the

Mediterranean itself was the great sea it used to be. Despite the changes the world has brought to it, though, Venice remains what it has been from the beginning.

'Yes,' I answered, 'It is romantic.'

A day later Jany was on a plane home to Aix-en-Provence and I was back travelling on *terra firma*. For me, if not for the trading ships of the Serene Republic, Venice remained a jumping-off spot for the East. Perhaps traces of that old cosmopolitan existence lay that way still. I was headed to Istanbul.

Thirty

In the Italian port of Ancona, 150 miles along the Adriatic coast from Venice, I bought a British Sunday paper. It was half a week old but hefty enough to keep me going all day. I had time to kill.

I'd spent the previous afternoon on a train plodding slowly across a wide, flat plain. Provincial, semi-industrial Italy had dragged by my window, its aging assembly plants and housing estates backing directly onto the rail tracks. Seen from its rear end, small-town life on the lower Po looked supremely dull and ugly. It was as dreary inside the train as out. Heads lolled and mouths fell open – even the locals preferred to sleep through it.

At Rimini things promised to pick up; the railway rejoined the Adriatic and ran for miles beside the open sea. But the resort towns were tacky and the water was cloudy and mud-coloured. At the Hotel Dorico in Ancona I asked for a room away from the noisy street. The hotel, though, was like the places I'd been passing through all afternoon – its back end was even less attractive than its front. After sunset a guard-dog tied to a chain-link fence began barking. The racket dragged on through the night, every link in the fence rattling as the dog hurled itself at shadows. After Venice it was all a bit of a let-down, and in the morning I discovered I had fourteen hours to hang around in Ancona. The next ferry across the Adriatic to Split did not leave until late evening.

It was a long time to wait. Even without luggage to haul around, the city, a traffic-ridden place pressed between high hills and the sea, offered few diversions. In the 15th century Pope Pius II, admittedly unwell even before he arrived from Rome on his way to yet one more Crusade, died of old age as he waited to sail from Ancona. My case wasn't as serious. But as I installed myself in a café near the water I looked at the long day stretching before me. Terminal boredom loomed.

I worked my way through the newspaper. I caught up on the latest royal indiscretion. I learned how to accessorise my garden pond with Japanese carp. I was warned off investing in vintage Bordeaux wines. By the time I came to the travel pages I was nodding. But I woke up when I turned to a colour-photo splash of an old stone house sitting over a bright blue sea. Never mind high-rise living on the Côte d'Azur, advised a fulsome feature writer. Forget golf-course residences in Marbella and luxury time-shares on the Costa Smeralda. There was a new place where the fashionable set was investing in the Mediterranean these days. There was still time, in fact, to buy affordable waterfront property there. But the prediction was that the supply wouldn't last – the quickening trail of investors along that hottest new Riviera, the Croatian coast, was turning into a horde.

The article bothered me. If the Croatian coast was in the Sunday papers it was far too late for me to be on the ground itself. I'd had about as much international tourism as I could stand in Venice. The idea of travelling a seashore gearing up for a summer onslaught was enough to give me hives.

What I needed was a tour of a touristless coast, a Mediterranean place no foreigner in his right mind would dream of visiting. It wasn't easy – even Colonel Qadhafi welcomed tourists with open arms these days. There was always Gaza, I considered as I flipped my way idly through the news pages. It wasn't quite what I was looking for. Gaza might be Mediterranean, but it was a Mediterranean of violent division and dissolution. What I was searching for were traces of an older sea, a place more integrated, more inclusive than it is now.

Of course tourist-mobbed Venice, and now the Croatian coast, were part of the Mediterranean, and part of today's larger globalised world. Even the fact that I could sit on the Italian coast and read about Japanese carp and Bordeaux wines in a locally-bought British newspaper were part of that. But ever since I'd arrived in Alexandria almost six months earlier I'd been coming across the remains of a much older globalisation. It hadn't just connected the known world through commerce – it had traded in an open market of ideas as well, invested in a mutually beneficial outlook. It had made the Mediterranean cosmopolitan. It was this Mediterranean, or at least what might be left of it, that I was hoping to find at the eastern end of the sea. In the meantime, though, the problem was getting there without being deluged in a tidal wave of tourism.

My eyes came to a halt over a short, two-inch news piece. A people-smuggling ring had been smashed in Germany. It was run by the same men who'd lately muscled their way into much of the organised crime in Europe. They were vicious, they were violent, and there was nothing to which they would not stoop. They were Albanian.

Now there was a thought. I'd never heard of Albanian tourism, never seen advertising luring visitors to the romantic and sunny Illyrian coast. Come to think of it, I'd never heard of a single Albanian attraction apart from Mother Teresa. Perhaps here was the solution to the summer crowds of the Mediterranean. But I hesitated. This was a British Sunday paper, after all. Off I trotted to verify the story of Albanian bad guys at an Internet café up the road.

Unsurprisingly, I found nothing about Albanian tourism. But the nasty character of the Albanian Mafia was unstintingly confirmed in dozens of web-pages. There was an Italian prosecutor who'd identified Albanian thugs as a major threat to Western society – 'The road for drugs and arms and people, meaning illegal immigrants to Europe, is in Albanian hands,' he'd said. In Poland Albanians had cornered the market in Ecstasy distribution. In former Yugoslavia they smuggled petrol. On the Georgian border, conducting business with the Russian army, they traded heroin for heavy weapons. Even in Soho, in the heart of civilised London, the Albanians were busy – the Metropolitan Police estimated that nearly three quarters of all women working in UK brothels were Albanians or Albanian Kosovars.

If the Albanian Mafia had been able to pull that off on the far side of the continent, I wondered, what kind of havoc they had they managed to wreak in their own backyard? Of course nobody went holidaying in Albania. It was the perfect Mediterranean stop *en route* to Istanbul.

I was at the ferry ticket office down in the port ten minutes later. There were at least half a dozen companies running in and out of Ancona – Jadrolinija to Split and Zara; Minoan Lines to Greece; the Blue Line; Anek; SNAV. The queue for the overnight ferry to Split wouldn't start forming for hours, but there was a line tailing back from the Superfast Ferries counter, and it was so restive that there was obviously a ferry about to leave.

'Where are you going?' I asked a short, grizzled man in a black suit standing at the back of the queue.

'Igoumenitsa!' he smiled broadly. He looked so happy about it that Igoumenitsa or parts thereabout had to be home.

'What time does the ferry leave?' I said, stepping into line behind him. I wasn't exactly sure where Igoumenitsa was, but the man was flipping a set of worry-beads. He looked Greek. That was good enough for me – anything was better than another ten hours in an Ancona café.

'Now! Now!' he replied, looking at his watch. My question only made him more anxious that he would miss the sailing. In fact there were still a few minutes left. From my bag I fished out my map of the eastern Mediterranean and searched for Igoumenitsa. It lay behind Corfu on the Greek mainland, just south of the Albanian border. A quarter of an hour later I was in front of the counter, asking about accommodation for the eighteen-hour trip. After a night in the Hotel Dorico I thought I deserved a small treat, and told the ticket lady so.

'For €271 you can have an outside cabin with double bed, television, fridge, hair dryer and in-cabin breakfast,' she replied. 'It's a good price. In high season it's €380. It's a luxury cabin.'

€271 would have bought me more than a month's stay in the Union Hotel in Alexandria. It was a little more luxury than I needed, I told her.

She shrugged. 'Then you can have a reclining seat for €61.' I shook my head. That didn't sound much better than the Dorico.

She lowered her voice. 'I wouldn't take either of them,' she confided. 'The boat is almost empty. Take a bed in a six-berth compartment. There will be no one else there.'

€98 and five minutes later I was climbing aboard the *Superfast XI*.

The ferry was red and white, newly built and squeaky-clean. There wasn't a scuff mark on it. There was chrome and mirrored glass everywhere. Acres of thick carpeting stretched away into the distance. The vessel was 656 feet long, towered ten decks high, and could carry 1,500 passengers and 900 vehicles. And it was, as promised, superfast – it shot up and down the Adriatic at 31 knots, more than 35 miles an hour.

But what the ferry was not, at this time of year, was busy. The lounges were empty, the cafeterias abandoned, the bars deserted. I dropped down a couple of decks to dump my bag. When I swiped my key-card in a door and entered a communal accommodation area not a soul had claimed any of the half-dozen compartments inside. I felt reprieved, like a long-haul air passenger who suddenly stumbles onto a whole row of empty seats to stretch out on.

I stood at the rails of the stern sundeck, watching the last vehicles roll into the *Superfast XI*'s hold. Tourists might be seasonal, but provisioning Europe's factories, firms and supermarkets was a year-round affair. There were ten times more commercial trucks and drivers boarding the ferry than private cars and passengers. Eurostar Transport, Continental Food and Flowers, Logistics Mars, Olympic Flame International, Floridis Meat Industries, Brinkman Trucking of Holland ... Ancona may have lacked interest for idlers like me, but for businesses across the continent it was a busy international transport-hub.

You only had to look at the couple of hundred trucks pulled up in the port parking lot, wavy lines of heat pouring from exhaust stacks above their cabs, to realise how connected the different parts of Europe had become. Politics was something else – the French could moan about the English, New Europe could stand up to Old Europe and the whole lot of them could bitch about Brussels. But in the meantime they were all happy to go on eating each other's food, wearing each other's shoes and buying each other's cars. You didn't have to ask the crew of brawny truck drivers ascending from parking bays silly questions about what was going to make Europe work or not work. They already knew.

My only complaint was that the whole thing was so completely aseptic. I wandered for a few minutes. There was a video-game area with banks of flashing screens and synthesized sound effects – they introduced passengers to light entertainments with names like 'Armageddon' and 'Death Wish III'. There was a casino with more serried ranks of machines – one-armed bandits and electronic roulette tables – also awaiting fresh infusions of Euro coins. There was an Internet Corner, a brightly-coloured children's playroom, a whole slew of sparkling-clean buffets, self-service cafeterias and *à la carte* restaurants. There were more television viewing areas than I could count. There were lounge-bars, a discotheque, a swimming pool, boutiques selling jewellery and name-brand fragrances. The *Superfast XI*, halfway between a utilitarian transport ferry and a sumptuous cruise liner, was anodyne and anonymous. It had all the character features of an international airport. Even its name spoke of something stamped out in series – presumably there were at least ten other similar vessels ploughing ferry routes on other seas.

I re-emerged onto the stern sundeck to see ropes being cast off and cables running through hawsers onto drums. Slowly the *Superfast XI* moved away from the quay and began churning water. We crawled past port installations running out on a long mole. There were tall yellow cranes, grain and cement silos, gondola-cars moving down a rail spur. A boat basin full of commercial fishing vessels came into view beside the ferry port, then a freight terminal piled high with shoebox-shaped freight containers. We passed the *Halo Cygnus*, a bulky black container carrier registered in Panama, being loaded by the quay. Behind her the *Romania II*, out of Monrovia, was lying low in the water and waiting to be unloaded. Finally we were away. The ferry picked up speed and the green hills behind Ancona began to grow smaller. Fifteen minutes from the port we crossed a line, so distinct that it might have been laid out with a pencil and ruler, dividing on-shore waters from the open sea. The first I'd already seen from the train – a mucky brown effluvium washed into the sea over recent days of heavy rain. But the water that lay beyond it was the purest Mediterranean blue, a clear, deep aquamarine whose surface now foamed to a creamy white froth behind us.

I sat out on the deck in warm sunshine and daydreamed most of the afternoon away. Occasionally there were glimpses of the low-lying Italian coast. Mostly, though, there was nothing, just bright sky and bright sea and an empty horizon. Few other passengers came outdoors. Of the truck drivers there wasn't a sign – they had their own designated lounges and as a superior class remained apart from the dross of ordinary humanity. I was happy enough just to watch our wide wake recede, a dazzling, spumey ribbon fading first to a velvety blue, then to nothing. We were eating up the miles.

Around sunset it grew cool and I moved indoors. I drank a beer at the bar and had dinner in a brightly lit, virtually deserted restaurant. After dinner I watched a middle-aged couple, the sole occupants of the dance-floor, revolve in the spangly light of a mirrored disco-ball twirling from the ceiling.

I turned in early, thinking about our 5.30 a.m. arrival in Igoumenitsa. And also because there wasn't a single television screen, video game, fruit machine or boutique service I wished to avail myself of. The sheets in my berth were snowy white and crisply ironed, the calm absolute. But I regretted that human cargoes were moved about these days with as much emotion as steel-bound container cargoes. For a moment I was tempted to think almost fondly of that other ferry I'd taken, the rusty Saudi hulk that made the run from Egyptian Nuweiba up the Gulf of Aqaba.

What the *Superfast XI* needed, I decided as I dropped off to sleep, was a surprise boarding by a thousand or so clamorous Arabs, wild-eyed and wind-whipped in their travel-stained *galabiyas*. They might not please the occupants of the luxury outside cabins as they lay on double beds blow-drying their hair. But they would certainly add a little zing to modern Mediterranean ferry travel.

Thirty-One

A highly developed sense of self and personal honour; a fierce alle-giance to family and clan; a strong attachment to tradition and the past – no one admires these qualities more than I. They are the founda-tion of Mediterranean society, the firm sea floor to which Mediterraneans anchor themselves as the currents of history slop and swirl about them. They give the people of this sea a certain stability and order.

Unfortunately, they also give it a certain disorder. For as often as not Mediterraneans couldn't care less about anything that falls outside these narrow allegiances. I needn't have lamented too much the passing of an older way of life aboard the *Superfast XI*. I was on my way to Albania, and the screw-you-Jack, what's-it-to-me unruliness of the Levant was even closer than I thought.

On the early morning bus from Igoumenitsa to Ioannina, the inland town where I would catch another bus to the Albanian border, we crossed a range of high coastal hills. Scattered with wildflowers in late spring, still fresh and green before the searing heat of summer, they were glorious. I am not sure the bus driver saw them that way. I am not sure he saw them at all. From his side-window he flung out into the morning, at intervals, his sty-rofoam coffee cup, a chocolate-bar wrapper, a handful of paper tissues and an empty plastic water bottle. Perhaps he didn't see the no-smoking sign above his head either, for next he lit up a cigarette and threw out the just-finished packet for good measure. Nobody paid any attention – the ditches outside were full of this kind of stuff. Things only got messier from there.

The men who boarded the next bus in Ioannina weren't just slovenly in their attentions to the countryside. They weren't too fastidious about themselves, either. Unshaven and sweaty, they wore grubby suits bagged out at knee and elbow, broken shoes and white shirts with grime-ringed collars. Some of them looked as if they had been travelling for days. At the border they pulled out Albanian passports and were treated disdainfully by Greek customs officials. They didn't look like violent and vicious Mafia thugs to me. They looked like tired, overworked migrant labourers anxious to get home.

We walked a quarter of a mile through a tree-stripped no-man's-land. 'Tourism,' an Albanian customs official intoned slowly, once I was on the far side of the barricades, observation towers and coiled razor-wire that made up the frontier. As if in some doubt he knitted his brows as he read and stamped the immigration card I'd filled in. It didn't look like he processed tourist entries very often. Overall, I got the feeling more people were trying to get out of Albania than get in.

The next man I spoke to was much more positive. 'Welcome in Albania!' crowed Ermir Bejkollari, a smile on his plump, moustachioed face as he opened the front door of his minivan. He meant it, too – he immediately hustled the old woman sitting beside the driver's seat into the back with the other passengers. It was no good protesting. I was his personal charge until we got to Tirana, and he wouldn't hear another word.

Albania, for a short while at least, seemed like a rural paradise. As we drove away from the border post there was no indication that the industrial age had ever penetrated these rugged hills. Beside meadows dark with blood-red poppies women turned drying hay with pitchforks. Men scythed grass or tilled patchwork fields with horses and iron ploughs. Dropping lines into torrents splashing with snowmelt from the mountains above, bare-footed boys fished from ancient wooden bridges. There were shepherds' huts of daubed wattle; curling rams' horns nailed to gateposts; scarecrow effigies hanging like talismans from the rafters of houses. Albania didn't appear merely pre-mechanical. It looked pre-Christian, pre-Muslim, pre- any institution that extended its requirements past basic survival and the husbandry of animals. Albania was barely formed, a pagan land buried back at the very beginning of things.

The illusion was captivating, but crumbled almost immediately. Further down the valley I could see giant puffball mushrooms two or three feet across growing in swathes. Closer up, they turned out to be low, half-domes of concrete, above-ground protection for gun-slitted foxholes buried in the earth. They were military bunkers, each built to hold a single man, and there were hundreds of them. They continued in successive defensive bands for miles down the valley. Peasant life – pastures, fruit orchards, herds of sheep – just had to work around them.

When I looked at Ermir Bejkollari for explanation he only rolled his eyes and tapped the side of his head with a forefinger. 'Big crazy!' was all he could say in English.

It wasn't long before I was beginning to think the whole country was big crazy. The first villages, no pastoral idylls, were built on the Stalinist social model – block after geometrically laid out block of flaking and decrepit cement-slab constructions. Towns were the same but larger. Garbage lay liberally strewn about. Roads were muddy and pot-holed. Traffic was held up by horses pulling overloaded carts of fodder.

Country people got on and off. Some were pretty ripe. Near the town of Gjirokaster one old gent climbed into the van exuding an odour of unwashed body so pungent, so fermented, cured and aged that we all rolled down the windows. But sometimes it was less fragrant outside than in. We drove into a long valley that had once been an oilfield. Rusty rigs and abandoned derricks littered its slopes and floor. They'd been clumsily capped – the air was heavy and acrid, and from the base of the derricks thick black oil oozed out into pools. It ran downhill beside orchards and fields of crops, dribbled into stinking ditches and finally emptied into a river whose surface was black and iridescent with petroleum rainbows.

We drove down out of the hills and onto a more populated coastal plain, now close enough to Tirana that the capital's FM radio stations filled the van with the slick voices of American-style DJs. The music was gangsta-rap sung in Albanian.

Outside the window the bizarre mix of primitive agriculture, abandoned industry and deserted military installations only grew more nightmarish. But as we drew near the port of Durrës Albania took on a contemporary note. The roads were now thick with jockeying traffic – in six hours we had gone from a wheel-less society to one that appeared bent on mass automotive annihilation. Odder still, most of the cars were the same make. In between Bejkollari's own attempts at suicidal passing I did a rough count – six out of ten vehicles were Mercedes. The landscape, too, assumed modern touches. There were still women out there ploughing with horses, but scattered among the fields, bunkers and smashed-up factories were new constructions.

Possibly they were resort hotels and holiday homes. They were so shoddy and gimcrack, so hastily thrown up amidst the detritus of a collapsed society that it was difficult to imagine anyone wanting to spend any free time in them. But as we arrived at the coast and ran north along the sandy sweep of the Bay of Durrës there could be no doubt – the cheap buildings erected side by side were beach hotels. Some were open for business even as earth and rubble from construction sites next door was being piled high around them.

Albania's hysteric building boom reached a paroxysm as we swung inland for the half-hour drive to Tirana. The approaches to the city were one vast construction site. It was anarchic. Buildings sprouted everywhere. Zoning had never been heard of. There was slum housing in narrow lanes running beneath half-completed flyovers. There were shiny new car showrooms lying amidst cabbage fields. Cement mixers, iron scaffolding and pallets of tiles lay strewn along the roadside. The roads grew more congested, drivers edgier. Car horns blared continuously. It was all getting out of hand – if these were just the suburbs, I wondered, what in God's name could I expect in the city itself?

But downtown Tirana, inexplicably, was a haven of order. There was a main square where a vast wall mosaic had once honoured the toiling revolutionary masses; now the red star of communism that had crowned it was gone and workers and peasants were conspicuously absent in the streets below. In their place prosperous-looking urban consumers went placidly about their business. There were grassy parks, promenades, broad avenues of government ministries decorated in yellow sienna and maroon trim. The whole city centre had been spruced up – in keeping with the mood even old-style communal housing had been repainted and now looked like a bright, multi-coloured experiment in Op-Art.

Ermir Bejkollari dropped off the last of his passengers and we drove around in circles looking for a hotel. Everything was in the luxury category. I was perplexed. Here was a country where things like soap seemed out of most people's reach, yet you couldn't find a room for less than $150 a night. Finally I paid Bejkollari off – he made me promise to telephone him if nothing came up – and began to walk. Five minutes later I was registering at the Dajti Hotel. Obscured by tall pine trees, it was so gloomily monolithic I had taken it for one of the last, unreformed institutions of the old dictatorship.

It was. Just down the street the former Enver Hoxha Museum, not long ago dedicated to the eternal memory of the Albanian dictator, had reinvented itself as the International Culture Centre. But the Hotel Dajti had been so steeped in the totalitarian spirit for so long it appeared unreformable. It had been built by other despots, Italian Fascists who'd occupied the country during the Second World War. But soon homegrown autocrats had taken it over and felt perfectly at ease in its Mussolini-inspired décor. Now one of the country's last state-owned establishments, it had been communist Albania's premier hotel for half a century. Pompous and ponderous in style, everything in it spoke of decades of crushing state bureaucracy.

The reception desk dwarfed the woman who stood behind it. A grand hallway almost a hundred yards long and covered in worn red carpeting ran off into dim obscurity on either side. Lined by massive square columns, it was supposed to be illuminated by chandeliers hanging from high ceilings, but most of the light bulbs were missing. There was a conspicuous shortage of guests, too – the only people in the lobby when I arrived were two shapeless women swabbing the endless marble lobby floor with mops and buckets.

Some of the rigour of the old days must have gone, for the receptionist was quietly quaffing an afternoon glass of wine. She wasn't above a little cash bargaining, either, and I ended up with a double room for the price of a single. The Dajti was a fraction of the cost of the new hotels, but I got what I paid for. The plumbing was quirky and the furniture threadbare; maintenance was so minimal the potted palms in the lounge appeared to be suffering the effects of long-term drought. But I liked the Hotel Dajti anyway. It was about the only place in Albania I could actually understand.

How did it all fit together? I walked through the city that evening, trying to figure it out. A stone-age countryside; industry in ruins; an out-of-control building boom; a military gone mad, then just plain gone. And now this – a mystifying prosperity that let hip young Albanians splash out on a lavish scale.

I strolled around 'the Bloc', once a barricaded residential area reserved for members of the communist elite. Green and leafy, it was still a place for the privileged. But now capitalists lounged around in ersatz French tea salons. They browsed pricy clothing boutiques and socialised in cafés with silly, hybrid names like the Cowboy Pub. The citizens that packed the sidewalk cafés were well-dressed and well-bathed and fragrant – there was no soap shortage here. They liked to show off other little luxuries – if there were half a dozen people sitting together in a café there were half a dozen mobile telephones piled on the table in front of them. Downtown Tirana was as trendy as any Western capital – it was just that nothing jibed with the appalling mess that lay all around it.

I considered dropping by the Boom-Boom Room, a place where live bands would keep crowds of Albanians rollicking until dawn. But it didn't get going until late, and after the long day's drive I was tired. Nobody else was. When I strolled home around midnight even the little park opposite the Hotel Dajti was still going strong. There, surrounded by illuminated splashing fountains, lay the latest in high-tech bowling alleys.

I thought bowling alleys were hang-outs for blue-collar buddies in the American rustbelt. But there was no one swigging Busch Lite from the bottle here. Inside, bowlers sat sipping exotic cocktails around tables whose glass surfaces showed their bowling scores racked up on electronic displays. A battery of wall-mounted plasma screens was tuned to Fashion TV. Justin Timberlake wailed 'Rock Your Body' through a dozen thudding multi-directional speakers. Out in the lanes, ultraviolet lights picked out eerily-lit teenagers whose orange and blue fluorescent bowling balls rolled towards pins glowing in the distance. Tirana was getting stranger and stranger. I needed some answers, fast.

I got them the next morning without ever leaving the hotel. At the rear of the Dajti lay the offices of Albturist, the Albanian state tourist organisation. The Hotel Dajti was not only Albturist's global headquarters; it was its sole public office. That didn't mean the world was beating a furious path to the Dajti's back door. When I asked to see Albtourist's general manager, Arjan Skenderi, I was shown in right away.

Mr Skenderi was a deliberate, methodical man with salt-and-pepper hair and a mustard-coloured jacket. He seemed delighted that an outsider might be interested in a concept as ephemeral as Albanian tourism.

'Of course it's difficult to understand Albania today. But it is even harder to understand Albania as it was before,' he said. He sat with his lips pursed and the fingertips of his hands lightly pressed to each other. He had the contemplative air of a man considering one of the great conundrums of his age.

'Hotels are meant to receive guests. But do you think the Dajti was run to encourage foreigners to visit Albania?' It was like a riddle from the sphinx. I didn't know how to answer. 'No!' Mr Skenderi answered for me. 'Everything was done to turn them away!'

Turning away foreigners seemed to be an Albanian speciality. Perhaps this was the moment to ask about those military bunkers.

Arjan Skenderi winced, rolling his eyes precisely the way Ermir Bejkollari had done. He seemed genuinely embarrassed. 'All dictators have their obsessions,' he said. 'Enver Hoxha's was fear of attack. Do not ask me who was going to invade us. Nobody ever knew. But when Hoxha studied in Paris as a young man he learned about the Maginot Line. Those bunkers were our Maginot Lines. There are still more than 600,000 of them scattered along our borders. We've got to do something with them. There has even been talk of a national competition with a prize for the best suggestion. Beach-front changing rooms, Enver Hoxha souvenir telephone booths ... everyone has a different idea.'

But there were still tougher Albanian puzzles to solve, the general manager told me. When the regime collapsed in the early 1990s mayhem had set in. A decade and a half later the country had yet to emerge from it.

'After fifty years of absolute state control suddenly we were free. We felt, naturally, we had the right to do anything we liked. So that's just what we did,' Mr Skenderi said. 'No one had ever owned anything before. But just owning things wasn't enough – in the middle of collapse everyone wanted to be an entrepreneur, a rich capitalist. It was impossible to control. There was,' he said, carefully searching for his words, 'an abusive interpretation of the market economy.'

It was masterful understatement. Out in the country, peasants appropriated the land they'd worked collectively and refused any kind of zoning or planning. More than 15 years later rural property disputes were still choking the courts. In the city things went even further out of kilter. Before 1990 only 200,000 of Albania's three million residents lived in Tirana. Over the next decade more than three times that number swamped the capital. Those who were able to get out of the country altogether did so. Soon almost a million overseas Albanians were repatriating funds and sinking them into an urban free-for-all.

'It was chaos – too much, too fast,' said Mr Skenderi. 'First it was bars, cafés and clubs. Then bigger things – the investors took over the whole city. You couldn't imagine what the downtown looked like. It's all been pulled down now, and the illegal operators driven out of the centre. Our next targets are on the city periphery. Control there has not yet been wholly re-established.'

More understatement. I mentioned the Mercedes-Benzes that clogged city streets and defied death out in the country. The manager winced again.

'Ah yes. The Mercedes ... It's a very, well ... a very *Albanian* thing.

Everyone wants to look important. Under Enver Hoxha we all pedalled around on bicycles – there were only three or four hundred cars in the whole city. They belonged to officials, and they were mostly Mercedes-Benzes. So now there's an endless appetite for second-hand Mercedes. It is the vehicle of choice – for a few thousand euros you can look like an influential man.'

Maybe that's why people drove so atrociously – a decade isn't long for an entire nation to learn to shift S-500 Mercedes Sedans around hairpin Balkan bends. But I refrained from asking the man from Albturist the obvious question – where had all the money for this conspicuous consumption come from?

The pinching of attractive motor vehicles from shopping-centre parking lots across Europe could only be just the beginning of Albania's abusive market-economy interpretations. What about the gangsterism run on a continental scale, the money laundering, drug dealing, gun running, prostitution, people smuggling and sundry other forms of racketeering? Poor Mr Skenderi, however, already seemed more than sufficiently pained – he'd already had to explain away a psychotic dictator, to say nothing of unsolvable land squabbles, urban anarchy and an unconscionable number of luxury motor cars. So I asked him instead about Albania's great hope for the future, Mediterranean tourism.

Immediately he brightened. Plans were already well advanced, he said. Of course, Greece to the south and Croatia to the north were far ahead. But the potential was there, and it was focused on Durrës. Those chaotic beach developments I had driven past were intended for domestic tourism, for Albanian and Kosovar package holidays. But there were many more miles of beautiful coast, still untouched, reserved for an elite foreign market. Even as we spoke plans were being drawn up for half a dozen tourist villages with a thousand beds each.

I hoped the entrepreneur with the concrete-bunker changing-room idea was not part of the tourism planning committee. What, I asked, was the biggest problem for the leisure industry – money?

Arjan Skenderi shook his head. Of course funding was needed, he acknowledged – foreign investors were more than welcome to come forward. But that was not the main challenge.

'What we have to do is get away from the lure of quick profit,' the man in the mustard jacket sighed. 'There is one thing Albania really needs – a new mentality.'

The next day I took a bus back out through the confusion of suburban Tirana to the old port of Durrës. Once it was the starting point of the Via Egnatia, the Roman road linking Rome to Constantinople. Much later, too, it was a major Venetian trading port. For a few years in the early 20th century it was even the capital of Albania. But all that, like the Durrës of the future, had to be imagined.

Behind the Durrës bus station a narrow lane ran towards the harbour. It ended in a kind of makeshift waiting area, an open, muddy place pressed up against a railway track and the high fence that surrounded the port. Flimsy chairs and refreshment stands thrown together from wood and plastic sheeting shared the area with piles of refuse. A guard stood at a metal gate in the fence, blocking the only way forward.

Where, I asked a man slithering through the mud on a bicycle, was the main passenger entrance to the Durrës ferry terminal?

Right here, he said.

Could this possibly be the first taste of Albania for sea-travellers arriving from across the Adriatic, I wondered? It seemed so doubtful I went back to the lane and enquired at a ticket kiosk there. The man behind the counter threw up his hands.

'What do you want?' he said. 'This port belongs to thieves and corrupt officials.' He didn't seem to share Arjan Skenderi's optimism for the future. 'When Hoxha fell 20,000 people sailed from Albania in any boat they could find.' He pointed out to sea and the Straights of Otantro. 'Brindisi lies just there, 120 kilometres away. Do you think 20,000 people are going to come sailing back from Brindisi tomorrow? Yes, this is where ferry travellers arrive.'

If Albania was going to open its doors to tourism Durrës would have to get a move on. I walked a mile or so along the street fronting the port.

Mottled and stained apartment blocks, their balconies bricked in to make extra rooms, ran along the harbour fence. Abandoned buildings, wrecked train carriages, piles of scrap metal and more concrete bunkers buried in the ground completed the air of seafront desolation. Further on, past guarded gates where transport lorries were entering the port, I saw new buildings going up. Waylaid by a drunk, I never got there. He was rheumy-eyed and crying and, latching on to my shirtsleeve, refused to let go. He'd been deported from Italy. 'Come and drink, just one drink,' he kept whining in Italian. I eventually pried his hands away and started back for the station. I'd had enough of Durrës. If there was an unhappier port in the Mediterranean I hadn't seen it.

That evening I sat on a sidewalk terrace in the Bloc drinking coffee and thinking about progress. All around me people were relaxing after a day's hectic efforts. Trying to get ahead in any way they could, Albanians were making progress. At least a sort of progress. A saner kind of Albania was slowly spreading out from the centre of Tirana, and one day its ripples would wash up against sad and dilapidated Durrës. In the end I liked Tirana, if for nothing else than a drive and energy so rugged you could almost touch it. Albanians, there was no doubt about it, were go-getters.

And that was a good thing, if they were going to sort out the looniness that results when human contact is stifled and people become cut off from each other. For half a century Albania had been the very opposite of cosmopolitan, a state in perfect isolation. That Albanians had in the last little while become not just more cosmopolitan but unscrupulous go-getters as well – pirates, to put it plainly – was not an insurmountable problem.

For there were other Mediterraneans just up the coast who had once indulged in wholesale piracy, too. If I remembered it correctly, a major naval expedition under the Venetian Doge Pietro Orseolo had been required to curb their enthusiasm for thievery, murder, rapine and all other manner of nastiness. So relieved were the Venetian population when it came to an end that they celebrated ever after with an annual thanksgiving. And where were those once-feared Croatians today? In the travel pages of the British Sunday papers, of course.

Thirty-Two

In the northern Greek port of Kavala I asked about sailings to Lesbos. The young man behind the counter, organised and efficient, barely glanced at his computer.

'There's a sailing to Mitilene tomorrow morning at five o'clock on the M.V. *Rodanthi*. It costs €23.60, and it stops at Limnos at eleven. You arrive at Mitilene at four in the afternoon.'

'But I don't want to go to Mitilene,' I said, thinking I'd been misheard. 'I want to go to Lesbos.' I pulled out my map and showed him the island, triangular and indented by a deep bay, lying just a short hop across the water from the Turkish coast. It was clearly marked 'Lesbos'.

He studied the map, then tapped it with his finger. 'Yes, that's what I told you. You arrive at four o'clock.'

'But why do you call it Mitilene?' Lesbos was how the place was marked on all the maps and guidebooks I'd looked at.

The ticket man was now looking both self-conscious and defiant at the same time. 'Lesbos was an early name. Tourists and foreigners still use it, but Greeks prefer to use the later name.'

'Why is that?'

'Because...' he said, hesitating over an answer. 'Because we are traditional.'

I was confused. 'But if you were traditional surely you'd use the earlier name, wouldn't you?'

He'd had enough. 'No, we are traditional because we don't want to be connected with the idea of sex between women. Some people like to make a big story about Sappho on Lesbos and the kind of woman she was. But we do not. The women who live there are ordinary Greeks, wives and mothers and family women. Why should they be called Lesbians?'

'Fine,' I said. 'You're right. Forget Lesbos. I'll take a ticket to Mitiline instead. And I'll also take a later ferry if you've got one – I find early sailings as offensive as early names. In my book five o'clock is a scandalous and indecent hour.'

The ticket man wasn't amused. But I thought his insistence on a sexually-neutral name for an island prudish. It was only a name. No one should subject old islands to modern gender issues. At any rate there were no other ferries to Lesbos/Mitiline so I settled down to spend a quiet time in Kavala waiting for the *Rodanthi*.

I didn't mind at all. I was travel-weary. I found a room overlooking the sea and with bright light bouncing up through closed shutters snoozed for half the day. The road from Tirana over the mountains into Greek Macedonia had been long. And Thessalonica, Greece's industrial second city, had been uncomfortably big and sprawling for a passer-through like me.

But Kavala was different. Too far north in the Aegean to be on the busy tourist circuit, it was one of those rare things – a Mediterranean fishing port that had kept its soul. Prosperous, relaxed and friendly, it was easy to feel at home in the little city. And it had a past, too. On the top of the hill overlooking the harbour sat a citadel with high stone towers and battlements. Over the centuries Kavala had served as the fortified base for the usual cast of Levantine defenders and attackers – Byzantines, Normans, Franks, Venetians and, of course, the longest-installed of all occupants, the Ottomans.

When I woke in the late afternoon I strolled the steep, narrow streets of the old town. There were still signs of those earlier residents. Here and there were old Ottoman private homes, the wooden lathes of their crumbling walls showing through like ribs. They were reminders, melancholy accusations against a departed but still deeply-resented occupier. Most evocative of all was a mosque in ruins, its minaret taken down and its doors closed tight with rusty locks and chains. Above, bright red wild-flowers grew on a rotted roof beneath a copper finial of a crescent moon, long ago bent out of shape and never straightened.

Such neglect was hardly astonishing. In the last century the relation-ship between Greek and Turk has been so bitter and vindictive that it's a surprise to see even faint traces of one people lingering on in the territory of the other.

But in Kavala there were Turkish remains that had not only survived, but prospered. On a small square I stumbled across a bronze statue of Mohammed Ali, the Muslim Kavala Albanian who had gone on to become the founder of modern Egypt. Bearded and turbaned, unsheath-ing a curved scimitar, he sat his fiery steed in front of the house he'd been born in. He was not the only one wielding the tool of his profession; behind him stonemasons were busy hammering and carpenters sawing – his stone house was undergoing major renovation.

There was another hive of activity further down the hill in a building known as the Imaret. Long and narrow, dimpled with stone domes and covered with carved calligraphy, it had once been an Islamic almshouse lodging students of Koranic theology. Judging from the expensive Italian kitchen ranges and cold-storage units being hefted through its doors by panting workmen, it was well on its way to a culinary future.

Down at the port, I shared the setting sun with a leisurely crowd of Kavala citizens on their evening promenade. The only really busy indi-viduals on the waterfront just then were hundreds of diving, looping swal-lows and the crews of two fishing boats preparing to head out to sea. The *Stephanos Manios* and *Constantinus B* were eighty-foot *lamparo* boats, the skiffs on their decks fitted with acetylene tanks and bright lamps for night-fishing. Dressed in tracksuits and cheap plastic sandals, their crews were loading ice and preparing for a long, cold night out on the open water. Not one was Greek. They were all Egyptians, Muslims from the coastal cities of Port Said and Damietta.

I stood watching their last-minute work with a knot of well-covered, elderly Greeks, men who fifty years ago would themselves have been setting out to spend the night fishing. One had a sister in Newcastle. 'Newcastle! Po! Po! Po!' he said to me. 'Too wet, too cold for Greeks!' I asked him about the renovations to the old Ottoman buildings on the hill above the port.

He laughed out loud. 'It is easy,' he said and, holding out his hand, rubbed his thumb and forefinger together.

'It's money. They are worth a fortune. No Greek can do such beautiful work in stone these days. You have seen the changes at the Imaret. And Mohammed Ali's house is being turned into a hotel by a wealthy woman – it will soon have a bar and a swimming pool and luxury suites. As for the Egyptian fishing crews, they go out in all weathers for long hours, summer and winter, and they are paid very little. Local men don't want to do that anymore. We Greeks say history is sacred. I say there are times when money is more sacred to us than history.'

The next morning the *Rodanthi* not only left at an indecent hour; she was, quite literally, a smutty old ship. Heavy black cinders flew from her rusty smokestack as soon as we cleared the harbour. At first I didn't see them in the half-light, but before Kavala was out of sight my shirt was covered with thick smudges. Soon the rear deck where passengers walked was a mess of long black streaks and I moved upwind to the bows to escape the hail of ash. I am glad I did. I had never seen Mediterranean porpoises before. Now they were dancing and diving before the ship's bow-wave, as old as mythical Greece itself and as fresh and bright as the morning that enveloped us. They made getting up early worth it.

The day was long, the *Rodanthi* late, and before I set out for Molyvos at the far north end of Lesbos the island's buses had stopped running. But hitch-hiking the forty miles of winding hill roads to Molyvos wasn't difficult. I had rides with a soldier, a salesman and – I dare not say three Lesbians – three island women returning home from a shopping expedition.

It was almost dark when I arrived. Molyvos was worth the effort, too. In no time I was sitting on a balcony high over the town, looking out at red-tiled roofs and a darkening sea to the shores of Anatolia. In the little walled and marble-flagged courtyard below me, Maria Karanikoli's husband was trimming garden-grown vegetables for the evening meal. The landlady herself was tending to her flowers – roses and geraniums, pansies and hydrangeas and fuchsias – all growing in big terracotta pots. The rooms she rented above her family's ground-floor quarters were comfortable and spotless, and apart from mine, empty. On the quay at Molyvos' miniature harbour that evening, with tourists bobbing by on one side and boats on the other, I drank retsina, ate calamari, and went to bed happy. There is nothing quite as Greek as a Greek port.

But in fact Molyvos's past was even less Greek than Kavala's. Molyvos was, quite simply, a Turkish town. Having wrested Lesbos from Genoese control less than a decade after the fall of Constantinople, Sultan Mehmet II used the island as a place to reward deserving Janissary troops with retirement and property.

In the late 1400s one of these resettled Janissaries married the widow of a Greek priest on Lesbos and there produced six children. Two of these offspring went on to change Mediterranean history. One of them founded the kingdom of Algeria far to the west. The other, known as Barbarossa, became Captain General of the Ottoman fleet under Suleiman the Magnificent. Drawing on years of experience in piracy – not only Croats were good at that game – Barbarossa transformed the Turkish navy. And with it he turned the central and eastern Mediterranean into a Turkish sea.

Molyviots could hardly hide the Turkish origins of their town. Touristy but well-preserved, shaded by trellised foliage, its streets were overhung by upper stories protruding outwards in typical Ottoman style. There were Turkish fountains, Turkish inscriptions carved in stone, Turkish baths that once formed the social centre of the town. But no local would ever tell you that the most feared admiral in Turkish naval history was the son of a Lesbos woman once married to a Greek Orthodox priest. Molyviots would rather die first.

From Molyvos Turkey may fill the entire eastern horizon, but islanders avoid mentioning it at all. Officially the country didn't seem to exist. In municipal tourist-office brochures the island sat not off Turkey but off the coast of Asia Minor. The failed 1922 Greek invasion of Turkey was the 'Asia Minor Disaster'. Local food, drawing heavily like all Greek food on Turkish cooking, had 'near-eastern' influences. And in a travel agency down by the port one didn't visit Turkey – one took, as a poster in the window coyly put it, 'a day-trip to the Orient'.

If the T-word was scrupulously avoided it was more difficult, despite the reticence of the ticket agent in Kavala, to avoid the L-word. In recent years the island has become a summer pilgrimage for European lesbians. Locals themselves may not subscribe to the sexual preferences of their 6th-century BC poetess, but Sappho has become an important source of island revenue. Beneath a rainbow flag in the same portside travel agency the Lesbos Pride Tour Company advertised same-sex holiday activities. They were Gay and Lesbian Mezze Get-togethers. For more adventurous and sporty types there was Gay and Lesbian Donkey Trekking. And for those with a bent for pilgrimage there was always Eresos, the birthplace of Sappho herself.

A word of warning to anyone looking for a little homoerotic diversion in sunny Greece: before packing a bag for Lesbos, think twice about gay and lesbian donkey trekking. It is awfully hot out there, even in the spring. I rented a motor-scooter in Molyvos and even with the highway breeze rushing by me all I could think of by noon was deep shade and cold water. As for nocturnal entertainment, consider other, possibly livelier places as well. Lesbian get-aways, like all other get-aways, fall into trendy and not-so-trendy categories. Molyvos was definitely in the latter group. It was a sort of family lesbian holiday place, if that makes sense. Many of the female couples sitting at restaurant tables in the evenings, German and Dutch for the most part, were middle-aged and had obviously co-habited a long time. An evening out with their partners was evidently about as exciting as shelling peas or assembling flat-pack furniture. They were barely looking at each other.

On the other hand, I did meet a young Greek woman who told me of a three-day lesbian festival held for the last few years in Molyvos in mid-summer. It seemed to have been hijacked by factional lesbian extremists. My Greek correspondent had lived most of her life in a Western European

254

capital, only recently returning to the island her parents had emigrated from. She regarded herself as liberal and enlightened, but the festival disgusted her. I shall call her X, in light of her outspoken opposition to it and threats from antagonists that she'd have the crap kicked out of her if there was any more complaining. Our conversation took this kind of turn:

X: Same-sex sex doesn't generally upset me. But you would not believe the kind of women who showed up here. They were hardcore lesbian militants. They had tattoos and piercings everywhere. And I mean everywhere. That didn't bother me so much. But some of them had their skulls shaved. They wore combat fatigues and army boots. They weren't normal people – they were intimidating and physically aggressive.

Me: They sound like Nazi paratroopers.

X: They were worse. They were Nazi heterophobe paratroopers.

Me: But what harm could they do at a festival?

X: Festival? They wanted to hold what they called an all-day Pussy Party. On the beach outside Molyvos. Three thousand fascist lesbians, unleashed in the full light of day! Is there no shame?

Me: God! A Pussy Party! What happens at a gathering like that?

X: I cannot possibly tell you. Unspeakable things.

Me: Go on, tell me – what happens?

X: No, I really can't, because the locals broke it up. It got very nasty. It caused a scandal here, and a scandal in western Europe. The press was full of headlines like 'Greeks Send Lesbians Packing', and 'Lesbians vs. Lesbians in Holiday Island Sex War.' It was horrible. Of course they want to stage it again this summer.

Me: Really? It sounds unmissable. Do you know the dates?

But the truth was that I was actually far more interested in the island itself than its invaders, either Turks or lesbians. In a few days I would be catching the little ferry that crossed the narrow straits between Lesbos and the town of Ayvalik in Turkey. From there it wasn't far to Gallipoli and then on to Istanbul, a megalopolis whose estimated population is regularly revised upwards by a million or so. The last thing I wanted at the moment was crowds of any kind. So every morning I would hop on my motor-scooter, whiz out of town, and wind my way through a thousand bends to the prettiest, most deserted places I could find.

It wasn't hard on Lesbos. After Crete and Évvia it is the largest island in Greece. Parts of it were covered in hilly oak and pine forests. There were also vast swathes of olive groves, fields of wheat, flooded salt-pans full of bird life, ranch-size stretches of cattle-land. The western half of the island was volcanic, a rugged near-desert, and ethereally beautiful. But in this season the whole island was fresh and inviting. Everything was alive with shifting light and colour, from the green olive trees that turned silvery-grey as I drove past, to fields of young wheat that streamed and rippled like waves in the breeze. Even the waste-ground by the side of the highway danced and fizzled, its swaying poppies tiny pinpoints of exploding colour.

Best of all was the coastline, steep and rocky almost everywhere. Riding through dazzling sunshine, I would roll along high over the sea. Calm and unruffled, the water changed colour as it ran away from the shore, turning from clear turquoise to opaque ultramarine. The sky, too, was made of graduated blues. Light and luminous at the horizon, it was as dark and deep as the sea itself by the time it was straight overhead. It was by the water, on the coast road running west to the beach at Sappho's Erressos, that I found one of the loveliest places on the island.

The unpaved track running down to Archea Antissa – Ancient Antissa – was steep and bumpy, and what lay at the end of it was so old there wasn't a great deal left. The first Aeolians to inhabit Lesbos arrived more than 3,000 years ago and built a colony on a small, narrow-necked head-land here. It was difficult to see the remains close up, so I walked back along the shore to a stone church, from whose vantage point I could see ruined walls and towers.

There wasn't a soul about, but the door of the church was unlocked. Inside, sitting beneath framed Byzantine prints and a wooden iconostasis, was a tray containing the accoutrements of an Orthodox service – candles, olive oil and a plate of aromatic incense. None of it was very formal. The candles, pink and with little plastic cups on their stems to catch the wax, were of the birthday-cake variety. They sat ready to be lit beside a Bic disposable lighter. The olive oil was kept in an old cough-medicine bottle. Short on ritual, the atmosphere in the church was all the more powerful for its simplicity, remoteness and silence. The only thing I could hear was a lapping of nearby waves.

Outside, I stripped off and slid into the water. It was cool and silky, and when I opened my eyes beneath the surface, clear enough to swim my way around rocks and weed-beds. I bathed for a long time and on emerging dried off in the sunshine. An onshore wind was picking up.

Even with my shoes back on I was afraid of snakes and scorpions in the tall weeds that grew in the ruins of Archea Antissa. Lizards sunned themselves on rocks and there were worrisome slithering noises as I climbed the hill that rose inside old, collapsed walls. But the wild fennel, tall and feathery, was so fragrant, the smell of the plants crushed beneath my feet so aromatic, that I kept climbing. And when I reached the top I found myself standing on a flat, grassy shelf with nothing between me and the water far beneath.

I didn't know anything about the Greek Aeolians, apart from the fact that they traced their ancestry to the mythical Aeolus, god of the wind. But it seemed to me the open place where I stood was as much an altar as the one that lay in the church below. Ahead, the sea was even livelier with light and colour than the land behind. Appearing as sudden patches of dark, fast-moving agitation, heavy gusts of wind tore across violet-coloured water. The Aegean might have looked empty, but it was full of an unseen, living force, one great breath after another sweeping over it to buffet the shore.

The wind kept growing in strength until it flattened the grass and was howling through the remains of crumbling walls. It was exhilarating and just a little bit frightening – I was alone, and yet not quite alone. In places like this it wasn't hard to believe that even now there might be something to those powerful old myths of gods and air-spirits. I left Lesbos a day later, wind-battered and content, having met the oldest island-occupiers of them all.

Thirty-Three

There is an odd thing about the seawater that flows through those narrow and spectacular Turkish straits, the Bosphorus and the Dardanelles. To non-scientific landlubbers like me it seems wholly improbable, but it is a fact that the current between the Mediterranean and the Black Sea flows in both directions at the same time.

It is a piece of information of no conceivable personal use, but I find it fascinating. Apparently it has to do with salinity levels. Being an almost enclosed sea in a warm, sunny part of the world, the Mediterranean loses more water through evaporation than it gains through rainfall or the discharge of rivers. It is thus a good deal saltier than other seas, and getting saltier all the time. The water that replenishes it through narrow entrances is colder and much less salty – the Black Sea, especially, is fed by large amounts of fresh water from rivers like the Danube and the Don. Compared to the Mediterranean it is merely brackish. For reasons beyond my comprehension these waters don't easily mix. In the Dardanelles, as at Gibraltar, fresher water rushes into the Mediterranean along the surface of the narrow straits. Far underneath there is compensating movement in the opposite direction – heavier, denser, more saline water creeps along the bottom northward into the Black Sea. So different is the salinity between surface and deep-sea waters there that the two levels never mix at all. Only the top 500 feet of the Black Sea contains marine life – never oxygenated because it never comes to the surface, the 5,000 feet of water below contain no organic life whatsoever.

End of discourse on marine hydrology. And all that simply to say that when the bus from Ayvalik dropped down the steep hills towards the Dardanelles on a hot afternoon in early June I immediately felt refreshed. So lively and bracing was the cold water that flowed past Çanakkale, so revitalizing were the cool fingers of air wafting through the streets of the town that I, too, felt suddenly oxygenated. After a bus ride through a wavy, heat-bent countryside that announced the coming of a harsh summer, life on the banks of the Dardanelles felt suddenly fresh and bubbly. The air was clean, colours were bright, and out on the water a steady northerly breeze was kicking up small whitecaps.

Çanakkale, not surprisingly, is a navy town. For anyone who controls the strait here – at Çanakkale it is less than a mile wide – controls a good deal. Not only are these narrows the defensive approaches to Istanbul and the gateway between two inland seas; the Dardanelles are a strategic link between East and West as well. Time and again the place known to the classical Greeks as the Hellespont has been a focus of conflict. In the more poetic accounts Trojans and Achaeans may have battled over Helen, the most beautiful woman in the world. The real fight on these narrows, though, was over control of the Black Sea grain trade. Here King Xerxes built his bridge of boats across the Hellespont in the 5th century BC Persian invasion of Greece. It was here, too, that Ottoman Turks were ferried for the first time from Asia to Europe – they came not to invade Byzantium, but as mercenaries hired by the Byzantine Emperor John Cantacuzenus to help put down an internal rebellion. Small wonder, then, that the Turks have maintained a strong military presence here ever since – in the middle of Çanakkale looms the grim stonewalled fortress of Çimenlik, one of eight waterside fortifications guarding the Dardanelles.

I'd been drawn to Çimenlik by a passing-out parade of naval cadets. Their buttons gleaming, their dress-uniforms and shoes of a whiteness only naval officers seem capable of attaining, they had marched out of the Military Zone surrounding the fortress and down Çanakkale's main street. You could tell – the jubilant brass-band aside – that they were happy. There were smiles on boyish faces, an extra spring in their step, and rolled-up diplomas in each new junior officer's gloved left hand. After months of training in a Turkish military installation I think I'd be happy, too.

Çimenlik is still an active defence zone but it also houses a naval museum, and after the parade had marched out I marched in through the fortress gates. Scattered beside paths on precision-mown lawns were more torpedoes and cannons than anyone but an ordnance expert would care to see. But the paths led down to quays where clear, cold seawater flowed by at what seemed an alarming rate. I could hardly imagine Byron or any other Hellespont swimmer launching himself towards the other side. Even the *Nusrat*, a much-revered First World War minelayer, now lay protected from the current and permanently anchored in a small, still sea of concrete up on the quay. I toured her with a party of Turkish school-children until the exuberant clamour got to be too much. Jumping ship, I stood outside enjoying the water and watching commercial traffic make its way through the straits.

I asked a marine guard standing nearby if he could read the port of registration painted on the back of the *Milos*, a gigantic, bright red tanker now disappearing southwards. Soon it would be in the busy Mediterranean shipping lane that the sooty, smoke-spewing *Rodanthi* had crossed on its way to Lesbos. But it was too far for his eyes also.

'How far away is it?' I asked.

'I will show you something,' said the guard, tipping back his sailor's cap. 'It is very useful, something every gunner knows.' His English was good; he said he'd learnt it on the internet. 'Hold your arm out to the *Milos*, raise your thumb and close one eye. Note the place you see behind your thumb. Now open your eye and close the other eye. Note this place too. Estimate the distance between the two places, multiply by ten, and that will give you the exact distance to your target. Try now.'

'Boom!' he said softly, going through the procedure with me, then lobbing an imaginary shell straight through the tanker's hull. 'What distance did you get?'

'A kilometre,' I said.

'No boom,' he said, looking crestfallen, as if an easy answer had unexpectedly evaded a star pupil. 'That ship is 1,700 metres away. You must practise.' I took my rebuke silently, like a soldier. Knowing how to shell giant oil tankers seemed like another useless piece of information, but one never knew. I would keep at it.

'And what about that?' I said, swivelling my thumb towards the far side of the Dardanelles. There on a hillside stood the gigantic silhouette of an infantryman, hundreds of feet long and outlined in rocks painted white. Beside it, also traced in white rocks, were four lines of Turkish script.

'Oh, that is easy,' said the guard grinning, himself the star pupil now. 'It is not necessary to look; I know every word with my eyes closed.' And screwing his eyes shut he slowly, dramatically recited the verse, beginning '*Dur yocul! Bilmedin gelip bastığın.*' After Greek the intonations were strange, soft and guttural at the same time, and full of odd vowels and dipthongs that sounded as if they should have come from Scandinavia.

'And in English now,' he said, delighting in his display. 'Every tourist wants to know. I learned it from the *Lonely Planet*:

Traveller, halt! The soil you tread
Once witnessed the end of an era
Listen! In this quiet mound
There once beat the heart of a nation.'

'Why is it in the *Lonely Planet*?' I asked.
'In Turkish the peninsula on the other side of the water is named Gelibolu. Every foreigner who comes here visits it. You call it Gallipoli.'

Towards evening I returned to my hotel. I had found it by following signs painted with an Australian flag and a legend that read:

Yellow Rose Pension
G'day Mate
Mr Ozal, Family Run.

And the Yellow Rose was indeed full of people who said 'G'day Mate'. Even the Ozals, big and little, talked like that. But by this point I was getting used to the accent. There were Australians everywhere – you heard them in the streets, in the restaurants, in cafés along the waterfront. But nowhere was Australianness more concentrated than in Anzac House, the teeming backpackers' hotel, restaurant and travel agency where I went that evening after dinner.

'Hey, Mate, what's the difference between a bison and a buffalo?' said the young Turkish clerk behind the desk. He didn't sound like a Turk. He sounded like he'd just surfed here from Bondi Beach.

'I don't know,' I said. 'Is there a difference?'

'Course there is, Mate!' he chimed. 'You ever tried washing your hands in a buffalo?'

Good on 'im – he must have cracked them up a thousand times with that one. But the Australians gathered at Anzac House hadn't come for the jokes. They'd come for the movies, and every evening for years it had been the same two. The first was an Australian documentary on the country's most famous engagement in the First World War. The second was more of the same in dramatic form – *Gallipoli* featured a young Mel Gibson, handsome and dashing in the uniform of the Australian Light Horse Brigade, heading straight into hell on earth.

I am not sure which film, emotionally speaking, the audience found more powerful – the solemn, measured tones of the documentary, or the sight of a naked Mel Gibson being shelled as he and his comrades tried to find a little relief from war with a swim on the beach beneath Turkish guns. But in the end the calamity of one of the First World War's bloodiest and most futile campaigns moved everyone in the audience. Of the 38,000 British Empire troops who died in nine months of trench warfare at Gallipoli 28,000 were British and 10,000 were Anzacs – soldiers of the Australia and New Zealand Army Corps. Fully half of the 500,000 Turks who fought there became casualties, and 55,000 were killed. For Australians though, it was a signal Australian event, a young country's baptism of fire. Going nowhere, achieving nothing, marked by poor planning and inept leadership, the campaign came to be seen as a tragic rite of passage from colony to nationhood. Eight thousand Australians were killed at Gallipoli. These days more than half as many again show up every year just to pay their respects.

After the films were over there was a flurry of T-shirt sales at the reception desk. The shirts showed a silhouette of Australian troops storming the heights of Gallipoli. Below was printed the second quatrain I'd seen that day. Banjo Paterson gave the same emotions a more popular cadence than his Turkish counterpart:

The mettle that a race can show
is proved with shot and steel
and now we know what nations know
and feel what nations feel

I was looking above the desk at signed photos of the Australian Cricket Board's Gallipoli visit when a voice behind me asked: 'Goin' on the Die Tour?'

God, I thought, they don't mince their words. 'Which tour is that?' I asked.

'Leaves here every die at nine o'clock,' said Cameron. Cameron was in his early twenties, wore baggy shorts and flip-flops, and had a large tin clutched in an even larger hand. He was a fan of Australian Rules football, a hanger-out at Brisbane beaches and an avid drinker of beer. Victoria Bitter being but a distant memory, he was doing his best to chill out with Turkish lager. It just didn't compare, he said. But when it came to patriotic pride beer brands faded into insignificance. Cameron was in Gallipoli to see where his great-grandfather had died fighting.

'Supposed to be a good tour,' he said. 'They throw in a late lunch, then run you up to Istanbul. You could probably get in a few cold ones along the way.'

Well, why not, I thought. Seeing Gallipoli is obviously best done in the company of Australians. So, like Mel Gibson, I signed up right away.

There were seven of us in the minibus the next morning. I'd never been on a battlefield tour before. I thought they were for older people, but none of these travellers were over thirty. It was a very casual, very Australian, very baggy-shorts-and-flip-flop kind of group. Just one man, Ali Efe, our guide, was middle-aged. His own grandfather had been killed at Gallipoli. He'd been a military man himself, a submarine commander before he'd retired, but his authority was natural and easy and he got along well with his group. He smoked like a fiend. It made me wonder what it would be like to be submerged in a submarine in a tricky strait with a Turkish crew of heavy smokers anxious about water flowing two ways. It didn't bear imagining.

But neither did Lone Pine, the first battle-site we visited. 'Here,' said Ali, as we walked along the top of a steep escarpment, 'is the only place where ground was ever won or lost from fixed positions in the whole campaign. It totalled thirty-nine metres. Four thousand Turks and 2,000 Australians died in a space the size of two tennis courts. They are buried in common graves beneath us.'

The thought of 6,000 dead men strewn beneath our feet was enough to calm the two blondes who'd been cackling ferociously in the back of the minibus ever since we'd boarded the ferry at Çanakkale. Cath was a short-order cook in North London and Viv an Earl's Court barmaid. They'd been sharing a £160-a-week bed-sit in the year since they'd left Australia. They couldn't stomach anything about the English, they said – not their food, or their manners, or their cost of living. They put it all down to the weather.

'It rains all the time. It's cold,' said Cath.

'When you spend that much time indoors you can't help it,' said Viv. 'It's either Playstation or drugs.'

But, they had to admit, they were having the best time ever. They loved the London scene. They loved parties and new people and clubbing and being away from boring Sydney suburbs and not having to see their families and taking off to places like Turkey on cheap holidays. Cath and Viv were bubble-brained ditzes and they found it hard to stop talking for even a minute.

But now they pulled out the little bunches of flowers they'd prepared and placed them at the foot of the white stone monument in the middle of Lone Pine.

'Now don't start me crying, Viv,' Cath said. Viv didn't say a word but Cath started crying anyway. Cameron and his girlfriend wandered off down rows of headstones, looking for his great-grandfather's name. He didn't seem too organised and I didn't think he stood much chance of success – there are thirty-one war cemeteries on the Gallipoli peninsula. That left Ali Efe to cope with Terry, a fierce Melbourne republican whose hatred of war was almost as great as her hatred of authority – British authority, especially. While the others were content to listen to Ali and then stroll about, Terry would sniff around Ali's historical commentary like a dog on a scent – wherever she smelled the slightest whiff of opportunity she was straight into the fight. She loved to hear about the imperial upper classes treating the working- class colonials under their command as inferior expendables.

'Bloody Poms,' she'd mutter with a dark scowl, 'Incompetent, arrogant, supercilious, condescending fucking Poms.' Ali's account only confirmed what she already knew about the entire British race.

And so the morning drew on, the minibus dropping us at cemeteries, grassy fields, landing beaches and half-filled trenches lying only yards apart. Chunuk Bair, Shrapnel Valley, Anzac Cove, Jonston's Jolly ... each place was more murderous than the last.

'Three days were lost after the British landed divisions at Suvla Bay,' Ali would say, pointing down the coast to a beautiful curving sweep of blue water. 'They had to wait for artillery to arrive from Egypt. It gave the Turks time to dig in and prepare.'

'Bloody Poms,' Terry would growl.

'Yeh, bloody Pommies,' Cath and Viv would echo.

They were delighted with Terry. Here was a new way to get back at shoddy public health services, underground train delays and £4.60-an-hour salaries.

'British High Command sent men to certain death in four successive suicidal attacks here,' Ali said as we stood at The Nek. 'The soldiers knew it and they went ahead anyway. They were very brave. The Turks called this place "the Hill of Courage" in honour of their enemy.'

'Ah, the Poms.'

'The bleeding Poms.'

'Those Pommie fuckwits.'

Terry's resentment was infectious – there was now general stirring among the whole party whenever the British were mentioned. It struck me that if retired Commander Efe was doing a fair job repairing Australian-Turkish relations, he was doing a superlative one sabotaging ties between Australians and Englishmen.

But of his overall belief in man's humanity to man there could be no doubt. After years spent reciting the same sad story, Ali Efe still respected soldiers' bravery. What he revered even more, though, was their brotherhood.

'These were ordinary men, Turks and Australians, doing their duty,' he said as we sat in shade in the heat of midday. 'But after much killing and suffering the soldiers realized the ugliness of politicians. They hated war. They stopped killing each other. They realised that, whatever race, they were all human beings.'

I wasn't entirely convinced of the historical truth of what he was saying. If Gallipoli was finally evacuated it was in order that British and Commonwealth troops be thrown into the even bloodier battlefields of northern Europe.

'The suffering and loss here was great,' Ali went on, 'but in the end both sides gained something. The Turks gained Atatürk, who became famous at Gallipoli as a fearless general and leader of men. Without him we would be like Iran or Saudi Arabia today. And the Australians gained the Anzac spirit, the birth of their belief in themselves. Not long ago Turks and Australians thought each other the most dangerous people on earth.' He searched for a symbol of compatibility. 'Now we mix together like sardines in a basket.'

And here Ali performed his own small commemoration ceremony, presenting each of us with a spent bullet dug from the earth of Gallipoli. We all applauded him. Cath and Viv enjoyed the presentation so much they began crying again.

An hour later we had eaten lunch at a restaurant beside the straits and were waiting for the bus to take us north. Cameron had not found his great-grandfather's grave, but he didn't seem upset.

'No worries,' he said, draining yet another beer. 'I wouldn't have missed it for anything. Great Granddad's not feeling any pain. Christ, but it's hot, isn't it? Do you think we could get some cold tinnies for the ride?'

We did, and so arrived six hours later in Istanbul, not feeling too much pain either.

Thirty-Four

It was midnight by the time the bus rolled off the Marmara coast highway and into Sultanahmet, the heart of the city. It wasn't late for Istanbul, but it was late for a tired and wobbly traveller unused to the beer-quaffing style of Australian Rules. I tried consulting the Sultanahmet map in my guidebook, but in the bus's dim lighting I could barely make out Aya Sofya and the Blue Mosque, much less the dozens of small hotels marked in surrounding side-streets. Instead I looked through the window and watched the minarets above the mosque, slender, brightly illuminated rockets aimed into the black night. They grew closer and higher. When they were near enough to be an easy walk, I got the driver to let me down and made my way to the first hotel I saw. Twenty minutes later I was asleep.

The Onur was not a grand hotel. It was a gangly hotel instead. Tall and thin, sandwiched into a row of other skinny buildings, its seventeen beds were distributed, two rooms to a floor, over five stories. The rooms were narrow. The stairways were steep. The showerstalls were slim. But when I woke in the morning and stumped up to the rooftop terrace for breakfast I was delighted with the Onur's gawkiness. Rising above surrounding buildings, it not only looked up a steep hillside to the dome and pencil minarets of the Blue Mosque. Downhill, it looked out over the Sea of Marmara and busy shipping funnelling past Seraglio Point into the throat of the Bosphorus. From the Onur Hotel all Istanbul appeared thin and attenuated.

All, that is, but Yilmaz, the hotel's proprietor. He was dark and bristly, a stocky, thick-set Kurd from Bingöl in eastern Anatolia. He looked like a country labourer, but in fact there was nothing rural about him. When he offered me an omelette it was with an accent that had the inflections of both England and America. Yilmaz had worked in the hotel business in Bath. He'd lived in New Jersey. He knew the United States better than I did – he'd made a living there towing a U-Haul trailer. He'd followed the motorcycle festival circuit from Orlando to San Francisco and from his stand sold black leather jackets, belts, chaps, studded wrist-straps and other fancy bikers' gear. He had, as you might expect, a breezy, confident air about him – you couldn't get away with less when you sold contemporary tribal-wear to Hell's Angels. Village Turkey lay a long way behind him.

Stirring sugar into a little tulip-shaped glass of tea, I was looking over the water at a dozen freighters riding at anchor when we were joined by a couple of hotel residents. They, too, had a breezy, relaxed air. They were so familiar with the place that they paid no attention to the sack-shaped, headscarfed cook in the kitchen on the floor below, but proceeded to rustle up their own breakfast. John and Jan had already been at the hotel for a few weeks, and were likely to stay on for several more. They were broke. They did their own shopping and cooked meals in the hotel kitchen. They commandeered the reception desk computer to write e-mails to their families. They scrounged cigarettes from the proprietor. They brought homey domesticity to the Onur Hotel.

'We're just like family,' said John, putting his arm around Yilmaz's shoulder as Jan set down a tray. Yilmaz grinned munificently. He had given John and Jan his lowest, extra-special discount rate.

John was American and his wife Thai. In his mid-thirties, John had a candid, open face and the unguarded ways of the Midwesterner abroad. But he had bailed out of conventional American life long ago. Not even the peripheral existence he had tried in Alaska and Hawaii had been far enough removed. He had left it all behind to study Mahayana Buddhism in Singapore. He had moved on to Hinhayana Buddhism in Taiwan. He had meditated outdoors under an umbrella for three months. He had undergone cures by traditional Chinese medicine. In Thailand he had met Jan and taken over a patch of her parents' hill-farm. It still wasn't enough. John wanted to get even further away from civilisation and all its works.

He and Jan had decided to travel the earth's biggest oceans, crewing their way around the world on other people's yachts until they could raise money to buy their own. As we sat on our rooftop perch, eating toast and watching ships sail into the Bosphorus, John told me about their sea voyage from Thailand – the plank-springing, Hong Kong-built wooden boat they had joined; its eccentric German owner and smelly, menacing Gypsy crewman, Giuseppe; the horrendous storms off Sri Lanka; their reception by hostile Muslim fundamentalists on the Sudanese coast; the venality of corrupt Red Sea customs officials; the decision, taken in Port Said, to abandon the boat before it sank beneath them. Now John and Jan were marooned in Istanbul, hard-up and biding their time until the late summer sailing season when they could find a boat to crew on from the Azores across the Atlantic to the Caribbean.

If John and Jan's confidence in the peaceful serenity of life at sea had been tested to the limit they remained committed to their new life. It was liberation for them. For Yilmaz, on the other hand, the life John had run from in despair was *his* liberation. He loved America and its opportunities. John would talk about the jungle farm in Thailand, encounters with Muslim Sufis in remote, forgotten seaports, the spiritually bankrupt state of the modern Western world. Yilmaz would respond with observations from another life, a world in which neon-lit roadside bars, all-night driving marathons and wild blonde biker-chicks figured large. The biker-chicks, especially – and the kinds of thing they're capable of when they meet truly hunky Kurds out on the blacktop wilderness of the Interstate highway – were a Yilmaz leitmotif. It was wacky dialogue, *On the Road* meets *Walden*.

'That's crazy and impossible,' Yilmaz would chuckle dismissively at some utopian world-vision of John's.

'That's immoral and disgusting,' John would react to Yilmaz's account of an especially depraved road-trip.

But each enjoyed the other's fascination with opposing cultures – it was the reason Yilmaz gave the couple a room practically free of charge. And I enjoyed it too. These were the kind of conversational exchanges that are only easily sustained in big, cosmopolitan cities like Istanbul, the meeting-places of the world.

So on my first day in Istanbul I, too, was contemplating settling down semi-permanently in the Onur Hotel. But around lunch-time a telephone call home to Aix-en-Provence changed everything. Being married to a teacher of languages had its benefits. Once again Jany's continent-wide network of contacts had kicked into life. Through her own cosmopolitan encounters Jany had met a teacher, who knew another teacher, who had a colleague who'd been seconded to work in a French-language *lycée* in Istanbul. The links connecting these individuals, a thin thread running eastwards from France to the edge of Asia, were tenuous. But they led to an irresistible destination – the oldest foreign school in Istanbul, established in a labyrinthine Jesuit monastery under Ottoman rule in the 16th century. Barring Topkapi Palace and a few other imperial piles, there was barely a more venerable address in the whole city to put up at. It would take a little arranging, but in a couple of days there would be a room available for me there. In the meantime I had the Onur, and the old quarter of Sultanahmet around it to explore.

In fact I didn't make it any further that day than a carpet shop up the road. John and Jan didn't have the money to run around town doing the things visitors to Istanbul usually do. Most days they spent time with yet other Turkish Kurds they had met, four cousins who ran a family business selling carpets from their home villages in eastern Anatolia. They invited me to the shop in a busy tourist area off the Hippodrome.

Hakan, the shop's owner, didn't appear terribly trustworthy to me – his smile was wide and his hand went over his heart in a gesture of welcome, but his look was slippery. None of his three 'cousins', slick and ingratiating young men in leather jackets, looked any too honest either. They put too much emphasis on their simple country origins, were too effusive in their vows of hospitality to strangers. They offered us cigarettes, brought cushions and sat us down in the midst of a spotlit showroom piled high with sumptuous fabrics. To me Hakan and his associates looked like carpet conmen.

But they had befriended John and Jan, entertained them, pressed food and drink upon them, made protestations of eternal friendship. Their relatives, they'd promised, would soon receive them in their humble peasant homes in the hills. The couple could stay and be fed as long as they liked, and not a single Turkish lira would change hands in return. It all put John, morally correct as ever, under a sense of inescapable obligation. But lately he'd been troubled – his friends weren't turning out quite the simple, stalwart villagers they claimed to be.

'I'm not sure they are 100 per cent honest,' John whispered to me when the Kurds went off to a back-room to prepare tea. 'First I discovered they're not really cousins at all. And I suspect one of them is a sort of stool pigeon – I think he sells information to the police. Another flies every couple of weeks to Amsterdam with large amounts of cash – I saw it in a suitcase before he went to the airport. And the third, I'm pretty sure, has a part-time career as an enforcer – I think he beats people up for money.'

Wanting to believe the best of everyone, John had to admit before mounting evidence that his friends might not be entirely virtuous. In the meantime he was doing his best to repay their hospitality by helping to sell carpets.

It was Hakan who had suggested it. When it came to Western tourists John was his front-man. With his innocent face and easy conversation, John could persuade any number of potential customers off the street and into the shop where Hakan sat like a waiting spider. Their defences lowered, their trust and confidence raised, passers-by were suitably softened up even before they got into the master's hands. And once there, few walked away unscathed.

The talent of the Istanbul carpet salesman is a wonder to behold. It is an ancient art combining a dozen disciplines. It entails the subtlest skills of communication. It calls on the greatest technical expertise. It requires assertion and insistence, flattery and compromise. It demands elegance, manners, and split-second timing. In its finest form it is a game of moral suasion – it depends on the seller obtaining psychological advantage over the buyer, drawing him by a dozen unseen tricks into a corner from which there is no way out. In the end, short of bringing his own honesty and goodwill into question, the customer becomes ethically bound to buy an object he was never really sure he wanted in the first place.

No doubt there are principled sellers and happy buyers of carpets. Neither was in evidence in Hakan's carpet shop. I watched four sales that afternoon, complex rituals of carpets thrown lavishly, one after another, at the feet of unsuspecting visitors – they ranged from a wealthy South African couple inveigled in minutes into buying a $6,000 silk prayer rug, to a British student backpacker who agonised for an hour over a bright and nasty $35 kilim. All of them, though, walked out scratching their heads in wonder.

How, they asked themselves, had this happened? How had they been strolling along the street one moment, and the next signing American Express travellers' cheques? Hakan, of course, knew the answer. It happened because John – consumer-society renegade, seeker of truth, student of the Eight-fold Path and the Middle Way – had helped them buy it.

Early that evening, a tidy profit realised, Hakan, John and the rest of us sat down cross-legged on a carpet to a small, well-earned feast. There were crisply grilled sardines, olives, slices of cucumber, crusty bread, and plenty of chilled beer and raki. The company was loud and merry – everyone was in a good mood.

I had arrived in Istanbul at street level, I thought – the meeting between East and West doesn't get any more basic than this. Hakan and his so called cousins were rogues, but cheerful rogues, and I didn't like them any the less for selling over-priced carpets to tourists on holiday. It was certainly a better way of making a living than beating up people who failed to pay their debts on time. Nor did I like John any less for assisting them – this was globalisation, too, the way one part of the world becomes familiar with another. Given the right circumstances John might even make a carpet seller himself, but an ethical one, and help bring decency and good practice to the trade.

In the meantime there was food and talk and wild Kurdish singing, a soulful lament for a distant, lost way of life. It was very late in the evening by the time we made our way back to the Onur.

Thirty-Five

I woke up in doubt the next morning. Where was I to begin, carpet shops aside, in a place like Istanbul?

This was not one city, but many. For more than 1,500 years it had been the dazzling capital of two successive empires. It had been a political and administrative hub, a religious centre, a military stronghold and the greatest commercial and trading emporium in the world. It was Greek Byzantium. It was Constantinoupolis Nea Roma, the new Roman empire of Constantine and capital of eastern Christendom. It was Konstantiniyye, the centre of a Muslim Ottoman empire that had stretched from Baghdad to Budapest.

And now it was Istanbul, the most varied, sophisticated and outward-looking city in modern Turkey. It was a port on the threshold of the Mediterranean. It was also an Eastern city and a Western city, European and Asian, imperial and republican, traditional and modernist, secular and religious. To ancient Byzantines it was the navel of the world, the place at which all things converged. To today's Istanbuliots it was still that, a galloping, unstoppable city twenty miles deep and a hundred miles wide, a megalopolis that refused to cease growing.

Where to start? Difficult as the question was, I only had to look out from the Onur's rooftop to know the answer.

Twenty-seven hundred years ago a Greek named Byzas, about to set off to found a colony on the Bosphorus, approached the oracle at Delphi and asked where precisely he should site it.

The oracle, so the story goes, answered, 'Opposite the blind', an answer that at the time mystified the colonists. But when Byzas and his fellow settlers sailed up the Bosphorus, they came across another Greek colony at Chalcedon, now Kadiköy, on the Asian side of the narrows. Gazing to the European side of the strait directly opposite, they saw that marvellous deep-water anchorage, the seven-mile-long Golden Horn. It wasn't hard for Byzas to decide that the citizens of Chalcedon must indeed be blind to ignore such a site. So at that place he founded Byzantium. The city began with the sea, and so would I.

It takes just fifteen minutes to walk from the tourist crowds swirling around the Blue Mosque to the still thicker commuter crowds swamping the Eminönü ferry quays on the Golden Horn. But as I walked down to the Horn the next morning neither tourists nor commuters were spending any more time than necessary strolling outdoors. Bad weather had blown in overnight – heavy with low, scudding cloud, the skies over Istanbul brought one squall after another sweeping across the city.

The weather wasn't enough, though, to discourage the Bosphorus ferry passengers making the day-trip up to the Black Sea and back. Joining a crowd of excursionists on a rain-soaked quay I couldn't help thinking of another sopping waterfront far to the west – for a moment I was back again in rainy spring weather on the Grand Canal in Venice. From the ferry's covered stern the city that rose beyond the quays resembled Venice all the more.

It was precisely the same dull colour. Everything blended soggily into everything else. The stone of the mosques, the walls of the spice markets, the old weathered roofs of merchants' warehouses – all matched the dirty grey wash of the sky. On the road running along the waterfront broad puddles were pocked with rain and the air was full of the sound of bus tyres hissing their way over slick black tarmac. Behind me on the Galata Bridge, men fishing in the Golden Horn wore water-streaked rain jackets and plastic bags pulled onto their heads. Pouring dark and intent off arriving ferries, Istanbul office-goers, just like Venetian office-goers, leaned their bodies and their umbrellas into the wet, gusty wind.

It wasn't just the rain that made the two cities seem alike. Nor was it the architecture, the random, vertical scattering of mosque and minaret that so resembled that of church dome and campanile. It wasn't even the general wateriness of the place – the prospect of flat, wet surfaces, silvery and rain-pitted, that ran away into the distance. It was none of these things alone. What made Istanbul and Venice similar was their liquid energy, the exuberant, exhilarating, endlessly-changing spectacle of life borne upon water. Both cities had the same relentless aquatic drive.

Wherever you looked there were boats – not leisure boats for sitting and resting, but busy boats for living and working. The coming and going of Bosphorus ferries, large, double-decked steel vessels spouting sudden palls of grimy smoke, was ceaseless. They arrived from Üsküdar and Haydarpaşa on the Asian side, from up the narrows at Beşiktas and Bebek and Yeniköy, from the Prince's Islands off in the Marmara Sea, with a hurried self-importance that was barely polite. Moored at deep-water quays at Karaköy on the other side of the Horn, ocean-going ships of the Turkish Maritime Lines were also preparing to leave – to the Aegean and Ionian, to the Adriatic and to other Mediterranean seas beyond. Ukrainian cruise-liners lay waiting to sail for the Black Sea. From landings near the Galata Bridge local water-taxis, as battered and humble as Venetian water-taxis were snooty, industriously chugged their way inland along the inner edges of the Horn. In the other direction small rowboats skittered like water-insects about the mouth of the Horn, their occupants pulling lustily on oars or jigging hand-lines from seats in the stern.

Even the little boat tied to the quay directly below me was busy. It wasn't going anywhere except up and down, a violent rocking in the surging wake of departing ferries. But with its open charcoal fire and hot, pan-swirling oil, it was voyage enough. Braced against constant pitching and tossing, raincoated and baseball-capped against blustery weather, its adventurous crew, cooks to a man, were settling down to another day of making the finest fried-mackerel sandwiches in Istanbul.

Soon the engines beneath me were thrown into gear, the foot-worn planking of the wooden deck juddered, and my ferry, too, was in motion.

Quickly the noise of honking traffic on the Galata Bridge faded and the yellow slickers of fishermen grew faint.

The tall, stone-built Galata Tower, a construction that would have looked more at home in Renaissance north Italy than here in Istanbul, slid by on one side. The pleasure-palaces and kiosks of Topkapi eased past on the other. And then the confines of the Golden Horn were behind us. Quitting the ferry terminal at Eminönü is a bit like exiting Santa Lucia railway station in Venice – suddenly the Bosphorus opens up before you like a wide, restless highway, and you are on the grandest of Grand Canals.

It is only when the passenger pulls away from the shore and looks back from mid-stream in the Bosphorus that the full magnificence of the port-city becomes apparent. From out there I could see a narrowing, hilly promontory pointing from the European side of the strait towards Asia. On its southern edge began the broad Sea of Marmara, on its northern flank the deep-water inlet of the Golden Horn. Along with the Bosphorus itself, these bodies of water surrounded Istanbul on three sides. They had long made the city a natural fortress. Nor were its narrow land-approaches any less well defended – for a thousand years they'd been protected by the most splendid stone walls ever built. Even in the 19th century, when the barrier raised by the Emperor Theodosius was crumbling and inhabited by goats and greenery, Byron enthused that in all his travels through the classical world he had never beheld a work of nature or art quite as imposing. Few cities have so often been the object of men's envy, or so successfully withstood their attacks. Nor, on the only two occasions when Constantinople actually was overwhelmed – the Venetian sack of 1204 and the Ottoman conquest in 1453 – was the destiny of the Mediterranean world so radically altered.

Human history may move in sudden, unpredictable lurches, but the progress of the ferryboat was stately and relentless. There was no time to think of the past. Istanbul dropped behind. Like Venetian palazzi on that other canal, successive waterside scenes now began looming left and right as the ferry threaded its way up the Bosphorus. Even in rain and drifting fog they delighted the passengers. Everything along the banks

– parks, pavilions, fishing ports, fortresses, forests, palaces, villas and villages – seemed to have found its perfect natural setting. Admirals of the world's navies could talk about the strategic importance of the Bosphorus. Maritime shippers could praise its commercial benefits. Geologists could discuss its tectonic functions, geographers its role as a divider of continents, climates and cultures. But we ordinary mortals immediately knew the Bosphorus for what it was above and beyond all those things: the loveliest, most enchanting sea-passage on the face of the globe.

Parties of foreigners from every corner of the world skipped across the decks of the ferry, from port to starboard and back again as the whim took them. There was an itinerant, fleet-footed assembly of Korean ladies, all in identical orange jackets, determined to photograph each other in front of every sight along the way. There were solemn families of Malaysian Muslims, the boys in embroidered skullcaps, the little girls wearing ankle-length coats and scarves tied beneath their chins. A festive group of Brazilians chattered their way up the Bosphorus. A cluster of French tourists, glancing repeatedly up and down in concerned, Cartesian manner, worried over their map and questioned its placement of Bosphorus sites. Hardy in shorts, socks and sandals, a pack of leathery Germans lunched on sandwiches pulled from rucksacks. Navigating between these groups were Turkish waiters elegant in white shirts and black ties. They kept their flashing smiles for the younger foreign female passengers, but briskly plied us all with glasses of steaming tea and little tubs of fresh yoghurt.

Proffered a plastic spoon, I ended up sampling some from a tub bought by a California couple.

'Matt always reads up before he goes anywhere,' said Susan, Matt's wife. 'The yoghurt on the Bosphorus ferries comes from Kanlica, a town on the Asian side famous for its high quality milk and dairy products.'

Her husband was probably right – it was pretty good yoghurt. If Matt went in for thorough briefings before he did anything on his holidays it was only because he stuck to the professional habits of a lifetime. Fair-haired, healthy and youthful, Matt had recently retired from a flying career. He'd begun jockeying American jet-fighters over south-east Asia and ended up piloting Airbuses across the Atlantic. Now he and Susan flew free of charge to holiday destinations around the world.

'What Matt didn't plan for was the weather,' said Susan. 'It's not supposed to be raining.' She seemed surprised Matt hadn't got Turkish meteorology better in hand. 'Tomorrow we're going yachting – we've chartered a boat for a week on the Turkish Mediterranean coast. Things don't look too good.'

Perhaps that was why Matt kept sweeping the horizon to the south with his binoculars – he was looking for a break in the weather. But all he kept sighting were Turkish navy ships.

'Destroyer,' he would say, passing me the glasses. 'See how her silhouette masses up high to the tower in the middle? You can't mistake a destroyer even at twenty miles.'

'Matt flew from an aircraft carrier in the South China Sea,' said Susan. 'In fact, he holds the record for the longest single aerial-combat engagement in the whole Vietnam War.'

'Yeah, but I wasn't alone,' said Matt. 'There were six F-4s against twelve MiGs. And it might have seemed to go on forever, but the whole thing lasted less than five minutes. Time gets sort of elastic up there.'

And so the morning and the world floated by. We looked at minesweepers and torpedo boats through Matt's binoculars. At Dolmabahçe and Beylerbeyi we cruised past imperial Ottoman palaces, sprawling 19th-century wedding cakes of marble. We slipped by waterside *yalis*, lovely fret-worked wooden houses once favoured by viziers and princesses, today the pride of Turkish millionaires and industrialists. We passed under the Bosphorus and Fatih Bridges, spans of flying steel and cable so high that the trucks and buses above us looked like toys. Beneath the first bridge a giant hanging banner of blue and yellow, the colours of the city's Fenerbahçe Football Club, swirled and fluttered in the rain.

At Kanlica Pier the socked-and-sandaled Germans disembarked beneath the dismissive gaze of even tougher, more resilient Turks – in a cold wind they were fishing from the dock in rolled-up shirtsleeves. At Yeniköy all the Malaysians descended. At Sariyer the Korean ladies disappeared. But we stayed on, fighting a fast current as tankers and tugs, container-loaded freighters and camouflaged submarine-chasers swept down past us. We finally got down at Anadolu Kavagi, the turn-around point where the Bosphorus widens to meet the Black Sea. We had a couple of hours to wait before the return journey.

We tramped up to the Byzantine-built fortress above the village, Matt and Susan holding umbrellas aloft against a steady drizzle, our feet slipping in mud by the roadside. The fortress of Anadolu Kavagi wasn't much to see in drifting mist. It wasn't much to see anyway. Sodden dogs, their coats stained dark by rain, had knocked over refuse bins in the picnic grounds outside the high stone walls and spread garbage far and wide. Inside, little toilet-paper-covered mounds in the corners beneath defensive towers discouraged further exploration. It was cold and windy, and only in a fish restaurant back down at the port did we warm up again.

The food wasn't wonderful. It didn't have to be; in good weather hundreds of ferryboat tourists pass through the fish restaurants of Anadolu Kavagi every day, never to return. But the wine was cheering and it was good to be dry again – we felt cosy sitting in front of a big picture window upstairs watching fishing boats bob in the little harbour in front of us. Just beyond them, big ships moved at speed in the narrow shipping lanes.

The sight woke a memory in Matt's mind. He began talking about an accident at sea – the running over of several Vietnamese fishing junks by the aircraft carrier he'd flown from during the war.

'We smashed into them like so much driftwood,' he said, looking at the brightly painted boats, their decks covered with nets and orange buoys. 'They fell into a thousand pieces.'

'Why didn't you just go around?' said Susan. 'You must have seen them.'

'Sure we saw them,' he replied. 'But you can't turn a 900-foot ship on a blowy day in the middle of a flight operation. Planes have to launch and land into the wind. So we ran them over.'

It sounded callous. I wondered if Susan had heard the story before and asked the next question to make it sound less callous. 'Did you pick up survivors afterwards?' she asked.

'Yeah, I guess we eventually picked them up and dried them off,' said Matt.

'Did you buy them new fishing boats? Did you kill any of them, drown them?' Perhaps Susan hadn't heard the story.

Matt only shrugged. We stopped talking about aircraft carriers, and a few minutes later heard the ferry horn hoot passengers back on board for the return journey.

Halfway down the Bosphorus again, at the foot of the Fatih Bridge, we passed Rumeli Hisar, the Fortress of Europe. On the way up we'd been gazing skyward at the bridge and hardly noticed it. But now here the fortress was, its rough walls running down uneven banks to the water, its stone towers looking wild and medieval beneath the smooth steel risers of the bridge. Long after Rumeli Hisar disappeared past our stern I was still thinking of it – behind its construction lay a violent meeting of two ways of life quite as different as American capitalism and Asian communism were to be 500 years later.

The fortress had been raised in record time by the Ottoman Sultan Mehmet II, otherwise known as 'el-Fatih', the Conqueror. So anxious was he to take Greek Constantinople, the city both his father and great-grandfather had besieged, that he had it thrown up in a mere four months. In 1452 he ordered each of his three Viziers to take responsibility for one of the fortress's three main towers – failure to complete them on time, the story runs, would have resulted in their execution. And when the Fortress of Europe was finished, Mehmet used it to block off this narrowest point of the Bosphorus – no longer could Constantinople be provisioned from the north by the sea.

Less than a year later, in 1453, his armies besieged the city walls. Two hundred and fifty years after its sack by Venetians and Crusaders, Constantinople was a mere shadow of itself. It possessed few of its former territories. Its population had shrunk from 400,000 to less than 50,000 – the once-great city was now a straggling collection of half-abandoned parishes separated by fields and pastures. Its monuments had been stripped, its wonders sold or stolen. Even the lead on the roof of Hagia Sofia, the

900-year-old church of Divine Wisdom, had been melted to mint coins. The only surprise was that the city had held on as long as it did.

Moribund, living on borrowed time, its 5,000 fighting men facing an army of 300,000, Constantinople put up great resistance by land and sea. Even its monks fought. In the end the city's conquest was aided by a vast gun, a taste of Ottoman military superiority to come. A novel weapon whose first testing had terrified peasants and caused women to faint, it was twenty-eight feet long, fired a half-ton cannonball for a mile and required a special carriage drawn by thirty oxen to haul it. The millennium-old walls of Constantinople were not designed for cannon. It had about the same effect on them as an aircraft carrier on a fishing junk.

Cannon at that time were relatively new on the field of conquest, and so were the Ottomans. When Mehmet II entered the city on a white horse through streets being put to bloody sack, he dismounted before Hagia Sofia, swept up a handful of earth and poured it over his turban. It was intended as a show of humility before God. But he and his ancestors had never displayed the same humility before men – their lurch to power had been proud and sudden.

The Ottomans, later such proficient saltwater sailors, had come riding out of the arid steppes of central Asia in the 1100s. Even there, rootless pastoral nomads, they'd seen themselves as chosen, a people of destiny. They were pulled westward by a better climate and the failing power of the Byzantine Empire. By the early 1300s the soldiers of Osman, the first in a dynastic line of Sultans, had reached the Marmara shores.

If military success followed fast and furiously, a lot had to do with Ottoman encouragement of Muslim *gazis*, combatants anxious to fight in holy wars against Christians. Such conflict brought great virtue, and even greater booty. By the mid-1300s the Ottoman capital had moved from Anatolia to Edirne on the European side of the Bosphorus. In the following decades Ottomans swept not just through Anatolia, but Bulgaria, Serbia and much of the rest of the Balkans as well. By the time Mehmet the Conqueror stood before the walls of Constantinople it was nothing more than a tiny island in an already wide Ottoman sea.

To the Ottomans, intoxicated by success, it appeared only right that the greatest city in the world should be theirs. It seemed tailor-made, a city shaped by geography and history to be the capital of world rulers. Constantinople commanded sea-lanes to the Mediterranean, Africa and the Black Sea. It lay on overland trade routes between Asia, the Near East and Europe. Nowhere else on earth seemed quite as central, as perfectly situated for the imperial domination of the four quarters of the globe. Constantinople's ambit was religious, too. In the city where Hagia Sofia was transformed into the great Ottoman mosque of Aya Sofya, the Caliphate – the world-centre of Islamic rule – installed itself and there remained until modern times.

I was so immersed in contemplating changes to the ancient city that I missed a change taking place immediately around us. It was hardly historical, but it put a smile on Matt's face.

'Check it out,' he said, passing me the binoculars and pointing southwards. I did, and towards the Sea of Marmara saw open spaces between the clouds, and beyond them clear sky. By the time we were nudging into the ferry-quay at Eminönü the sky had cleared still further. A late afternoon sun was now out, and I understood for the first time why they called it the Golden Horn. As far down the inlet's surface as I could see, the water and every human being near it was lit by a warm, bouncing glow of reflected light. Before turning back to Sultanahmet and home, I walked out to the middle of the Galata Bridge just to stand in the Horn's glittering reflection.

Anyone could see why Mehmet, and every other strongman before or since, had wanted this city.

Thirty-Six

A couple of days later I was back on the Galata Bridge. This time, my bag over my shoulder, I crossed its entire length and kept on going.

I climbed through a warren of streets rising steeply away from the water on the far side, puffing my way past busy artisans' workshops and the premises of minor traders. Halfway up the hill, where stray dogs slept sprawled about a small park at the foot of the Galata Tower, I turned onto a residential side-street. Three large Turkish women, sitting on front door steps in long, flowered dresses, watched idly as I dropped my bag before a gate sunk into a high wall. I fished in my pocket for the ring of heavy brass keys Madame Annie had given me. I was at the rear entrance of my new lodgings, the Lycée Saint-Benoît.

You had to go a long way back, almost to the beginnings of Galata itself, to find the origins of Saint-Benoît. If the hillside above the Golden Horn is still a quarter of traders and small-time commerce, it has been so for more than a thousand years. In Byzantine times a community of foreign merchants – Genoese principally, but also Venetians, Florentines and other Western Europeans – grew up opposite walled Constantinople. The Franks flourished on the East-West commerce that placed the city at the very heart of things. Perhaps not feeling entirely protected by the trade agreements they had signed with the emperor – Byzantines did not have duplicitous reputations for nothing – they raised their own walls, erected the tall stone defensive tower that still stands there, and proceeded to build warehouses, churches and homes. In Galata they created what was virtually a small north-Italian city, and inside closed communities lived prosperous lives according to their own ways.

There was little resemblance to the great eastern city that lay just across the Horn, and that difference remained remarkable throughout Ottoman rule as well. Today Galata and the wealthier and even more westernised quarter of Pera on the hilltop behind it are called Beyoglu – son of the *bey*, or lord – after one of its best-known 16th-century residents. Excluded by his illegitimacy from any suitable career in Venice, Alvise Gritti, bastard son of the Doge Andrea Gritti, settled in Galata instead. He'd been born there – as a young man Andrea Gritti had been a Galata merchant and fathered Alvise by an Ottoman concubine. There the son of the lord dealt in jewels and acted as a diplomatic agent for the Sultan's Grand Vizier. Like thousands of other westerners over the centuries, he not only made a fortune in Constantinople but became a go-between for two cultures. He was also famous for his lavish entertainments, inviting Turkish nobles to huge banquets and treating them to displays by Galata's notorious dancing girls, specialists, as one knowledgeable observer noted, in 'such lascivious movements that they could make marbles melt'.

For general wantonness and debauchery Galata's countless taverns and brothels remained celebrated among the world's sailors right into the 20th century. But the community's more genteel residents were catered for as well. Among Franciscan, Cistercian and other religious orders, there were Benedictine clerics from the great French abbey of Cluny serving on the Bosphorus even before the Frank's sack of Constantinople. But when in 1204 the Latin invaders took control of the city's 12,000 Greek Orthodox churches and 300 monasteries, efforts to draw them into the Roman fold brought new waves of monkish orders to the city. They built their own churches, too. In the mid-1300s the Republic of Genoa, Venice's great trading rival in the East, was renovating the Galata Tower and expanding city walls; at the same time it also undertook to pay for a new church and monastery to be built by Benedictines just below the tower. This was the institution through whose creaking back gate I now let myself.

I barely knew my way around. I had only gotten my keys from Madame

Annie, the school secretary, after meeting Saint-Benoît's principal the day before. Now it was a Saturday and there wasn't a soul around to ask directions. With a large key I opened a heavy wooden door into a main building, swung it closed behind me, then plunged forward through near-obscurity down a high, echoing hallway.

The place soon had me spooked. The only light came from windows lying beyond open classroom doors on either side of the hall. Each time I poked my head into one of these rooms I would be met by the same cold gaze – since the early years of the republic a portrait of Kemal Atatürk has hung in every classroom in Turkey. His eyes were piercing, his gaze cold and forbidding. He made the old building feel more ghost-ridden than a hundred monastery crucifixes could.

It was like a bad dream – the dark hallways went on and on, turning left and right but never leading anywhere. Once I found myself in a dusty storeroom piled high with books centuries old, their ancient leather binding disintegrating, their Greek and Latin print shot through with wormholes. Once I encountered a ceiling-high display case, the pelicans, storks and other large stuffed birds inside it fixing me with beady glass eyes as I passed. I negotiated a series of interior courtyards and several sets of gloomy stairwells. I tried other floors that turned out to be just as con-fusing as the ones above and below. After twenty minutes of rising panic, I at last found the locked metal door I was looking for.

Sitting beneath high antique beams, the air-conditioned guest accom-modation that lay beyond was opulent for any school. The armchairs were deep, the hardwood floors polished, the lighting soft and indirect. There was a wide-screen television the size of a small car. Not far from a stone fireplace, rising unexpectedly out of the floor and protected by heavy glass, was the complex spring-and cog mechanism of a 19th-century clock. On its frosted glass face, incorporated into the wall and overlooking the school quadrangle on the other side of it, I could read, letters inverted, the words 'Collin, Paris'.

In the 500 years since Saint-Benoît had opened a school for the chil-dren of Galata Catholics it had not always been as prosperous. Fishing for

Catholic converts amongst the Sultan's Orthodox subjects was hardly a wise public relations gambit. There had been worse. In the 16th century the monastery's Brother Joseph de Léonisse, charged with seeing to the spiritual salvation of the Sultan's Catholic galley slaves, was so inspired by them that he impulsively sought an audience with the Sultan himself and called on him to embrace Christianity immediately. Restrictions on Catholic monks were tightened and Brother Joseph, for all his effrontery, merely thrown into prison – he might have ended up with his head impaled on the walls of the first courtyard of Topkapi Palace.

Benedictines, Dominicans, Jesuits – and finally, after the French Revolution, French Lazarists – administered the monastery. All knew uncertain times. Often short of funding from home, the Lazarists were obliged to raise revenues locally. They published a Turkish grammar in French. They established an Armenian language press. They even cultivated a commercial jasmine plantation in the monastery courtyards. And their diligence paid off – today the Lazarists still run Saint-Benoît. Their prosperity is assured by the fees paid by the wealthy parents of their Turkish students. And if they are prohibited from inculcating any kind of faith in their charges, their secular teachers turn out the next-best thing to Turkish Catholics – Turks instructed in the ways of the French. *La Mission Civilatrice* continues.

It certainly continued in the suite of rooms I had been assigned on the far side of the spring-and-cog clock. It was entirely civilised, its furnishings pleasing from both Eastern and Western points of view. In my study I discovered a 19th-century print of the Bosphorus at sunset. Entitled '*Palais du Sultan et Bateau de Parade*', it showed the Sultan arriving at Dolmabahçe Palace in his royal *caique*. Long and narrow, its high prow carved and gilded, the vessel was powered by thirteen pairs of rowers dressed in red fezzes, white uniforms and black waistbands. Lounging beneath a richly-decorated canopy at the stern, his chin bearded and his turban feathered, an imperial potentate took his leisure. It was a scene of pomp and ceremonial splendour, and it looked all too familiar – here was an eastern Doge sitting before an Ottoman Ducal Palace in an oriental state-vessel. Sea-sovereigns never change.

But maybe in the end they have to. In the bedroom beyond I came across a second, very different picture. It, too, was a waterscape, and also 19th century. But it was a blown-up, panoramic photograph of the Golden Horn and it showed another Istanbul. It had none of the first picture's Oriental decadence – this was a vista of industrial-age transport, an image of funnelled steamships, smoky skies and the new, floating steel-pontoon Galata Bridge. The ships were massed side by side and the bridge jammed with pedestrians in a hurry. You could almost hear the bellowing of porters, the klaxon of horse-drawn trams, the chattering of telegraph lines. All Western energy and vigour, Constantinople was no less frantic than the ports of New York or London at the time.

And this was what had made the port-city so extraordinary – the fact that *caique* and steamship existed alongside each other at the same time. Saint-Benoît was an early example of attempts to bring European ideas to an Asian metropolis. But it was only one initiative in a long process in which East and West met and mingled in Constantinople, and in many cases fused.

Neither side, of course, was fired by mere altruism. As elsewhere around the globe, France's civilising mission was never lacking in self-interest. In Constantinople France found an ally against her European arch-rival, Spain. And when in the late 1600s long-successful Ottoman institutions began failing an empire that had outgrown them, a reverse process set in – the Ottomans began looking westward for their own advantage.

Their empire needed modernisation and France, at the forefront in great-power relations with Turkey, was only too happy to oblige. Like other nations of the European Concert during the age of nationalism, she was poised in a delicate balance of power – each country, afraid that Turkey and its imperial possessions might fall into the hands of the others, cooperated in a collective effort to prop up the famously 'sick man of Europe'. Who could have put it more candidly than the Duke of Wellington? 'The Ottoman Empire stands not for the benefit of the Turks,' he pronounced, 'but of Christian Europe.' Without European assistance it would have fallen far sooner than it did.

From battle tactics to ballet techniques, the French were everywhere in the effort to reform and westernise the ailing power. They taught modern artillery to its armies, European construction to its engineers, Western surgery to its doctors, continental administration to its bureaucrats and French poetry to its students; by the end of the 1800s more than 5,000 French words had become Ottoman words. But a Gallicised elite was not enough to help the Ottomans survive – in the end Western knowledge came too little and too late to allow them to adapt to a fast-changing world.

Today the French still delight in instruction, but now, it seemed to me, they came to Istanbul to learn just as much as to teach. Soon after settling into Saint- Benoît I was invited to a party in the suburb of Bebek, halfway up the Bosphorus. Normally I think I would have hesitated over an evening hosted by a *professeur de mathematiques* for a group of science teachers. But Farida and her guests were about as unconventional as French *lycée* instructors can get.

I took a taxi to the soirée early one evening with Florent, the Saint-Benoît teacher who'd arranged my rooms at the old monastery. Florent taught information technology, and after a year in Istanbul he had no desire to return to the same job in France. In fact he had no desire to return to France at all. He was learning Turkish, a hard slog in a tongue that resembles no Indo-European language whatsoever. He played the *darbuka*, a Turkish drum, and rather than spend his holidays in France went trekking in remote mountain ranges in Anatolia. He had fallen in love with Turkish carpets. Florent was going native, as far as that is possible in a city that in some measure has been European from the beginning.

It was the same with the other foreigners there. The taxi skirted the edge of the Bosphorus and just before the Bebek ferry pier, in an affluent suburb between the strait's two bridges, climbed upwards to a house poised high over the water. Tables and chairs had been set up under fruit trees in the garden outside. The plums there were still hard and green, but the cherries were ripe and red and began to glisten in the light of the candles flickering beneath them. From the edge of the garden you could see freighters churning their way up the Bosphorus – they were so close you could almost spit cherry pits at them. Who could blame the French gathered in the garden at sunset for not wanting to leave the city? They had fallen in love with Istanbul, and made of their lives in it a happy mix of East and West. All of them told me the same thing. With their Turkish friends there was a directness of engagement, an ease and comfort in daily human contact they hadn't known before. Was it perhaps a holdover belonging to what was left of an older, more cohesive society? At any rate it gave them a sense of complicity that had long ago been swallowed up by modern French life.

And what of Farida, Saint-Benoît's young and pretty mathematics teacher? She had a natural warmth, a level, curious gaze, and an immediate sincerity, even with strangers, that was disarming. But beneath the candour there was a tough, uncompromising resilience. She had made some hard choices.

Farida was light-skinned and clear-eyed, a Berber born in a remote town of the Middle Atlas mountains in Morocco. Her grandfather had been a traditional hill-chief, an adamant, unbending tribal elder with a strong religious bent. He had trained his son to be a Muslim imam, but Farida's father had fled the town's poverty – and its overbearing patriarch – choosing instead the life of a migrant labourer in France. Farida had arrived there as a baby.

Farida's younger sister Naïma was born in France, and had chosen the more extreme option available to those cut off from their roots – religious reaction. In some ways she was a modern, professional woman – she worked in the marketing division of a French car-manufacturer. But she had also taken the Islamic headscarf and lived the conspicuous life of a devout Muslim. Growing up in the same high-rise, low-income immigrant suburb outside Paris, Farida had gone a different route. She'd studied hydro-electric engineering.

'I wanted a modern, liberated life. I wanted freedom and equality,' she told me as the night drew on and we watched Florent light a charcoal grill. 'And I couldn't find it in France. I was the Muslim fundamentalist's

291

sister, the Arab factory-worker's daughter who had found her way up and out. I'd become a proper Frenchwoman. But I didn't want to be a social phenomenon – I wanted to be myself.'

She'd sought escape in rural village life in southern France, looking for neighbours, human ties, close-knit community. 'I realised later,' she said, 'that what I was looking for were the same connections, the same kind of social fabric I might find in a more traditional life – in Berber life, for example. It doesn't exist in France any more. So I moved again. I came to Turkey.'

And did she find those connections in the sprawling, modern megalopolis of Istanbul, I asked? Farida shook her head.

'No. But I've found a kind of mental space in which at least I feel comfortable. Turks have the same doubts I do – they feel divided about religion and secularism. They're unsure about being both Western and Eastern.' She laughed. 'So I'm a fish in water here. Teaching school maths isn't what I imagined for myself and it won't last forever. In the meantime I can cope with all the questions and still get on with life.'

Was this the Mediterranean at work again, that inter-connective, cosmopolitan influence that blurred origins, that made for a wider sense of identity? In Alexandria I had found the last remaining traces of that kind of society, but it was close to dying. Was it still possible, even today in Istanbul, to share in more than one identity? It was dark now and the grill had burned down to a red glow. More guests arrived – other French and their Turkish friends, couples who lived neither European nor Oriental lives, but both.

We dined on tabouli and grilled lamb and Turkish wine. After there was dancing. I stood on the parapet watching the lights of ships describing slow, broad curves through the dark straits – if a few stars burned faintly in the clear sky above, entire bright constellations of lights were passing by on the decks of giant tankers below. Every now and then a ship's horn gave a long, loud blast and an echo would reverberate up the hillside to the dancers on the lawn.

And so we sat by the Bosphorus, refugees all, listening to ships and drinking wine into the night. Later the music and dancing stopped, people began drifting home, and finally there was only the sound of Florent softly playing his *darbuka*. I sat with Farida, sometimes talking, sometimes thinking about her group of friends. What was the lure that attracted such people to Istanbul? I left an hour before dawn, and by the time a taxi dropped me at the foot of the Galata Tower there was light to the east over the water.

Thirty-Seven

I tried to get a feel for the capital of the Ottomans through its most famous monuments, but it wasn't much good. If there are a dozen buses parked outside it doesn't matter which place you're visiting – inside it's always the same place.

Istanbul was not far now from the full-blown summer tourist season and the palaces, mosques and jewelled treasure-collections of Sultanahmet were overrun. I have nothing against such visitors. There is no reason why a couple of dozen excursionists from, say, the Göteborg branch of the Swedish Association of Dental Hygienists should not admire the Iznik tile-work of the Blue Mosque. I have even less against the hawkers who make their living selling trinkets in the street. Is there any denying that the world of Swedish dental care would be a happier place if only its practitioners brought home a few embroidered caps with swinging tassles? What wrecks everything is when twenty or thirty such tourist groups descend on one place and attract entire marauding bands of streethawkers. It all becomes pointless noise and confusion. In the midst of it the fainter voices you've come to listen for simply slip away, back into the past.

So it was with relief that I came to the end of several rounds of intensive sightseeing. My one real satisfaction had been in seeing the tomb of the Venetian Doge Enrico Dandolo, who died in Constantinople after overseeing its sack, left forgotten and ignored in an obscure corner of the Aya Sofya. I finished up just down the road with Istanbul's most popular tourist-scramble. Why exactly the Sultan's harem in the heart of the Topkapi Palace should have such drawing-power was a mystery. Did the crowds surging around the ticket office in the third courtyard think they were buying admission to heaven on earth? Were they surprised to discover there were no Circassian slave-girls with alabaster skin and perfumed thighs reclining in the cramped little rooms at the top of narrow palace stairs? The chambers were hardly redolent of seduction – the press of flesh the tourists themselves produced there was merely sweaty and clamorous. Duty done, I took myself off to quieter, calmer places.

I spent a day strolling beneath the sixty-foot height of the city's Byzantine walls. There were no tourists milling below the wall's ruined Tekfur Palace. It was a remote part of the city – the only hygienists were bus drivers who used the waste-ground there as a place to wash their buses. Borrowing a ladder from one of them, I scaled a break in the palace fortifications, climbed to the roof of a tower and gazed down onto an old field of battle. Tranquil now, it wasn't hard to repopulate it with a massed and heaving army of Ottoman soldiers – it wasn't far from here that after seven weeks of siege Mehmet the Conqueror's Janissary troops had breached the city walls and entered Constantinople.

I spent another day walking the narrow streets of Fener and Balat, quiet quarters a couple of miles up the Golden Horn. Most old residential areas of Istanbul disappeared long ago, their wooden houses victims of modern property development and the great fires that regularly used to sweep the city. But these areas, traditionally the homes of Ottoman ethnic minorities – Balat is Jewish and Fener Greek – remain poor and largely undeveloped. Dodging kids playing ball in the street, I walked into an earlier century. Crooked stovepipes protruded from the sides of sagging and ramshackle wooden houses. Hanging laundry swayed in the breeze. Shady vines sprouted in tiny gardens and ran up trellises over the street. It was quintessentially Mediterranean – this could have been backstreet Naples, a hillside in Marseilles or a waterfront quarter of Tunis. But here I didn't have to strain at all to catch the voices of the past – in Balat an elderly man approached and addressed me in Ladino, the Spanish dialect that has been used by Jews in Constantinople since their eviction from Spain 500 years ago. We just about managed.

There were scores of old places like these, peaceful and uncrowded, scattered all over Istanbul. One of my favourites I discovered on an airless, sultry afternoon when the heat of the streets had become too much. What I craved was a bit of freshness and greenery, and I found it in Ihlamur Kasri, the Kiosk of the Linden Tree, preferred retreat of the 19th-century Sultan Abdulmecid.

The entrance ticket I bought at the gate to Ihlamur included a guided visit of the Sultan's kiosks. But as I was the only visitor around and the custodian on duty was a sociable type with nothing else to do, the tour was downgraded – it turned into a leisurely stroll around the grounds with plenty of conversation thrown in for free.

The park was charming, a jewel hidden amidst concrete apartment blocks and growling traffic. I was led over crunching gravel paths through well-kept rose gardens, over manicured lawns and past a stone-lipped pool where carved lions sat looking at their reflections. We walked on through a less formal, hillier part of the grounds, where fragrant stands of linden, magnolia and pine trees gave us deep shade. The custodian, a large, paunchy man in a grey uniform and peaked cap, enjoyed the cool as much as I did – beneath his visor his face was florid and overheated. He didn't look Turkish at all. His hair, light brown, would have been straw-blond in his childhood. His eyes were an icy, penetrating blue. His name, like the Conqueror's, was Mehmet. And if he looked more like a Hungarian or a Pole than he did a Turk, he had definite views on his countrymen's past and their origins.

'Where you think the Turks came from?' Mehmet asked me conversationally as he stopped to mop his face. I could see he was going to tell me no matter what I replied, so I shrugged.

'A long time ago,' he said, walking on, 'there were two brothers. They lived by the water at Çanakkale. One was named Turka, and the other Franka. Each wanted to be a big man. They wanted land, a lot of money and many, many women. So they decided to go in different directions. Turka went east into Anatolia. Franka went west to France.'

I blinked, never having heard a folk-tale of Turkish beginnings before, and said nothing.

'They were the first Turks,' Mehmet said. 'Who do you think the Kurds, the Armenians, the Egyptians, the Syrians and all the other people of the empire were? They came later, they were the Sultans' conquests.

'Franka was very handsome, with blue eyes and yellow hair. He had many pleasures with ladies,' Mehmet continued, giving me a man-of-the-world wink. 'And he made many children as he went west. Most Turks came from Romania, Albania, Kosovo, Bulgaria, Greece. This is God's truth. They were top-quality, number-one people. Original people! This is why the French are good people, too. Their ancestor is Franca. This is why they are strong and clever. This is why they are good soldiers. Napoleon, you must know, was a Turk.'

Here I couldn't help interrupting. 'Are you sure about that? The French say he was a Corsican.'

Mehmet was having none of it. 'No, no!' he insisted. 'Intelligent men, professors from big universities, have looked at this question, and decided it is so. There are many books on it, thick books.' He held up his hand, his thumb and index finger as far part as possible.

The books I'd read weren't thick and hadn't said anything about two brothers, but I couldn't help getting Mehmet's point. Never mind all those dark and foreign-looking Eastern people, he was saying – we Turks are really much more European than Oriental. And for a blue-eyed Turk with a job looking after a building that was beyond all doubt European it was, in the end, an understandable point of view.

We had looped through the woods back towards civilisation. By the side of the path delicate wrought-iron lampposts now appeared. Discreetly equipped with hi-fi speakers painted forest-green, they were emitting the dulcet strains of a Mozart string quartet. The stands of wood thinned, the lawns grew broad again, and soon we were in front of the Kiosk of the Linden Tree. Who, standing before Abdulmecid's sylvan getaway, could doubt that Turka's brother Franka had made it not just to the Balkans, but all the way to the far end of the continent? Whoever had ordered up this stone-carved fantasy surely had to have had a little Gallic blood in his veins.

The kiosk was a French folly, an impossibly romantic mix of baroque and Second Empire neo-classical architecture. A pleasure-pavilion wrought in marble, it dripped ornamentation – it was heavily loaded with half-columns, Corinthian capitals, urns, medallions, acanthus leaves, floral decorations, scalloped shells and bas-relief pyramids of fruit. It looked like a crazed *pâtissier* had squeezed it all out of an especially extravagant piping set. It was delicious and ready to eat.

The interior decorator had done himself no less proud. The salons inside – you simply couldn't call them rooms – were lavished with every European refinement. The vast chandelier was of Bohemian crystal. The vases were Sèvres. The Louis Seize chairs were upholstered with fine brocade. The coal-grated fireplace was enameled and covered with detailed floral decoration. Almost as much gold-leaf as glass, there was a gilded Hall of Mirrors that would not have shamed Versailles. Only the Imperial Water Closet featured recognisably eastern, squat-down design, but you couldn't accuse the Sultan of scrimping – at the time there wasn't a Western-style lavatory between London and Vienna that would have met his approval. If his toilets were not elevated, the Sultan's standards were.

With a triumphant, I-told-you-so sort of smile on his face, Memed left me to ponder his interpretation of the Turkish past. Once again history, that inevitable companion of any traveller in the Middle East, had caught up with me and I was going to have to try to sort it out. I sat down on the edge of the stone-carved pool and gave myself up to the luxury of the surroundings and the warmth of the afternoon.

Mehmet's past was a past reduced to myth, but what he was saying wasn't all that wild. The story of two ambitious brothers riding out in opposite directions from the edge of the Bosphorus was no less expansionist than that much better-known Ottoman myth, the Islamic conquest of the Red Apple.

For the Ottomans the Red Apple, a metaphor for world domination, was originally the city of Constantinople. It was said to stand for the globe once grasped in the hand of a giant statue of the Emperor Justinian outside the Hagia Sophia. 'We shall meet at the Red Apple,' generations of Ottoman sultans declared ceremonially to their Janissary generals as they assumed the reins of power, girding themselves with that other symbol, the sword of their ancestor Osman. But as the sword did its work and their dominion expanded, so the Red Apple changed – it remained a goal lying always just out of reach. For early Sultans sitting in the newly-built Topkapi Palace the Red Apple was the original western Christian capital, Rome. It later transformed itself into Vienna. Beyezid, son of Mehmet the Conqueror, confidently expected to move on past Vienna to Paris itself. What remained constant was the idea of continual military advance until war had subsumed the entire world into a single Ottoman commonwealth.

Nor, I thought, was Mehmet the Custodian wrong about the imperial enterprise being largely European, at least in its leadership. The Ottomans were never a nation, as the Turks were later to become. Issued from Muslim Turkish clans, they were a hereditary dynasty ruling over an empire in which Turks were just one component – to the elites of Ottoman culture 'Turk' was a disparaging term applied to unwashed Anatolian farmers. Not even the old Turkish clan nobility was enlisted as a base of support – it was seen as potentially troublesome. Instead, the Sultan's rule depended on the service of a foreign-born military and administrative class. Known as *kapi kulu*, Slaves of the Gate, such men were precisely that: imperial subjects whose lives from an early age belonged exclusively to the Palace. The 'Gate' referred to Topkapi's Cannon Gate, where the Sultan's justice was dispensed; it later evolved into the symbol of government known as the Sublime Porte. But the Slaves of the Gate were never Turks. Because the Koran forbid the enslavement of born Muslims, the Ottomans had to look further afield for each new generation of servants. Recruits came from Christian Europe.

It was a system that worked supremely well for almost 400 years. In Greece, Albania, Serbia, Bulgaria, Romania – any place in the Balkans that the Ottomans had recently conquered – a 'boy tribute' was levied

on the rural Christian population. Converted to Islam in Constantinople, the youths were placed where they would best serve the Empire. The
brightest were given intensive educations at the Palace or under a Pasha's
supervision. The best of them would eventually rise to the highest levels of
administration – of the first forty-eight Grand Viziers heading Ottoman
governments after the conquest of Constantinople, just eighteen were
native-born Turks. Other boys were destined to become Janissaries, the
Empire's elite corps of fighting men. Numbering some 20,000 they, too,
were highly trained and held crucial positions of power. Their zealous and
unflagging service was one of the secrets of the Ottomans' astounding
military advances. But when as a sign of dissatisfaction the Janissary regi-
ments overturned their pilaf cauldrons, the Sultans themselves trembled.

Ottoman 'slavery' is not entirely translatable, and the term did not
carry the same significance it does in the West. The Sultan himself, after all,
was the son of a slave, often one of those alabaster-skinned Circassians so
favored in the harem. For a Slave of the Gate submission to empire meant
escape from a life of rural Balkan poverty and ignorance. Becoming, in
effect, members of a privileged extended family of which the Sultan was
patriarch, the *kapi kulu*, sons of peasants, left the restrictions of feudalism
behind. Subject to a rigorous process of selection, trained to the limits of
their aptitudes, they entered a meritocracy in which intelligence, ability
and loyalty were valued above all else.

Thus the children of mountain shepherds became viziers exalted above
all ordinary men. Such opportunity, a direct contradiction of the principles of entrenched power and privilege sanctioned in the West, produced
great motivation. It also, quite naturally, horrified Europe's medieval aristocracy. It proved that the much-vaunted virtues of hereditary nobility
were a nonsense. Here was a system, wholly dismissive of feudal conven-
tions, which in feeding off its triumphs was capable of advancing ever
outwards. In the same way that the latest conquest provided the spoils of
war necessary to fund the next military campaign, so too did it provide
the personnel who would go on to execute the following stages of expansion. *Kapi kulu* could not pass on their slave status to their Muslim-born

children, but as long as conquest was possible new recruits were available. Until it began to unravel the system provided the empire with an unending supply of warriors and administrators. Efficient and self-perpetuating, it gave the empire both dynamism and stability for centuries.

Seen by anyone standing in its way, the Ottoman empire was a formidable machine harnessed for endless conflict. Not for nothing were the lands outside its jurisdiction known as the *Dar al-Harb* – the Abode of War. But viewed from inside it was called something else: *Dar al-Islam* – the Abode of Peace. Unlike many other imperial conquerors, the Ottomans had no interest in forcibly making the peoples under their rule become like themselves. No one was commanded to speak Turkish or Ottoman Turk, the language of the elite. No one had to renounce the customs and habits of centuries. No one had to convert; eventually the promised Mahdi would come and put the world of the infidel to rights. In the meantime the Ottomans had themselves and an empire to maintain. What they needed were not Muslims. They wanted taxpayers instead, and non-Muslims paid top rate.

And so from the beginning the *millet* – that method of multinational management which even much later cast its afterglow on 20th-century Alexandria – was a convenient and natural way to rule. It wasn't simply a matter of ensuring revenues. When the Sultan recognised any group's religious and ethnic identity he undertook to protect it and guaranteed its right to look after its own affairs. In return, however, he demanded every *millet*'s absolute loyalty to the empire; the principles of collective responsibility accepted by each community's leaders meant it was they, and not the Sultanate, who undertook to keep unruly internal factions in line.

I watched as Mehmet returned to the kiosk with a mixed party of visitors – Germans, Italians, and some Eastern Europeans. Not everyone understood Mehmet's English explanations, and he was having a tough time keeping the bored ones from wandering off on their own. It made me think of the problems history's great imperial rulers must have had in imposing order on their varied possessions. The practical advantages of the *millet* system of administration in a vast empire had been enormous.

Mobile as they were, Ottoman armies could not march off at the drop of a hat to police distant corners of huge and mountainous territories. And as they grew larger the Ottomans' holdings grew infinitely more complex. Multicultural Alexandria was only a dim reflection of a far greater intricacy. Vlachs, Laz, Tartars, Bogomils, Bedouins, Serbs, Uzbeks ... at its height the Empire was said to be composed of seventy-two-and-a-half nationalities, the half-nationality being composed of Gypsies. In such a complex world, interconnected but self-contained communities made the only sense. Here were the origins of a cosmopolitan society unlike any in the West.

Attracting talent and ambition from every part of the empire, Constantinople became the heart of this interdependency, the only multinational capital in Europe. And its diverse and contrasting ways of life became the essence of the city. When Mehmet the Conqueror came on the scene the majority of his subjects, not just in the city but in the empire as a whole, were Christian. Anxious to repopulate and restore the metropolis to its former glory, he immediately set about attracting merchants, artists and craftsmen from all over. Some were Muslim Turks, some Jews, some Christians – Greeks, Armenians, Slavs and Levantines. He also reinstated a Greek Patriarchate, a religious body which had overseen Orthodox affairs from Constantinople since the 4th century. It was the beginning of a process of reciprocal bargaining, persuasion, threats, cajoling and political horse-trading which was to characterise ethnic relations inside the Empire until its very end.

Even at the best of times there were strains and tensions. Not all elements in Ottoman society were in favor of a multicultural ideal – from the beginning the *ulema*, the empire's community of Islamic theologians, professors and practitioners of Koranic law, often opposed the privileges accorded non-Muslim minorities. But the Ottomans' great gamble, that an ethnically disparate collection of peoples would function better under co-option than suppression, generally paid off. And for centuries Constantinople, the meeting place of many worlds, enjoyed a truly cosmopolitan existence. In the same way the Sultans combined European and

Islamic and Ottoman identities in their own person, so was it possible for their subjects to have dual or even multiple identities. A Constantinopolite could be a Greek Jew, a Syrian Christian or a Hungarian Muslim. At the same time, however, he could still feel himself thoroughly Ottoman.

Why did cosmopolitanism stop working? Why did the Ottoman system of multicultural co-existence fall to pieces? Why was blue-eyed Mehmet now the grey-uniformed guardian of a superannuated pleasure-park when a distant forbear, resplendent in red boots and white linen hat, might have stood at the head of a battalion of triumphant Janissaries? For an answer I only had to look up from the rippled reflections in the pool to the extravagant building that lay beyond it.

Western Europe had had its own power and glory at the same time, too. And if its various states were fractious and quarrelsome, disputes between them had given the continent a combative vigor. In the centuries-old contest between East and West Europe had developed something that was wholly anathema to its Ottoman rivals – nationalism. As a creed it had become successful and attractive from Portugal to the Ottoman frontiers. By the mid-1800s even Venice, once the proudest and most independent of city-republics, had opted for union with Italy. Faced with the fervor of nations held together by patriotic myth – the vision of people of a single blood united in defense of a single language, history and sacred soil – the cosmopolitan ideal of a state based on plural cultural identity became a fast-fading irrelevance.

But in fact the Ottomans had built anachronism into their empire from the very beginning, and it began showing itself long before the age of nationalism reached such heights. The multi-ethnic state worked superbly from the 1300s through the 1500s, when the reign of Suleiman the Magnificent saw unparalleled successes in conquest and the consolidation of empire. Perhaps he was too successful. By the end of his rule a major sea-change, barely perceptible at first, began to set in. The empire was reaching its natural limits.

If Ottoman power was based on an economy and labour market driven by war, then continuing conquest was essential. But there came a time when logistics alone began to make successful conquest more and more difficult. With an empire now stretching from Algiers to the Don River, from Budapest to the Persian Gulf, the Ottoman armies could no longer race like lightning as they once had across the confines of the Balkans; simply getting to the peripheries of their territory inside a single campaign season became a challenge. Warfare became a much slower and more exhausting activity.

Once the Ottoman armies had seemed unstoppable; with the war against Austria at the end of the 1500s the Ottomans' outward expansion finally and painfully creaked to a halt. In the peace accords that followed, the Sultan had to recognise his rival, the Austrian emperor, as an equal. Never before in Ottoman history had such a humbling admission been made. Even more of a climb-down, the Red Apple, the tantalising goal always just beyond reach on the far horizon, now slipped from view forever. World dominion, the ambition that had fuelled Ottoman confidence for so long, was now just an historical mirage.

There were crucial material consequences, too. There was less and less booty to pay the salaries of the vast Ottoman armies and bureaucracy. Inflation was rampant. Taxes became unbearable. With budgets and stipends wearing thin, bribery and the selling of office became widespread. Out in distant provinces venal and self-serving officials brought misgovernment and misery to new lows. Resentment and violence grew correspondingly. Failing in their multicultural ideal, the Ottomans provoked their own virulent, homegrown form of nationalism.

Inevitably, the Empire was sucked into its own downward spiral. Its sense of direction was lost, its people abused, its institutions riddled with sloth and corruption. Only when it was too late did its conservative elite begin to look to technological and political change as a means of shoring things up. I only had to look at the little pleasure-pavilion before me to see that there had been aspects of brilliance in the Ottomans' long, slow decline. But an ornate façade did little to prevent the final collapse of the Ottoman house. In many parts of the eastern Mediterranean they are still trying to clear away the resulting mess of political rubble today.

It was late afternoon and beginning to cool off by the time I rose from the pool. The same Mozart piece had wafted out over the lawns a dozen times now. I gave Mehmet a wave goodbye as I walked out of Ihlamur's gates. But he was too busy to notice – he was accompanying a newly-arrived French couple and I imagine he was explaining to them why Europeans were really Turks. I have no idea how they received the news about Napoleon.

Thirty-Eight

Not far up the hill from where I stayed, on the other side of the Galata Tower, began the street called Istiklal Cadessi. I started going that way more and more because it was the opposite of everything I had seen so far – it wasn't Istanbul's past, but its future.

It didn't seem to matter what time of day I let myself out of the rear entrance of Saint-Benoît – the large ladies were almost always there, sitting barefoot on their doorsteps or on a carpet spread out on the sidewalk. I don't think I ever saw them without spoons in their hands. Either they were feeding numerous small children, or helping themselves from a communal bowl placed in the middle of the carpet. They were stolid, heavy women, prematurely aged by childbearing and domestic labour. They weren't beautiful, but their long, voluminous dresses were. The curlicue vines and tiny coloured flowers printed on the dresses' jet-black background were so bright they jumped out at you. Walking past these women was like walking through rural Anatolia, a place, presumably, they'd come from not long before. We never exchanged words, or even glances. Talking to strange men wasn't part of rural Anatolian protocol.

The dogs in the little park at the foot of the tower were always there, too. There are stories of dogs ruling the streets in the old days of Istanbul, large packs of howling, semi-wild brutes each controlling their own quarter and fed by a population who both feared and loved them. The half-dozen dogs I passed were big and rough-coated and still lived on handouts, but they didn't look as troublesome as they once might have

– most of the time they simply blocked the sidewalks as they lay snoozing in the sunshine.

The steep street that led upwards from the tower specialised in Turkish music. Its shops were filled with delicate and exotic-looking string-instruments – *baglamas* and *tamburs*, *kanuns* and *ouds* – and up and down its sidewalks odd, exotic sounds floated out into the air. The street attracted musicians from outside the quarter, but it still had an intimate, almost village-like feel to it. At its foot you might meet a horse-drawn cart offering piled watermelons for sale, or carrying dense little forests of fragrant potted basil plants. Higher up, on gradients too steep for any animal, you'd come across a handcart heading the other way. The man in front of it would be leaning far back in the cart's shafts, pushing hard with his shoulders as he struggled to ease the load gently down the hill.

And then, abruptly, the ascent would be over, the hill from the Golden Horn finally scaled. Broad and level, Istiklal Cadessi began its unhindered procession along the hill's crest towards Taksim Square, the heart of modern Istanbul. Gone were the anachronisms of an older world, the quaint scenes imported from dusty towns on faraway plains. There was no place for them on Istiklal Cadessi, the busiest, most sophisticated pedestrian thoroughfare in the entire eastern Mediterranean.

These days it is filled with the kind of establishment you'd find in any modern downtown shopping area: clothing boutiques and sports shops, restaurants and multiplex cinemas, bookshops and cash distributors and ice cream stands. A century ago the street had aspirations to much higher levels of fashion. Known as the Grande rue de Pera, it self-consciously styled itself on the great boulevards of 19th-century Paris. Pera matrons frequented shops like Bon Marché and La Maison des Modes Françaises. Pera husbands frequented brothels graced by grand stairways, wigged and powdered manservants and courtesans reclining on divans of red velvet. Together, husbands and wives frequented Taksim Gardens, a sort of Levantine Tivoli at the far end of the Grande rue; there they could sample the pleasures of a restaurant, an open-air cinema, a variety theatre, a cabaret and – as breathlessly described at the time in a local paper – a '*bar ultra-select frequenté par le high life de la capitale*'. Separated only by a quarter-mile of water from the still cramped, unlit streets of the oriental city across the Horn, the district was a modern marvel.

Like the population of Alexandria, the 180,000 residents of Pera living under the protection of foreign embassies had come to make money through trade. Like the Alexandrians, they too profited from tax and tariff exemptions, part of the Ottoman system of international 'Capitulations' granted from the 15th century onwards. And so from a very early date the capital was populated not just by the empire's many *millets*, but by numerous communities from beyond its borders as well. By 1718 Lady Mary Wortley Montagu, wife of the British ambassador to Constantinople, could write that 'in Péra they speak Turkish, Greek, Hebrew, Armenian, Slavonian, Wallachian, German, Dutch, French, English, Italian, Hungarian; and what is worse, there is ten of these languages spoke in my own family. My grooms are Arabs, my footmen, French, English and German, my Nurse an Armenian, my housemaids Russians, half a dozen other servants Greeks; my steward an Italian; my Janissaries Turks.'

Today the foreigners, like their languages and their footmen, have gone. But any number of European churches remain on Istiklal Cadessi, as do palatial former embassies. Brave efforts are also made by the few restaurants and hotels surviving from the turn of the last century. Not far off the street lies the Pera Palace Hotel, once Istanbul's finest. It is now a little less fine, perhaps a touch musty even, but nonetheless dear to wistful admirers of a privileged age of travel. No. 411, the room in which Agatha Christie is supposed to have written *Murder on the Orient Express*, has become a small museum. There are other establishments in the quarter, aging, washed-up remnants of that great tidal wave of White Russians fleeing revolution, where you can still get caviar, ice-cold vodka and a decent bowl of borscht.

But such places, it must be said, have become marginal curiosities, kept alive by travel writers drumming up nostalgia for Sunday papers. If a hundred years ago these institutions brought a vital Western energy to an Eastern city otherwise failing and moribund, things are different now.

The present generators of Istiklal Cadessi's energy, the source of the vigour and liveliness that flows along the street like an electric current, are the people of Istanbul themselves, Turks.

And they are neither Eastern nor Western. How, after such a history, could they possibly be just one or the other? Whenever I walked among the tens of thousands of Istanbuliots who streamed along the street such distinctions didn't seem to make any sense at all.

These were people who've become as we've all become – borrowers and adaptors, assimilators and synthesizers of every trend that circles the globe. They were both Eastern and Western at the same time. There were young Kurdish shoeshine boys, smart, skinny street-kids whom I might have labelled 'non-Western'. Then they offered me a shoeshine with a guarantee – three days or ten kilometres, whichever came first. There were pretty, dark Turkish girls who you could have dressed in chadors or head-scarves and called Eastern. But they were wearing low-riders and silver jewellery in their belly-buttons. Printed on their T-shirts were Western, in-your-face messages I'd never even seen in the West: '100‰ Hetero'; 'Give Me More'; 'Fabulous Cleavage Under Kit'.

They were part of a constant parade of Turks in whom you could sense a near-infinite genetic mix – it stretched one way through the Balkans and the other way to the Tartar Steppes and a third way through time itself as far as Byzantium. There were a hundred different shapes of eye, tints of hair, curves of cheekbone and nostril. But these were Turks in whom variety went far beyond mere natural selection – they had also made selections from a near-infinite range of big-city lives and lifestyles.

Under sumptuary law in classic Ottoman times each community had worn dress distinguishing it from the other – ethnic Turks wore yellow slippers and red trousers, Greeks black slippers and black trousers, Armenians violet slippers and purple trousers, and so on. Now the ethnic distinctions were gone, replaced by more subtle gradations of cultural difference. Some revolved around bleak questions of survival – even I could spot the newly-arrived migrant job-seeker with his three-day beard and cheap suit. But the Beyoglu side of the Horn tends, as it always has, to sophistication and complexity – there is no part of Istanbul culture as intricate as those sub-genres of youth-culture whose every piece of dress, language and gesture is still part of a code you have to know how to read. Outside certain Beyoglu bars there were people with big Adam's apples, five o'clock shadow and dresses every bit as gorgeous as the ones worn by the ladies opposite Saint-Benoît. But beyond that particular bit of deciphering I was quickly out of my depth.

No matter. Istanbul had a place for everyone, and I soon made myself comfortable on Istiklal Cadessi and the side-streets that run off it. When Mustafa Kemal proclaimed a republic in 1923 thousands of Beyoglu homes were abandoned by departing Greeks and other minorities. Stuck in legal limbo, some of Istanbul's finest 19th-century architecture was left to rot. There are still blocks of buildings with dark, grimy windows and refuse-covered doorsills, but today their ownership is being renegotiated and all over the quarter smart new art galleries, cafés, bars and clubs are springing up. The after-dark crowds of Beyoglu are even more mixed than the daytime shoppers they replace. It doesn't matter what their varied origins or lifestyles are. It doesn't matter that Beyoglu no longer proclaims itself ultra-select. When drinkers and diners and night-time strollers invade the quarter they invest it with garrulous sociability – they bring back much of the Mediterranean passion and *joie de vivre* it knew a century ago.

And so amidst the outdoor tables that cluttered street after narrow street, surrounded by fish dinners and spreads of *mezze* and waiters rushing to replenish glasses of cold beer, I joined them. With Florent I discovered obscure bars – kitsch, over-the-top places frequented by a hip, arty crowd. With Farida I explored restaurants in Cihangir, a bohemian quarter of antique shops, elderly ladies feeding stray cats, and some of Istanbul's last wooden houses. Along with a couple of hundred admirers of the avant-garde I went with French friends to watch a local dance performance – it was so experimental I didn't understand a thing. A few nights later, on the other hand, I was sitting sipping raki on a sidewalk terrace when not far away at a dinner-table a woman began to sing. It was a slow, sad dirge – it was sung in Turkish but was so poignant, so expressive of the losses and laments known to everyone, that it needed no translation at all. The entire street was held in silent thrall and everyone had goose-bumps, including me.

One evening I spent closer to home, in front of a stage set up at the foot of the Galata Tower. A local music group had laid on a free concert. It was as if an Irish rock band had met a Sufi mystic's ensemble head on – the music was an indefinable mix, somehow wholly familiar and utterly strange at the same time. But I had no problem recognising the atmosphere that along with circling seagulls drifted around the spot-lit tower. It was relaxed, sophisticated and tolerant. Spectators lounged on benches, enjoying the cool evening air after the heat of the day. Children played amid sleeping dogs. A young couple, wholly absorbed in each other and oblivious to the world outside, twirled slowly in each other's arms in front of the stage. Was the 800-year-old tower, symbol of a long co-existence, casting around itself some sort of urbane and harmonious influence? The Istanbul that lay below was a cosmopolitan, welcoming place, and I decided I would have no difficulty spending a lifetime there.

But the harmony, I knew, was deceptive. You only had to listen to other voices calling from beyond the tower. Some Turks were knocking hard at the door of Europe; other Turks were urging them to stop and turn back to Islamic ways. East and West, new and old, did not always lie so easily together – all around were other Istanbuls where conflicting strains and tensions were pulling hard in opposite directions. I lay awake a long time in bed that night, watching the seagulls circling the tower through my window and wondering how far its benign influence really extended.

Thirty-Nine

A day or two later I met a man so pulled by those conflicting strains that they had virtually brought him to a halt. Bekir Cantemir was chief researcher at the *Beyoğlu Arastirmalon Merkezi* – the Beyoglu Municipal Research Centre. It sounded imposing enough, but titles were the most impressive thing about the entire operation. Apart from the polished brass plaque at the door of a building just off Istiklal Cadessi, the place had little to boast of: three narrow floors of mostly bare office space, a few sticks of furniture, a telephone and a handful of staff-members with little to occupy them.

I'd gone there on a wild goose-chase. I was hoping to find an Armenian Turk I'd met at a bus stop on Taksim Square. Waiting together, we'd begun to chat and he had intrigued me immediately. Elderly, a small man with sharp, bright eyes, he was a Catholic priest.

He'd been born in Istanbul, grew up in an Armenian monastery in Vienna, and spent a difficult life in voluntary exile abroad – like Jews in Germany a generation later, few Armenians after the great slaughters of 1915 chose to remain in Turkey. Recently, he'd said, he'd finally returned to Istanbul to serve his church as he'd always wanted.

If anyone could tell me about a once-cosmopolitan world attempting to reconstruct itself it was people like this. But before I could ask his name his bus had arrived and he'd been swept off. All I knew was that he officiated in a church in Beyoglu. That didn't make it any easier – if there are few Armenians left in the city there are many Armenian churches. No one

I'd spoken to had heard of him. Shrugging his shoulders, one priest had suggested I try the Beyoglu Research Centre.

So now I found myself on a midweek morning in front of three men idly gathered around a desk. Ferruk Arslan, director of the Centre, was a large, powerfully-built man with a broad forehead and a bristly walrus moustache. Even inactive, he radiated physical energy and enthusiasm. Bekir Cantemir was his clever, over-qualified, under-employed right-hand man. Slighter, younger, he was more cerebral than Ferruk – his graduate thesis for the University of the Bosphorus had been an analysis of the Ottoman conception of time. On his dark face there was always a troubled look of polite scepticism, as if he badly wanted to believe but could always find a reason not to. The third man was yet one more Mehmet. He was sharp and quick, but often there was nothing on his face at all – you could feel ennui, an immense, crashing boredom, radiating from him in waves.

No one in the room was about to set an employee-of-the-month performance record. Currently the main interest in the office seemed to be a basil plant sitting in a pot on the desk. Ferruk had bought it at a street cart on the way to work that morning. Turks enjoy greenery and fragrance, and things like basil plants are small treats. Every couple of minutes Mehmet would drape his prayer beads over the rounded top of the plant, taking several runs through the aromatic leaves before languidly sniffing at the beads. Ferruk would occasionally pause in mid-conversation, drop his nose to the plant and take a deep lungful of air. Bekir would run his hands over it, patting delicately as he went, then smooth them over his hair.

'You must smell,' he said when he noticed my curious staring. 'Is it not delicious?' I inhaled and pleased Bekir by agreeing that it was delicious. But I could hardly believe that three grown, educated men were entirely happy to spend their professional careers sitting around sniffing at greenery. There had to be an explanation, and slowly, as I got to know them better over several visits, they gave it to me.

The Research Centre was an office set up and funded by Beyoglu's city hall. 'It is a wonderful project,' said Bekir. 'We are supposed to be

313

collecting the social memory of Beyoglu.' No other place in Turkey, after all, had the same complex, cosmopolitan history. And Ferruk and Bekir had devised many projects to keep that memory alive – everything from archival research facilities to minority language lessons and recitals of traditional Pera music. The Centre had been intended as a hands-on repository of a multi-ethnic Turkey – the basis of Beyoglu's existence under Ottoman rule.

And there lay the problem. I had been in Izmir when elections had brought AK, the conservative Justice and Development party, to power in municipalities throughout Turkey. It had brought them to power in Beyoglu, too. And no matter how far away AK claimed to have moved from its radical Islamist roots, a multi-ethnic Turkey was not part of its vision. AK was more interested in garbage collection than cultural collection, and it had cut back drastically on the research bureau's funding. The whole enterprise was barely limping along. 'Look at our library,' Bekir said gloomily. In the bookshelves above Ferruk's head there were less than a dozen volumes.

But that didn't stop the Beyoglu Municipal Research Centre from searching for a missing person. Ferruk spoke little English and Ahmed none at all, but Bekir conferred with them, explaining my problem. They would be happy to help me, he said; Ferruk knew everyone in Beyoglu, including its Christians. It might take a day or two to trace the Armenian priest. Would I, in the meanwhile, like to join them for a glass of tea?

And so began a string of mornings in which I would sit around sipping tea, patting the basil plant and discussing the world with Bekir and his colleagues. And for them the world, not surprisingly, had Turkey at its centre – what concerned them most was the way it was changing as the opposing forces of globalisation and Islam bit ever deeper all around them.

We circled each other a little warily at first. Turkish politics are complicated, emotional, sometimes dangerous and never, even in friendly conversation, entered into lightly. Turks take their political engagements personally and passionately.

And no wonder: just eighty years ago a radical moderniser had turned an old dynastic world upside down virtually overnight. Suddenly the fez was banned, Arabic script went out the window and Atatürk was foxtrotting around ballroom floors in Western evening wear. Suddenly Turkish women were given the vote years before it came to their French or Italian sisters. All this was dramatic enough. But at the heart of Atatürk's revolution lay two principles that shattered the foundation of Ottoman thought. The first was that all Turkish nationals were only that, Turkish nationals, with no claim to any kind of subsidiary ethnic identity. The second was that religion had no part to play in the public life of a democracy. Few countries have taken a gamble on such rapid and thorough transformation, and the world has watched the Turkish experiment with fascination ever since.

It hasn't always worked smoothly. The Kurds, the country's largest minority, have never been persuaded that they are Turks like any others. And while secular democracy has created a wealthy, Westernised middle-class, the god of Islam will not go away; a much larger number of Turks, left far behind and feeling resentful, look to religion for an answer. Sometimes the debate grows hot and heavy – in the last half-century the military, invoking the spirit of Atatürk, have stepped in numerous times to dispense to both radical left and religious right some heavy-handed guidance in the ways of democracy.

Turkish politics flip-flop in all directions, and my new friends had flip-flopped with them. In his socialist youth Ferruk Arslan had been imprisoned, and the other two had been left-wing activists. But now all that was over. To me the greatest irony in the AK's disapproval of the Beyoglu Research Bureau was that all three of these men had now become fervent, practising Muslims. The only time we stopped talking was when they removed their shoes, pushed back the office furniture, and prostrated themselves in the direction of Mecca.

I was taken aback. Ferruk, Bekir and Mehmet had nothing to do with the skull-capped imams I'd heard preaching at Friday prayers in Alexandria. They shared nothing with the peasant-farmers I'd watched emerging from dusty, clay-built mosques in small-town Anatolia. They were modern and educated and they'd undertaken the job of preserving Turkey's cosmopolitan past. But at the same time they were unhappy with the direction the country was heading in.

'Do I surprise you?' Bekir asked me one day. 'Can I not believe in democracy and Islam at the same time? In the West you are free to proclaim your religion if you like, as you are free to proclaim your ethnicity. Can't Turks do the same?'

What worried Bekir as much as a disregard for the Turkish past was what he saw as a misappropriation of its future. The more that Turkey became part of the larger world the less control ordinary Turks had over their own lives. For them, he insisted, things were not becoming easier, but harder.

'You've seen the Bosphorus, the beautiful 10 per cent of Istanbul – have you seen how the other 90 per cent of the city lives?' he asked me. 'Every day Ferruk, Mehmet and I sit here debating globalisation, Westernisation, big business, power and profit. Of course Turks want to open up to the world – they have been excluded for a long time. But do you think joining Europe will solve our problems? Europe cannot solve its own problems. Social engineering is not enough. We need social justice.'

I liked Bekir, and at the same time he perplexed me. He was serious and principled and believed in the need for redress in the world. He had none of the bigot's zealous faith in dogma. But sometimes I thought his idealism hid a deeper fundamentalist streak. One day I asked him if he considered himself an Islamist.

The question made him smile. 'Once I used to dream of a truly egalitarian Turkey.' he said. 'No more. Now I think, Islamist or socialist, it's all the same. The socialists put the people's money into the left-hand pocket. The Islamists put the people's money into the right-hand pocket. It all goes to the same place – to politicians who use power to lead lives of privilege and wealth.' He paused and his tone grew a little wistful. 'What I am,' he said, 'is a Muslim utopian. I am content to believe in ideals that cannot be put into practice. At least not now.'

These were the kinds of discussions we returned to day after day and it wasn't long before I was feeling as befuddled and batted about as the poor basil plant on the table between us.

One afternoon when Bekir and I stepped out of the office our conversation took a more personal turn. If he could pay more rent, Bekir told me as we sat in a sweet-shop eating plates of halva, nothing could induce him to stay on in Gaziosmanspaşa, the distant western suburb where he and his wife and baby daughter lived.

It was a poor place with few jobs and much frustration. Bekir and his family lived in an apartment, a fifth-floor walk-up that was cramped and hot and noisy. There was no water for most of the day. Bekir wanted to move to a better suburb on the far side of the Bosporus. He would have liked a car so he and his family could escape the city on weekends. And what he really daydreamed about, he confided, was a plot of land in the country where one day he could start an organic fruit and vegetable farm. He shrugged his shoulders – it was just a dream, he said. Muslim utopian or not, Bekir that afternoon seemed to me pretty much like all the rest of us.

The only things he really valued in his apartment were his books. He housed them in custom-built, glass-fronted wooden bookcases. 'You cannot buy bookshelves in Gaziosmanspaşa. I had to have them made,' he told me ruefully. 'Nobody where I live reads. We work if there's work available, we watch television, and we sleep.'

I asked him about the books. He had Islamic histories and sets of religious encyclopaedias printed in Turkish. But for years he'd combed through the flea-markets and second-hand bookstores of Istanbul and also had a surprising number of Western books in English. They included a collection of Marx and volumes by Foucault, Edward Gibbon and Bertrand Russell.

He was especially attached to his works by Marx. 'A great man, a great philosopher,' he said almost fondly as we spooned up sweet semolina patterned with swirls of bright green pistachio. 'In his economic interpretation of history he was the last great spirit in the West to have a complete world-view.'

'Hang on,' I said. 'That's a bit much. Don't you think there have been other thinkers since Marx who ...'

Bekir raised his spoon to stop me.

'It's nothing against the West,' he said conciliatingly. 'We are no more productive of new thought in the East. The last really original Muslim thinker lived 500 years ago. But that's OK. I enjoy him as much as Marx.'

We talked about political extremism and Turkey's frequent recourse to military rule. We talked about Islamists, socialists, communists, nationalists, Kemalists, syndicalists, neo-fascists and Kurdish separatists – all of them active in Istanbul politics. It was hectic and muddled, but Bekir believed that the Turkish obsession with ideology would eventually lead somewhere.

'Positive change will come out of it one day, I am sure, ' he said. 'If the East is merely in the same game as the West, then the only thing that counts anywhere is power and money. But we have other things to offer. If we can contribute our own learning, what will perhaps emerge is a global society, prosperous, but also guided by two things it now lacks – ethics and judgement.'

I had to sit and think about that for a while. I wasn't a Marxist and I wasn't a Muslim, but Bekir was trying to say something important about the way he saw complex and apparently contradictory ideas coming together to produce new ways of thinking.

In the meantime, though, even simple contradictions were enough to slow Bekir to a halt. He was attracted to Western democratic institutions but appalled by the economic excess and greed that came with them. He was enticed by the social justice preached by Islam but repelled by its lack of intellectual freedom. He couldn't give himself entirely to either. In the end, it seemed to me, Bekir was a reflection of something larger – Istanbul itself.

What was an outsider to make of it, this port-city of political ferment and uncertain direction? No one could know the soul of any metropolis after a few weeks' mere strolling around. But at least you could get a working notion of places like Alexandria and Venice. Both were cities of the past. One, ignoring its historical resources, was being swallowed up by it. The other had done something altogether neater – by trading on its past it was holding it at bay.

Istanbul, though, was different. It did not belong to the past alone. It was too vibrant a city, too full of energy and dynamic possibility. It had changed before and it would change again. But it was hard to see which way it was going. There were plenty of signposts indicating the way to Istanbul's future; the problem was that they were pointing in every possible direction. And Bekir was only adding to my confusion. Each time I walked out of the Beyoglu Research Centre I felt more confused about Istanbul than when I walked in.

Forty

Crash courses in Turkish politics are taxing, and I often felt the need for a quiet place to let things settle. I found it on the Bosphorus just five minutes' walk down the hill from Saint-Benoît.

The Nusretiye, or Victory, Mosque, was clean and peaceful, and even on the warmest afternoon refreshingly cool. I doubt that another tourist had set foot in it for ages. It was a tenth of the size of the Blue Mosque, and squeezed into an old complex of customs buildings not far from the Prince's Islands ferry pier. Outside, endless streams of traffic moved slowly to and from the Galata Bridge on both road and waterways. Inside, seated on the floor beneath a high dome, I had all the calm and open space I needed. The only traffic here came in one concentrated rush, for afternoon prayers, and the muzzein's call to prayer gave me plenty of time to get out of the way.

I liked the mosque for the comfort of lolling about shoeless on a vast expanse of red carpet. But I also liked it because the place sat there like an answer, a concrete resolution of the perplexing contradictions that not just Bekir Cantemir, but the entire city, had thrown up for me.

One had to, granted, overlook the Victory Mosque's original inspiration. Raised long after the great age of Ottoman mosque-building was over, it commemorated a later Sultan's grisly triumph over his own Janissary troops. So resentful were they of the European-style modernisation being imposed on the military, so undisciplined and rebellious had they grown inside the shaky empire, that in 1826 Sultan Mahmud II oversaw the brutal hunting down and extermination of some 5,000 of his elite corps. With their final disbanding, he heaved a sigh of relief and christened the massacre the 'Blessed Event'.

But there was no hint of dissolution about the building itself – it was an extraordinary synthesis. By that point Western influence in Constantinople had become so pronounced that the mosque's builder had decided on a complete blending of what had become two interdependent traditions. Gone were the austere lines and perfect circles, symbolic of the Islamic infinite, once employed by Sinan, the empire's greatest architect. Instead, like tulip stems growing from their bulbs, minarets grew out of globular, fleshily-rounded stone bases. Pepper-pot towers stood above domes whose lower edges were scalloped into undulating waves. Mullioned windows emerged from curved walls like the poops of Spanish galleons. It was a mosque out of a fevered dream. It was organic, baroque and sensual, a bizarre but happy mix of Islamic asceticism and Counter-Reformation exuberance. It was Santiago de Compostella gone to Mecca.

The builder of the Victory Mosque had been as sophisticated a mix as his creation. Krikor Balian came from a long line of architects serving the Ottoman sultans. From the early 1700s on into the 1900s the Balian family had, generation after generation, changed the face of Constantinople. They built vast palaces, theatres, schools, military barracks, hunting lodges and kiosks – most of the royal architecture, in fact, that can be seen along the Bosphorus today. And they did it in an eclectic, international style. Imperial builders, they were not Turks, but members of one of the most accomplished of Ottoman ethnic minorities, the Armenians.

The Balians intrigued me because they were representative of a cosmopolitan strain present throughout minority groups in the city. From the early 1600s Armenians had arrived in Constantinople in large numbers from eastern Anatolia. They had begun as broom-makers and porters, risen through commercial trade, and a century later attained some of the highest posts in the empire. Architecture aside, they replaced Jews as the city's chief bankers. One Armenian family, the Duzians, were appointed superintendents of the royal mint and kept the post for more than a century. Granted the Ottoman privilege of wearing quilted turbans and riding horses in the city, the Armenian elite oversaw tax collection and government expenditure. They served in the professions, dominated the customs service and became the empire's first modern industrialists – beginning as the Sultan's Chief Gunpowder Makers, the Armenian family of Hovhannes Dadian went on to supply the Ottoman Grand Armies with most of their needs, manufacturing everything from belts and boots to heavy ordnance.

One of Christianity's easternmost peoples, the Armenians were among the empire's most active propagators of Western culture. Ethnic Turks themselves had less interest in trade and the wider contact it brought – they excelled at war, bureaucracy and peasant farming. But the range of minorities promoting exchange between the Ottomans and the rest of the world was as wide as their field of conquest. And like the Armenians, other mercantile minorities not only made up the commercial backbone of empire, but also attained its highest posts.

I'd heard the story, for example, of Constantinople's Jews, a rare and happy one on a continent where violent anti-Semitism was pervasive. Bringing with them expertise in trade, finance, medicine and law when they were evicted from 15th-century Spain, many Jews rose to prominence in imperial service. Chased from Castile in 1492, the Nasis, to name one prominent family, faced continued exclusion as they moved over the next three decades from Portugal to Antwerp and on to Venice, originator of Europe's Jewish ghettos. Joseph Nasi's final move to Constantinople in the mid-1500s changed his fortunes. Developing interests in banking and trade, he became a supplier of both cash and wine to Prince Selim, heir to the throne. On becoming sultan, Selim awarded him the rule of Naxos, a Greek island wrested from Venetian hands and still occupied by a Catholic landowning nobility. Great must have been Joseph Nasi's satisfaction, after a lifetime of humiliation in Christian Europe, to be able at last to call his own tune there.

Or what about Alexander Mavrocordato, an Orthodox Greek born in Constantinople 100 years later? The Greeks were renowned as the craftiest, hardest-driving merchants in the entire empire; Mavrocordato turned out to be one of its finest diplomats. The first of the city's inhabitants to be sent for an education in Western Europe, he became a physician, a scholar and Grand Logothete in the Greek Patriarchate. His talent with languages soon ensured his promotion to Grand Dragoman. As the Sublime Porte's chief interpreter, he played a vital role in imperial foreign relations. When the Ottomans failed to storm the gates of Vienna at the end of the 1600s it was Mavrocordato who with consummate skill engineered a peace with the Habsburgs – with great tact he made each empire believe that a submissive entreaty for negotiation had been the initiative of the other.

Alexander's son Nicholas, also a Grand Dragoman and fluent in seven languages, went on to assume the throne of Wallachia, an Orthodox Ottoman principality in the Balkans. Like many other prominent ethnic-minority families, the Mavrocordatos had no qualms in serving an imperial master as long as it advanced their personal and community interests. Whether as Greeks, Ottomans or Wallachians, they played whatever card suited them, and sometimes two or more at once. As cosmopolitans, nationality was for them more a professional than a political choice. Possessors of several identities, they would have seen that later historical phenomenon, aggressive and undivided allegiance to a single nation, as limiting and pointless.

All this, of course, took place long before Ottoman institutions had grown rotten to the core, before calls for nationalist insurgence began making violent inroads into the multicultural state. After the Greek revolt the hundreds of thousands of Greeks who remained inside the empire never regarded it in the same way. After the great massacres of civilians in eastern Anatolia during the First World War, Turkish Armenians lost faith in their very survival, much less the possibilities of a larger identity shared with Turks.

In the end nationalist conflicts between the Ottomans and their Greek, Armenian, Serb, Arab and other minorities finished off the empire. Now, as I sat on the carpet beneath a dome that was neither Baroque nor Islamic but both, a question came to mind. What would the Balians or the Mavrocordatos make of today's efforts to build a globalised, multi-national world once again? I couldn't ask them, but the thought occurred to me that I could still ask their cultural descendents. If the Beyoglu Research Centre had as yet failed to trace down one elderly Armenian priest, they had other cosmopolitans on tap.

A day later I was knocking on the door of an upper-floor apartment in the steep streets of Beyoglu below Taksim Square. The man who answered was thin and bald and wore heavy-framed glasses. A springy mass of grey beard tumbled over his chest. He held one hand awkwardly in front of himself, and walked with a limp.

'Partial paralysis of the left side – a recent stroke,' he said, leading me into a living room where books, papers and newspaper cuttings cluttered every surface. 'I've had to stop the cigarettes altogether – four packets a day nearly killed me. But I don't want to slow down too much on anything else.'

I could see he meant it. He was a writer bursting with projects, some nearing completion, some well under way, others just taking shape. On a coffee table lay his most recently published book – a thick tome, full of grainy photographs, on the history of Turkish cinema. On the computer screen where he'd been working was the text of one of the three novels he was currently writing.

'And I'm just planning a new collection, short stories of macabre fantasy. I'm calling it *Beyoglu Nightmares*. What do you think?'

What I thought was that Giovanni Scognamillo had more energy and ideas fizzling in his head than most writers half his age. I asked if he thought of himself as a Turkish or Italian writer.

'I write just as easily in either language,' he reflected. 'But as to whether one is more mine than the other...'

He shrugged a shoulder. 'My grandfather was a Neapolitan chef. My mother's family was Greek, but originally came from Genoa. My parents were born here. I was born here. I'm Levantine.

'A lot of people like me don't like the term Levantine. Do you know why? In their minds it's another word for shifty – it's a label attached to someone who cannot be trusted. But I am Levantine, the product of Western Europeans long settled in the East. I don't have a problem with it.'

I, for one, I told Scognamillo, was having plenty of problems. I couldn't get a grip on things in Istanbul. I was confused about the city's cosmopolitan identity, about where it was heading. It seemed to have had one character under the Ottomans, another under Atatürk's republic, and now, as Turkey took up with the wider world, it appeared to be changing again.

'Ah,' said Scognamillo, wagging his beard. 'That's something different, a much larger problem. You're not alone. Every Istanbuliot has the same problem. *I* have the same problem. Some years ago a few fellow-writers and I got together and started a city magazine called *Identity*. But when we got going we realized there's almost nothing in Istanbul that *isn't* a question of identity. So we started to write about everything and anything – impossible, of course – and the magazine soon folded. The city still confuses me.'

I followed the writer into a tiny kitchen where he prepared coffee so black and strong I started worrying about my own heart. As he rattled cups and saucers I asked him about his interest in Turkish cinema.

'Oh, I've been writing about Turkish films for some while,' he said with a smile. 'I began in 1948 and I'm still at it. My veins are probably made of celluloid by now.'

It had all come naturally, he said. His father had been an importer and distributor of foreign films, and his uncle the owner of a cinema. He virtually grew up in front of a movie screen. He had started as a correspondent for the Italian film press and a decade later, writing for an Istanbul newspaper, become one of the city's most-read film critics.

'Those were busy days in cinema,' he said as I carried a loaded tray out. 'All through the 1960s Turkey was making 180 to 250 films a year. I'm not saying every one was a masterpiece – a lot were B movies. But the industry was thriving, everyone went to the cinema, and it gave Turks a channel for expression they don't have today.'

'Don't Turks watch Turkish films now?'

'Some do. There are some world-quality Turkish directors these days, but only about fifteen Turkish films a year come onto the market. There used to be small independent cinemas in every town and suburb, but they've almost all disappeared. When American studio distributors push 250 copies of the same film into Turkey it is difficult for small movie-makers and small cinemas to survive.'

'Is that what globalisation means for Turkey?'

He sipped coffee and thought about it. 'It means that Turks don't have much choice about becoming more and more like everyone else. It's an inevitable part of the process. When I was younger I used to sell European advertising through the Turkish film distribution system. I stopped it. Why encourage people to buy things they don't need and then work harder and longer to pay for them? They could be enjoying themselves at the movies instead.

'At least at the cinema you are sharing something with the other people there. With computers we are learning to live on our own. Istanbul is still a place where the tradition of close relations with relatives and neighbours is strong. In this building I can ring the bell at any door on any floor – the whole apartment block is one big family I can count on. There is solidarity, communication, participation. Once I was offered a very good job in London, but I soon came back. That kind of exchange has disappeared in other places. It is beginning to disappear here, too.'

We drank coffee. We discussed Beyoglu's once-famous courtesans, the subject of another book the author had written. We watched a torrential summer downpour turn the steep streets outside into raging spates. And when in due course the rain was over and I was at the door shaking his hand, the writer had a last word to say on globalisation. Honest Levantine that he was, Giovanni Scognamillo did not want to leave false impressions.

'I know that many negative changes are on their way to Istanbul,' he said. 'But look.' He lifted his useless arm. 'I can no longer cope with a manual typewriter. So at the same time I am very grateful to my computer. How could I write my friends and colleagues if it weren't for e-mails?

How could I compose *Beyoglu Nightmares* without a word processor? So I have to admit there are good things that come with change, too. Maybe it doesn't matter if it's the cinema or the computer. Maybe it depends on how these things are used.'

It was hardly a ringing and unqualified endorsement of the global community. Were other Istanbuliots as skeptical as the Italian Turk? The next morning I was at a door in the Syrian Passage, a covered sidestreet off Istiklal Cadessi. Inside, a Greek Turk named Mihaïl Vasiliadis was putting together *Apoyevmatini,* one of the last two last Greek-language newspapers in Istanbul.

Computer technology had not yet come to *Apoyevmatini.* Vasiliadis, his thinning hair slicked away from his forehead, his sleeves rolled up, was leaning forward over a back-lit, plastic-topped counter and laying out his pages with scissors and paste.

'I am a one-man show – I am everything from editor to tea-boy,' he said grinning as I gazed around the two small, bare rooms where he produced the paper every day. 'The only thing I don't have is an editor's or a tea-boy's salary. I don't have any salary at all. Still, the paper keeps going. When I arrived circulation was down to eighty copies a day, the lowest in its eighty-year history. Now we're back up to 500.'

Eighty years, I began to see as we chatted, was nothing in the Vasiliadis time-scale. Even the sack of Constantinople was a relatively recent event in his view.

'To mark the 800th anniversary of the event, the Pope apologised for the greatest disaster ever to hit this city,' said Vasiliadis. 'That's fine. We accept his apology. We do not bear a grudge.'

But Vasiliadis's own family predated the sack by a thousand years. 'My mother's people were not from here. They were Greeks from Macedonia – very tough, very authoritarian. But my father's family!...' He blew out his cheeks and threw up his hand as if even attempting to count the years spent here were useless. 'They were on the Pontic even before the Greeks founded the Pontic Empire. You'd have to go back almost to Adam to find their roots.'

And that was why, he told me as he carefully cut and fitted small bits of paper together, it was important to remember history. All of it – the disasters, the wars, the bloodshed. If he wanted to preserve the past it was not for the sake of revenge, he said, but to remember its lessons. And remembering sometimes came at a high price.

In 1964 Vasiliadis had been sports editor at the Greek Istanbul newspaper *Eleftherifoni* when it was taken to court for an article it had published on Greek Orthodox minority rights in Turkey. The owner of the paper escaped to Greece. Vasiliadis, who remained, was charged with making propaganda and attacking Turkish national unity.

'The trial lasted ten years,' the editor said wearily. 'Ten years! Two times I was acquitted, and two times the Turkish government brought the same charges against me. Finally, on the third adjudication, I was acquitted for good. I left for Athens and stayed there for twenty-six years.'

'Why bother coming back?'

'Because a century ago our community numbered 200,000. Because today there are only 2,000 ethnic Greeks left in all of Turkey and only 700 left in Istanbul. If we don't make the effort to keep our language alive and our community connected the numbers will dwindle to nothing. Without things like this paper we will disappear.'

Was the task easier or more difficult, I asked, than it was back in the 1960s?

'Oh, it's much better now. Turkey is getting closer to Europe all the time. That is not because the Europeans accept and welcome Turkish culture, but because the Turks accept to become more like Europeans. And one thing Europe demands is the protection of minority rights. When Turkey learns to accept its own minorities, then it, too, will be accepted as a minority.'

So overall, I suggested, globalisation was moving things in a positive direction.

'Perhaps not,' Vasiliadis replied, removing his mock-up from the counter and inspecting it beneath the room's fluorescent lighting. 'It's becoming harder to hold any small community together these days. We

Greeks have bad teachers right in our living rooms – our televisions. They tell our people to do the opposite of what our traditions tells us. Action movies, MTV, narcotics, sex, one generation set against another – none of these are going to help the last Greek Orthodox families of Istanbul.'

And was there nothing, I asked, to fight back with?

'Of course. There is a very old, very powerful weapon against all cultural transformation,' the editor said. 'It is the manipulation of race and religion by violent extremists. And we have all seen what it can do. When you are faced with two evils you choose the lesser. So we watch Pamela Anderson.'

Here, then, was one more doubter, another man not entirely convinced of the benefits of an ever smaller and more connected world. Mihaïl Vasiliadis left the office to take the day's edition of *Apoyevmatini* to the printer's, and I strolled back to Bekir Cantemir wondering if Istanbul really had any cosmopolitan future at all.

'Good news!' said Bekir over a now mangled and fast-wilting basil plant. 'Ferruk has found your priest. His name is Father Aygaram and he can be found at the Saint John Crysostome Armenian Church. He holds a communion service there every day and a full mass on Sundays. I hope he can tell you what you want to know.'

There was deep silence when I slipped in through the doors of the church the next morning. Not far from the Palais de France in old Pera, it was an elegant building, the dome over its apse decorated in glowing blue and gold. There were columns with imitation marble veining, a crowned Christ over the altar, and a crystal chandelier hanging from a great height. It wasn't lit, but instead caught the rays of morning sun that penetrated the church's tinted windows. Every piece of glass scintillated. The only thing missing was a congregation. There wasn't a single church-goer in Saint John Crysostome to take part in Father Aygaram's service.

But there was the man I had met on Taksim Square, the small priest with the sharp, bright eyes. Alone in the midst of all this splendour, he looked smaller still. He stood at a side-chapel beneath an oil-painted Pieta whose Virgin Mary bore a raised heart of embossed silver. He paid no attention to the empty church behind him, but, back turned to the pews, proceeded with a communion at which he was the only celebrant. Dressed in a white robe with a high collar and a gold cross embroidered on its back, he read in a firm, strong voice from an Armenian text sitting on an altar. He polished chalices, poured wine, broke and offered himself the host with all the decorum of a man officiating before a great crowd.

I thought he was magnificent, more impressive in his own way than Krikor Balian himself. Here was a man who'd been isolated from his community all his life. He had returned to serve a church so decimated by a bloody, genocidal past that not a single worshipper had turned up for a weekday service. And yet he carried on regardless, so persistent in his own conviction, sure enough in the spirit if not the substance of his people, that he considered the whole effort worthwhile. If this man could start trying to rebuild a once flourishing, multicultural world in which community identity was the touchstone, then anyone could. Without asking anything, I stole quietly out of the church before the service was over. Father Aygaram had answered my questions without having to say a word.

Forty-One

B arrel-chested Ferruk Arslan, I discovered, had two passions. One was the history of Beyoglu. The other was fishing.

I discovered this on a Monday morning when I was telling Bekir about the fishermen I'd seen on the Galata Bridge the day before. On weekends it isn't just the bars and restaurants on the bridge's lower level that fill to capacity. The sidewalks on each side of the tarmac above them get crowded, too. From early morning until after sunset the bridge bristles with fishing rods. Istanbuliots are among the most enthusiastic big-city catchers of small fish in the world. It isn't just the urban poor seeking inexpensive leisure who indulge – all sorts of people stand elbow to elbow at the bridge railing each weekend. Nor are they put off by the modest size of the catches on offer at the mouth of the Golden Horn. The little creatures they collect in bowls and plastic tubs to take home alive are scad, a saltwater fish also known as horse mackerel. Sea-going tiddlers, they measure between four and six inches each.

Nobody cares. When scad are running up the Bosphorus from the Mediterranean to the Black Sea you can haul up half a dozen on a multi-hooked line at one time. Watching little fish rise wriggling and flashing, one after another, only to mysteriously disappear into the heavens above is one of the privileges of the beer-drinkers lounging on the level below. There had been so many fishermen on Sunday afternoon that as I crossed the bridge I'd made a count – there were 327 of them on my side of the bridge alone, and at least as many on the other.

'Just imagine,' I was saying to Bekir as we sat over glasses of tea with Ferruk and Mehmet the next morning, 'that's about 650 people on the bridge fishing for scad.'

Ferruk, who usually sat through our conversations impassive and understanding nothing until Bekir made a translation, suddenly sat up.

'Scad,' he said, beaming. 'English, scad. Turkish, "*istavrit*." Latin, "*trachurus trachurus.*"'

Ferruk seemed to be a linguistic master when it came to fishing.

'How about mullet?' I said, testing him.

'English, red mullet. Turkish, "*barbunya*". Latin, "*mullus barbatus.*"'

This was astonishing. 'What about "lure"?' ' I said, switching to fishing tackle in a effort to throw him. 'Do you know what a lure is?'

'Lure!' he crowed. 'Red Devil, Mister Twister, Shad Rap, Silver Minnow, William's Wobbler, Rappala Husky Jerk, Blue Fox Super Vibrax Spinner, Bionic Bait Jig Combo...'

'Ferruk!' I said, interrupting a non-stop flow, 'You're an expert!' His face broke into a wide grin. If I hadn't stopped him he might have gone on forever.

It turned out he really was an expert – there was little Ferruk didn't know about Mediterranean fishing. If he knew English fishing terms it was because he corresponded with various scientific fishing research institutes and had a fishing library much larger than the Beyoglu Research Centre's cultural library. But his interests weren't just academic. Ferruk had actually built ancient Mediterranean fishing craft. He had experimented with antique methods of fish-netting and trapping known in classical times. And he loved to eat fish and seafood – Ferruk caught and consumed everything that finned, wriggled or crawled its way about the water.

Was there something hidden deep in his genetic memory? Ferruk wasn't descended from the horse-riding plainsmen of the Asian steppe. His ancestors were true Mediterraneans, shore dwellers from the coast of Albania. Whatever it was, his enthusiasm was infectious. Through Bekir we talked fish for half the morning, and by 11 o'clock he had set me up with a fishing trip.

He had wanted to send me to join the fishing fleet down on the Turkish Mediterranean coast, for it was now swordfishing season there. 'Big fish,' he said, holding his arm in front of his nose and making a spear of it. But that would mean an outing lasting at least a couple of weeks, and it was more time than I had. In the end Ferruk telephoned Ismail and Mumtaz, both friends of his and assistant managers at Istanbul's wholesale fish market. I was going fishing on the Sea of Marmara.

Early next afternoon I walked back over the Galata Bridge, across Seraglio Point and along the Marmara shore towards Kumkapi. There were fish everywhere – fish piled on ice in the display cases of waterfront restaurants, fish flipping in baskets beside wrinkled old men casting from the rocks. They were even fish lying fifty yards offshore in the bottom of a styrofoam shell, once protective packing for a refrigerator, today an improvised fishing boat used by two small and intrepid boys jigging with handlines.

I met Ismail and Mumtaz in an echoing hall, white-tiled and brightly-lit, where much of Istanbul's commercial catch is sold to fishmongers and restaurant owners. Workmen were hosing down floors and walls and the two assistant managers were removing the white coats that made them look like lab researchers. They were just as professional-looking in the crisp white shirts and ties that lay underneath.

I thought Ismail and Mumtaz were going to pass me on to some regular fishermen, for they were now at the end of a long workday – in Istanbul the boats arrive at two o'clock in the morning and the market opens at four. But instead they changed into old work clothes and we drove a couple of miles down the shore to a small boat-harbour. There we hopped into the *Oguz,* a 26-foot wooden vessel with a small forward cabin and a thumping diesel engine.

'Before we fished,' said Ismail.

'Now we work in an office with pens and telephones,' added Mumtaz.

'Wives and children at the weekends,' intoned Ismail.

'We miss the boats and the sea,' lamented Mumtaz.

Both looked far happier in old clothing covered in engine oil and dried fish scales than they had in their lab-coats. There was a strong breeze blowing down the Bosphorus and it whipped up their neatly combed hair and the little star-and-crescent Turkish flag blowing from the boat's bow. Mumtaz gripped the wheel and Ismail and I wedged ourselves into corners in the stern – as soon as we left the harbour the *Oguz* began ploughing into white-capped waves.

'This wind is from the north – it is called the Poyras,' Mumtaz turned back to me. With the wind singing and the engine banging away below he had to shout. 'It is the best wind for Istanbul fishermen. After blowing out of the Bosphorus it has no time or space to become rough. The other wind, the Lodos, is from the south. It is dangerous – long swells, big waves. It can sink fishing boats even in port and blow big ships onto the shore.'

I didn't mind the fresh and lively Poyras even if it was bucketing our little boat up and down. It was good to get away from the unending crowds and the heat of the street. It was good to get away, too, from all the difficult questions hanging over the city. From here Istanbul looked like what it had always been, one of the great seaports of the world. Each year 50,000 ships steered a course straight through the middle of the metropolis; slowly we were now making our way among a couple of dozen of them, moored tankers and freighters with their anchor-chains hauled tight and their bows pointed into the wind. Behind them I could see Istanbul, its minarets rising above the city, and beyond, higher still on the far side of the Bosphorus, the green hills of Anatolia.

Half an hour later we had drawn even with Yedikule, the stone-towered fortress that sits where the city's old Byzantine land-walls meet the sea. A mile offshore, Mumtaz set the *Oguz* turning in wide circles and Ismail went into the little cabin to get the equipment.

What were we going to fish for, I wondered? It wasn't going to be swordfish, but in Istanbul markets I had admired other large and handsome creatures. Was it going to be bluefish? Bonito?

Ismail came back on deck with a couple of blocks of wood around which were wound thin nylon line carrying dozens of miniscule feathered hooks. Bonito would just laugh at this kind of gear. I had the sinking feeling that I had seen this kind of equipment before.

'*Istavrit!*' smiled Ismail. 'We will catch many, many fish!'

I smiled bravely back. We might as well be jigging from floating refrigerator-packing. It was not going to be a trophy-fishing day.

But Ismail was right. There were scads of scad. We seemed to be in the middle of thick schools running intermittently for the Bosphorus. First there would be nothing, then we would be hauling line madly for a few minutes, pulling in eight or ten fish at a time. Then all would go all quiet, giving us a chance to collect the little creatures flopping about the floor of the boat. The wind blew, the boat circled beneath a bright sun, the fish came in fits and starts and I forgot our prey were scarcely larger than minnows. I was having fun. Before I knew it the afternoon had melted away and we were headed back to the harbour. At the stern of the boat lay a basket filled with hundreds of little silver fish. What were we going to do with them? To me they looked too small and bony to make eating anything but a problem. But I had not reckoned on the talents of Mumtaz and Ismail.

A few yards from where we docked the *Oguz* we set up chairs around an empty drum of heavy-duty electrical cable laid on its side. This was a working-man's harbour and the waterside looked like a marine junkyard. Around us were men fiddling over the open bonnets of their cars, men messing with outboard motors, men tinkering with fish-finders and other electrical equipment. Greasy bits of machinery and old engine parts lay scattered everywhere. There were dented barrels of marine fuel stacked on an oil-stained quay and socks and wet-weather gear strung on lines to dry. I might even have seen a rat or two climbing about some coils of old rope. As dining décor went it hardly matched the elegant fish restaurants that sat beside the water around Istanbul.

We spent half an hour gutting. It's not difficult snapping scad-heads off between your thumb and forefinger and gently pulling out their innards. After you've done four or five dozen it doesn't seem such a bad job at all. Still, I didn't think these little animals were going to make much of a meal. But from his storage shed Ismail dug out a small gas canister and ring, a frying pan and some cooking oil, and set to. Having heated and salted a good amount of oil, he quickly rolled a batch of twenty or so fish in a plate of flour before dropping them into the pan where they sat sizzling and turning gold. In the meantime Mumtaz set out a tablecloth from the pages of *Milliyet*, the Turkish daily, on the cable-drum table. From the boot of his car he returned with loaves of fresh bread, and into a tin plate he cut tomatoes, onions and dark purple shallots. There was also a cooler containing bottles of ice-cold Efes beer, and once he'd snapped off the caps of three of them we were in business.

I couldn't remember a fish dinner I'd enjoyed as much. Almost too hot to hold, we squeezed lemon juice onto the little fish, dipped them in salt, and popped them in our mouths. They were crisp outside and tender inside, and full of delicate flavour. Now I knew why so many fishermen stood on the Galata Bridge each weekend and carefully guarded their little prizes until they could carry them home still swimming. There is nothing quite as good as fresh scad you've caught and cooked yourself.

A bite of fish, a little salad, a sip of beer, a hunk of bread torn from a loaf ... as soon as we'd polished off one batch of scad the next was being fished from the spitting pan. Not only was the meal memorable – it wasn't long, in fact, before I decided that I couldn't think of surroundings more congenial to consume it in.

The cluttered concrete quay, the sheds and drying clothes, the boats flying their red Turkish flags ... all these ordinary things took on animation and life as other small-boat fishermen returned from a day on the water and began filling the port. There were still plenty of fish to eat, and soon our round table was surrounded by a half a dozen bristly-chinned fishermen. They were rough and raw and full of broad banter, but more than friendly to the foreigner who couldn't speak three words of their language. They slapped my back and encouraged me to take more food and drink. Here, of course, was the real attraction of these surroundings – generous, ordinary working people happy to share their lives with an unknown stranger.

Could they be called cosmopolitans? Hardly. Did it matter how Ismail and Mumtaz and their fishing friends fit into the complex puzzle of

Istanbul politics? Not really. As I finished off my last little scad the labels seemed unimportant. What counted was the exchange.

On the point of leaving, I received an invitation from a friend of Ismail's, a brawny, ham-handed man named Namuk. He was leaving the next afternoon on a four-day fishing trip to the distant middle reaches of the Sea of Marmara. I was welcome to go with him. '*Büyük balik*!' he said, using one of those calloused hands to measure on his other arm an imaginary fish running from fingertips to biceps. Big fish. Brave on beer and bonhomie, I was all ready to accept Namuk's offer when Ismail took me to one side.

'How did you like the sea on the *Oguz* today?' he asked.

'It was fine,' I said, remembering the boat pounding hard enough into each wave to make the hull shiver.

'Good,' said Ismail. 'Because Namuk's boat is even smaller than the *Oguz*. But the waves out in the middle of the Marmara Sea are bigger – much bigger. You will be three nights out there. And a Poyras does not hold forever – the wind can shift and become a Lodos. Then the sea is something else. Then I am happy I am not a fisherman with nets and a boat, but an assistant manager with pens and a telephone. Think of a little boat in big wind before you decide.'

So I did, and it sobered me up. It also made me think that Istanbul must be a strange and powerful place. It affected everything, even the wind that blew over it. The weather here was like the city itself. It was changeable and difficult to predict. It had two dispositions. It could veer between extremes. If I was going to sit and quietly contemplate the city one last time, it was probably better not done from the heaving deck of a small boat in a fierce blow. There was another place on the water I knew of, and not even the fiercest gale could capsize it. It was a bridge.

Forty-Two

Like maritime trading routes, those invisible bridges that have spanned the liquid continent for centuries, the Galata Bridge spans the Golden Horn and holds the city fast. And like those routes it, too, carries a wealth of freight, much of which is not material at all, but symbolic of the greater life of the city.

By 1845, the year the first Galata pontoon-bridge was opened, its pedestrians were already long accustomed to their cosmopolitan existence. Among the crowds that bustled daily along its floating, bobbing length, an endless variety of peoples could be seen. They were resplendent in every gradation of colour, from the white kilts and velvet waistcoats of the Albanians to the black tunics and tall sheepskin headdresses of the Circassians. There were still Ottoman officials from distant places, provincial dignitaries visiting the capital to inspect its wonders, who strolled over the new bridge swathed in turbans and flowing, floral-patterned robes. But already official Istanbul had abandoned traditional wear – the carriage-borne emissaries who clattered over the water from the Sublime Porte to the embassies of Pera now wore the stambouline, the dark, form-fitting frock-coat that made them look more like English country parsons than Ottoman functionaries.

More than a century and a half later, the Galata Bridge is still the focal point of the city and a barometer of both its constancy and its change. Enlarged in the 1860s, rebuilt with a row of shops and restaurants slung beneath it in the following decade, rebuilt yet again after the turn of the new century, the bridge remained a floating bridge, supported on steel pontoons, long after such constructions had disappeared from other ports around the world. And if the much-used eating and drinking places on its lower level became more ramshackle and less elegant as each decade went by, they were cherished by Istanbul's fond citizens as institutions that had become part of the very essence of their city. No evening was as cosmopolitan as a conversation-laden evening spent at a well-garnished table suspended over the waters of the Golden Horn.

In the early 1990s the old bridge was finally done away with. Its pontoons interfered with the flow of Bosphorus waters in and out of the Horn, and steadily rising levels of pollution threatened to turn the inlet into a sewer. The new Galata Bridge, a larger structure raised on fixed pilings, was perhaps more efficient in allowing the free passage of water. But not only did the blocky span of battleship-grey steel fail to charm Istanbuliots; it threatened the free flow of other liquids. No sooner were the new fish restaurants and bars built on its underside opened than the city's first Islamic municipality pledged to have the serving of alcohol in the city's public places prohibited. It would have meant the end of life as it had long been known and loved on the Galata Bridge.

But Istanbul's long tradition of tolerance continued to hold sway. In the end the alcohol ban, along with a series of other anticipated Islamising measures, failed to materialise. The new mayor ended up infuriating his hard-line supporters. Instead of bringing on the minor Islamic earthquake he had promised he did his best to present Istanbul as a modern, broad-minded, international city. It was one more example of old, moderating Mediterranean influences still subtly at work. Finally it wasn't the Islamists who were conquering Istanbul, exalted the city's more liberal inhabitants, but Istanbul which was conquering the Islamists.

So it was that on my last afternoon in Istanbul I could stroll down the hill from Saint-Benoît and in the middle of the Galata Bridge order a tall, cold glass of beer. I had my air-ticket to Marseilles and home. My bags were packed. I had made my goodbyes to Bekir and Ferruk and Mehmet, to Farida and Florent and their friends. I had a taxi booked to drive me to the airport for a 5.00 a.m. flight the next morning. And now I had the leisure to watch the afternoon sun sink into the Horn and the night to steal one last time over the city.

On late summer afternoons most people like to sit on the terraces on the shady, eastern side of the bridge, the side open to the Bosphorus. It's cooler, and there is the constant spectacle of big boats ploughing their way up and down between the Mediterranean and the Black Sea. But on this afternoon I chose a waterside table and the spectacle of little boats on the western, sunset side of the bridge. I wanted to see what I had seen on my first afternoon here.

And I wasn't disappointed. As I sipped beer and watched little fishes rise wriggling and flashing on the lines of the fishermen above me, the wind slowly died and the air became still. Growing larger as it dropped, a tangerine-coloured sun dipped to the horizon and the water and the world surrounding it were caught in glittering, rippling light. The Horn was golden once again. The small boats crawling their way from one side to another; the rounded domes of the mosques; the little figures strolling on the Horn's banks – all glowed bright and luminous, as if lit from inside. Everything was in stasis, each object centred around its own pulsing, interior life. A calm, or a least the only kind of calm a place like Istanbul can know, descended on the city. For a brief instant it looked like nothing in the city had ever changed or ever would.

It was all illusion, of course, a play of light upon water. Istanbul was always changing. I had finally decided that it was all right to feel perplexed by the city. So frequent and widespread were its mutations, so great its contradictions, that the city felt constantly perplexed about itself. Istanbul had been too many different things, was too many different things now, for it to have a single, fixed identity. Anyone who arrived at a set definition of the place was missing its point. Continuous exchange, transformation and diversity are its point. In that it was no different from many other cities around the liquid continent.

But Istanbul had been something else as well. It had been the very heart of the cosmopolitanism that had once made up the eastern Mediterranean.

From here a type of globalisation profoundly different from our own, the Ottoman *millet*, had radiated out to make up one of the world's most sophisticated and accomplished societies. It was all very long ago. Did it mean anything at all now, I wondered? Did a system of multinational management that guaranteed identity in return for cohesion hold anything for us today?

I thought of New York and London and Paris, of sidewalks and subways packed with people of every race on earth. In so far as most of us in the Western world have largely given up religious and ethnic identification and no longer bow to autocrats, such a system has nothing to offer us directly. These days we define ourselves by our economic standing and the cultural life we share with our peers, regardless of origins. And that, we say, is one of the great benefits of globalisation – at last we are getting over the crude differences of race and religion. And in terms of the worst excesses of nationalism, perhaps we are. But as I sat there watching the glow over the Golden Horn slowly subside I could think of a few things the old Ottoman cosmopolitans might be whispering to us if we chose to hear them.

Over the last half-century, they'd be saying, we have at last seized a Red Apple of our own – in our modern way we have conquered the world. We've evolved global financial institutions that make the wealth-creation of the Grand Viziers look paltry. We've devised global communications that are faster than any crack unit of Janissaries on the march. And we have developed a world-wide network of trade and commerce that even the most ambitious merchants of Istanbul would have never believed possible. All have permitted huge advances in a process of human interconnection that the Ottomans themselves long ago dreamed of in other forms and for other purposes.

But if we are coming close to creating a truly global economy, the old Istanbuliots would say, we've messed up badly in creating a global identity to go with it. There our thinking is not world-wide at all, but reverts to the same state of mind, compartmental and ethnocentric, that has formed our outlook for the last 300 years.

In the developed West we have reached a point of economic well-being where appeals to the security provided by shared race and religion no longer promise much benefit. It is harder for us to see the reassurance that such promises still provide in other, not-so-prosperous, non-Western societies. Not only does the rationale of the global marketplace allow us to reshape traditional economies without batting an eyelid. Without even noticing it we allow those same forces to run rough-shod over traditional identities – not over an economy-based identity like our own, but over religious and ethnic identities. And when those religions and ethnicities turn in on themselves in an attempt at self-preservation we say we don't understand why they hate us.

'Just think of it!' I could imagine a party of cushion-bolstered *kapi kulu* saying as their *caique*, lit by flickering lanterns and propelled by fez-topped rowers, slid through the waters of the Horn in the growing dusk. 'It would be like the Turks expecting all the empire's different communities to abandon everything and behave like just them. Can you imagine an Orthodox Christian Montenegrin fasting at Ramadan?' Can you see a wild Nubian from the upper Nile wearing flowered muslin? A Crimean Tartar speaking Ottoman Turk? A Bedouin nomad giving up his flocks? An Albanian mountain brigand abandoning his code of honour? No self-respecting Ottoman would dream of asking such things. Small wonder there's rebellion in the ranks.'

But suppose for a moment, just suppose, a cosmopolitan Krikor Balian or Alexander Mavrocordato might say, that something like the *millet* was operating in the globalisation process today. What if different communities in a fast-changing and unpredictable world were encouraged to hang on to what they feared for most, their identities? What if the recognition of those identities, accompanied by genuine participation in the larger world community, permitted the sharing of a larger, compound identity as well? And what if the economic and other rewards of that participation were sufficient that every group was prepared to answer to an authority superior to them all?

I realized, as I sat there daydreaming and watching night slowly fall on the city, what I was imagining: an authentically cosmopolitan world, a system based on a single global commerce and multiple global identities. Was the idea of world government – for that, in effect, is what it would amount to – too starry-eyed and innocent of the realities of international capital and power to be plausible? In our own particular vision of globalisation, fuelled by the hardnosed *realpolitik* of commercial competition alone, nothing has been easier than the violent manipulation of racial and religious fears. Has *that* been practical? It is not just exotic and distant populations who can answer that question. One could also ask the people of New York, London and Paris, those who have known the blind destructiveness of modern terrorism.

It is not only disintegrating societies that need a stake in a changing world. Today all of us are uprooted, all of us are potential cosmopolitans. The Ottomans would have seen plurality as a natural answer in the present world, insisting that if one identity weren't enough, well then, two or three might resolve the problem. But as I sat there listening to night whispers, my ear cocked for what the old city's sophisticates might have said, there were other, cautionary voices as well.

'We just weren't careful enough. We let ourselves become greedy,' I seemed to hear, although it could have just been the tipplers behind me pondering, too late, the wisdom of drinking double rakis. 'Obviously there is a certain style to live up to in a world capital like Constantinople. *Caiques* and *yali*s and pleasure-kiosks cost money. But we became self-serving. We sucked up the empire's wealth. We paid no attention to poor and distant rural areas. We stepped too hard on the peasantry. We ignored local needs. We forgot civic institutions. Naturally people got fed up. In the end the Ottomans got what they deserved.'

'We weren't as bad as the Alexandrians,' I heard a dissenting voice cut in. 'They bought all the cotton they could get their hands on and got rich selling it to the rest of the world. Did they ever think about cutting the Egyptians in? No wonder that fellow Nasser looked so good. Everyone gets their share, or things fall apart. And speaking of sharing, pass back that hookah, would you?'

Were the voices rising into the cool night air coming from somewhere beneath the underside of the bridge? Maybe it was just a few fishermen, happy to be rowing home at the end of a long afternoon's scad-fishing. Now another voice rose out of the darkness.

'If only we could start all over again,' it said wistfully. 'We didn't know it, but of course we were doomed from the beginning. Continual war and conquest – that's what the whole thing depended on. These other globalists, the ones chasing after markets, buying and selling every resource they can lay their hands on – they think they can carry on indefinitely. It can't be done – we reached our limit and at some point they'll reach theirs. You can only take something out if you put something back in. I believe these days they call it "sustainability".'

'Gentlemen!' there was a sudden loud harrumphing, although once again I couldn't be sure – perhaps it was only a ferry horn announcing an evening departure to Üsküdar. 'Gentlemen! All this talk of putting in and taking out is a waste of time. We're old men. We couldn't keep anything sustained for a single minute. But at least we have our old men's fancies. The night is young – what do you say we ride around Seraglio Point and float down to my cousin Yusef's *yali* at Yedikule? He tells me he's got the most delightful new dancing-girls, one from Tabriz, the other Crimean. It might be amusing. What do you say?'

There seemed to be a clamour of general accord, a splashing of oars, and with that the voices faded away. The only noise now was the noise of the modern Istanbul night.

Does any generation listen to any earlier generation, whatever the issue? Perhaps we are so certain that the world we're rushing into is so new and so different that the past cannot possibly hold anything for us. I didn't believe it. More than ever I had the certainty it was the same old world. But I was under no illusion that ancient Ottoman voices would ever have the ears of today's movers and shakers – even if the entire A-list at Davos were to come and sit themselves down on the Galata Bridge and listen hard I doubt they'd hear anything at all.

I reached the end of the bridge and began climbing the steep hill to

Saint-Benoît. In some ways it didn't matter if Davos listened or not. A cosmopolitan attitude to the world cannot simply be dictated. But then neither can its opposite. I thought of Mimi Awad and the winged god Nike perched on the statue of Alexander; of Lotfi the Tunisian racing sleepless night and day for Damascus; of a Syrian sea-captain ranting wildly into the Latakia night; of bear-like Gianfranco Vianelli rising to the defense of the Venetian gondola; of a French mathematics teacher travelling to the far end of the sea to recover her identity; of a small, sharp-eyed priest disregarding the emptiness of a large church to assert his own identity. The Mediterraneans I'd met in the last six months had too much vitality to let their world become the place we fear it might. For them it was still rich in variety and human possibility. Didn't the culture of the old Mediterranean we so much admire today grow out of times as unpredictable as our own?

And the greatest unpredictability lay right in this city, at the place where one day many worlds might meet and, again, fuse. Where is that place? I am sure it isn't, as the guidebooks insist, merely the spot where two continents come together on the shores of the Bosphorus. What did Bekir Cantemir mean when he talked about a global existence guided by two things it now lacks – ethics and judgement? Perhaps that is the place. I thought about it walking slowly up the steep hill, and I think about it still.

Reference Notes

Part of the vast literature of the history of the eastern Mediterranean, I have quoted from the following handful of books, indispensable to any sensible view of three global cities.

1   E M Forster's initial lukewarm response to modern Alexandria is cited by Michael Haag in his introduction to E M Forster's *Alexandria – A History and a Guide* (Michael Haag Ltd., London: 1982). Despite the city's long past, few notable books on Alexandria have emerged since its mid-20th century decline. A recent exception is Michael Haag's *Alexandria: City of Memory*, published by Yale University Press in 2004. Urban growth has made Forster's guide, which cross-references city-sites and historical events, often impractical; it nonetheless remains a penetrating study of Alexandria, and a favourite reference for lovers of the city. Still the best single tool for understanding the spirit of the place, I made liberal use of it.

2   Works on individual scholars who studied at the ancient Alexandria Library tend to be lengthy, antiquarian affairs. Harpocrates Publishing of Alexandria has produced a manageable English-language edition of a 1992 single-volume collection written largely by French academics: *Alexandria, third century BC – the knowledge of the world in a single city*, edited by Christian Jacob and François de Polignac, includes studies of the Library and its scholars, as well as the ancient city's rulers, religions, society and economy. My acknowledgements to Luciano Canfora for

his comments, in that compilation, on the Septuagint translation in *The World in a Scroll*. Also to Jean Lallot for his study on Zenodotus; to Christian Jacob's work on Eratosthenes and Callimachus; to François de Polignac for his summing-up of Alexander's legacy; and to Paul Goukowsky on Ptolemaic pomp, including the description I used, taken from the 3rd century BC writings of Callixeinos of Rhodes, of Ptolemy Philadelphus's procession along the Canopic Way.

3 There are several books on modern discoveries in Alexandrian archaeology; one of the best is *Alexandria Rediscovered* by Jean-Yves Empereur (British Museum Press, London: 1998), a coffee table-style volume with informative text and excellent illustrations.

4 Harpocrates Publishing has also issued a one-volume compilation of monographs on modern Alexandrian history. *Alexandria 1860–1960 – The brief life of a cosmopolitan community*, edited by Robert Ilbert and Ilios Yannakakis (1997), focuses on the plural, multi-ethnic nature of pre-Suez Alexandrian society. Especially useful were Robert Ilbert's observations on *millet*-based communities in *A Certain Sense of Citizenship*. The 1872 shipping schedule of sailings by the Messageries Maritimes from Alexandria to Constantinople was taken from the Appendices of that same volume.

5 *Venice* (Faber and Faber: 1993) is Jan Morris's paean to the island-city. It is lush, literate and invaluable, a treasure-trove of both Venetian arcana and style as ornately decorative as the city itself. In addition to quoting her lyric description of Venetian lions I have made use of her knowledge of the Venice state archives, the visit to Venice of the French king Henry III, Venetian streets and canals, and the legend of Saint Mark. A second volume by Morris, *The Venetian Empire – A Sea Voyage* (Penguin: 1990) left me indebted to Morris for her insight into the Venetian commercial ethos, Enrico Dandolo's sack of Constantinople, and the strategy behind the establishment of Venice's maritime empire.

6 Nicetas Choniates' account of the Frankish profanation of Hagia Sophia in 1204 is cited by John Julius Norwich in *A History of Venice* (Penguin: 2003). For decades the standard English work of Venetian

history, its 650 pages are replete with ambitious Venetian personalities, labyrinthine domestic politics and complex international relations. Among other stories I am grateful to Norwich for his accounts of the theft of the body of Saint Mark from Alexandria, the origins of the Sposalizio del Mar, the presence of Miguel Cervantes at the Battle of Lepanto, the functioning of the Venice Arsenal, the death of Pope Pius II in the port of Ancona, and, seen from a greater height, the historic shift in world power from the Mediterranean to the Atlantic.

7 A historian of court-life and dynasties, Philip Mansel excels in describing the cosmopolitan nature of Ottoman rule in *Constantinople – City of the World's Desire, 1453–1924* (Penguin: 1997). The Duke of Wellington's pronouncements on the empire's usefulness to European powers, which I have quoted, appear in Mansel's pages; so do Lady Mary Wortley Montagu's comments on the ethnic mix of her many grooms and footservants. I have also borrowed from Mansel's depiction of Galata social life and entertainment in both early and later Ottoman times; from his descriptions of mid-19th century sartorial fashions to be seen on the Galata Bridge; and from his accounts of Armenian, Greek and Jewish ethnic-minority families in the public life of Constantinople.

8 I also owe a debt to Jason Goodwin, author of *Lords of the Horizons – A History of the Ottoman Empire* (Vintage: 1999); in poetic, kaleidoscopic fashion he captures not only the history but the minds of the Ottomans. Especially helpful were his accounts of the myth of the Red Apple; of the Ottoman conception of war; of the ingenuity of the *Kapi Kulu* system; and of the reasons for the military and administrative decline of the empire.

About the Author

Nicholas Woodsworth was born in Ottawa, Canada in 1953 and grew up in a diplomatic family in Africa and Asia. He graduated in Asian history. He began newspaper freelancing after settling in Aix-en-Provence in his mid-20s. Woodsworth became the *Financial Times* Africa Correspondent in the late 1980s, and was later *Weekend FT*'s staff travel writer from 1989 to 2003. His interest in the Mediterranean, since expanded to include the entire region, began with his marriage to his Provençal wife. He is the author of *Seeking Provence* (Haus, 2008) and *Crossing Jerusalem* (Haus, 2010)

Also by Nicholas Woodsworth

Seeking Provence
Old Myths, New Paths

'What was a year in Provence compared with three thousand years in Provence? Peter Mayle had hardly invented the place – surely it has to exist in another, more authentic version. No place remains a centre of Mediterranean life for that long without leaving something of itself behind.' With these musings Nicholas Woodsworth peers deeply into the Provençal life and soul. He had with him the key to much of it; 'In fact I had to look no further than my wife Jany and the large Provençal family I had married into to see hints of its ongoing survival in everything they did and said. Buried, sometimes obscured, often mystifying, an older Latin experience still lay deeply anchored in them and the places they inhabited.'

This is the Provence that lies beyond the notion that it is really just the stockbroker belt moved south for the Summer, one more invitation to the Good Life. And that it is different to be a Mediterranean, an older, more fundamental way of life that is still worth learning and living today. Nicholas Woodsworth sets out on a journey to discover another Provence, a region of obscure and out of the way places.

AVAILABLE NOW

£12.99
978-1-905791-55-2
Hardback

Also by Nicholas Woodsworth

Crossing Jerusalem
Journeys at the Centre of the World's Troubles

Jerusalem is not an ordinary city and *Crossing Jerusalem* is not a standard telling of a city's story. While the author himself is deeply sceptical of religion, this book is both a portrait of a spiritual Jerusalem, and a recounting of the effect the city has on the spirit of one visitor who discovers its ongoing distress - through it he discovers some sort of spirituality in himself.

At the same time a travelogue, a questioning of spiritual values, and an examination of the beliefs that have sustained Jerusalem's populations through centuries of conflict and division, *Crossing Jerusalem* offers an unusual and penetrating perspective of the city. While many of the themes the author touches upon are inevitably sensitive and controversial, *Crossing Jerusalem* is intended to provoke thought rather than antipathy. At a time when both Jewish attitudes and the West's foreign policy options on a Middle East solution are evolving, *Crossing Jerusalem* is now especially relevant.

AVAILABLE AUGUST 2010

£9.99
978-1-906598-82-2
Paperback